Conflict, Insecurity and Mobility

TRANSNATIONAL PRESS LONDON

Books by TPL

Little Turkey in Great Britain

Overeducated and Over Here

Conflict, Insecurity & Mobility

Politics and Law in Turkish Migration

Göç ve Uyum

Family and Human Capital in Turkish Migration

Turkish Migration, Identity and Integration

Journals by TPL

Migration Letters

Remittances Review

Göç Dergisi

Journal of Gypsy Studies

Kurdish Studies

International Economics Letters

Border Crossing

Transnational Marketing Journal

Conflict, Insecurity and Mobility

Editors:
Ibrahim **Sirkeci**
Jeffrey H. **Cohen**
Pınar **Yazgan**

TRANSNATIONAL PRESS LONDON
2016

CONFLICT, INSECURITY AND MOBILITY

Edited by Ibrahim Sirkeci, Jeffrey H. Cohen, Pınar Yazgan

Copyright © 2016 by Transnational Press London

All rights reserved.

First Published in 2016 by TRANSNATIONAL PRESS LONDON in the Ukinted Kingdom, 12 Ridgeway Gardens, London, N6 5XR, UK.
www.tplondon.com

 Transnational Press London® and the logo and its affiliated brands are registered trademarks.

This book or any portion thereof may not be reproduced or used in any manner whatsoever without the express written permission of the publisher except for the use of brief quotations in a book review or scholarly journal.

Requests for permission to reproduce material from this work should be sent to: sales@tplondon.com

Paperback

ISBN: 978-1-910781-09-8

Cover Photo: Altay Manço

Cover Design: Nihal Yazgan

Contents

About the authors..iii
Chapter 1. Introduction...
    Ibrahim Sirkeci, Jeffrey H. Cohen, Pınar Yazgan, Natalia Zotova..........1
Chapter 2. Marginalisation and Copenhagen gang wars ....
    Pınar Yazgan and Therese Svensson 7
Chapter 3. Distance beyond the border: Kurds of Syria and Turkey in Istanbul...
    Souad Osseiran 19
Chapter 4. Border people's border perception: The case of Shemdinli (Shemdinan)..
    Ferhat Tekin..35
Chapter 5. Development, security and the role of Frontex on the Turkish-Greek border ....
    Burcu Toğral Koca 43
Chapter 6. Contributor or barrier: The role of Kurdish Diaspora in Turkey's European Union accession process ....
    Şevin Gülfer Sağnıç 61
Chapter 7. Perspectives on conflicts and potentials in a changing neighbourhood: Berlin-Neukölln and the role of urban governance ....
    Manuela Freiheit and Kristina Seidelsohn.................................77
Chapter 8. The Kurds: "A history of deliberate and reactive state-lessness"
    Hanifi Barış 89
Chapter 9. *As if all life had vanished...* The return of Kurdish villagers to their hometowns..
    Şemsa Özar..101
Chapter 10. Negotiating identity and coping with urban space among young Kurdish migrants in Istanbul..
    Karol P. Kaczorowski 115
Chapter 11. Perspectives on communal violence against Kurds in Turkey...
    İmren Borsuk 131
Chapter 12. Military service-migration nexus in Turkey.......................
    Ulaş Sunata 147
References..159

About the authors

Hanifi Barış is a PhD candidate at Centre for Citizenship, Civil Society and Rule of Law, University of Aberdeen, UK. He graduated from Baskent University School of Law, Ankara, Turkey in 2003. He practiced law as an attorney in Istanbul, Turkey, until 2009. Barış conducted his MA research between 2009 and 2010. His main research area is political theory. The social contract, multi-culturalism, political community, sovereignty, citizenship, nationalism and constitution-making are particular themes and components of his research. The root causes of the Kurdish Question, the ongoing constitution-making process in Turkey that has identified solving the Kurdish Question as one of its objectives, constitutional drafts prepared by four major political parties and their approach to the Kurdish Question are analysed and critiqued in his ongoing research project. His recent article titled "Dengbêjs on borderlands: Borders and the state as seen through the eyes of Kurdish singer-poets", co-authored with Wendelmoet Hamelink, appeared in *Kurdish Studies*, 2(1): 34-60.

İmren Borsuk was a Visiting Researcher during September 2013 – July 2014 at the Centre for the Studies of Ethnic Conflict, Queen's University Belfast, Northern Ireland. She conducts a comparative case study in her dissertation that interrogates which ethnic dyads are likely to come into conflict with one another. She is also interested in collective violence against minorities in Turkey and in Europe. She is working on an original dataset reflecting collective violence particularly regarding Kurds and Alevis in Turkey during the period of 1999-2012.

Manuela Freiheit is a Sociologist (Dipl.), studied Sociology, Communication Studies and Art History in Berlin and Konstanz. She is a PhD candidate and former fellow of the German Research Foundation training group 'Group Focused Enmity' (2008-2011) which is institutionally affiliated to the Institute for Interdisciplinary Research on Conflict and Violence (IKG) at Bielefeld University and the Philipps-University Marburg/Germany. Since 2012 she is working as a research associate at the IKG. Her specific areas of research include antisemitism and prejudice research, social and spatial inequality, qualitative methods in social research, as well as selected questions on conflict and violence.

Jeffrey H. Cohen is a Professor of Anthropology at Ohio State University, USA. He is currently on Sabbatical at Manisa Celal Bayar University, Turkey. Professor Jeffrey Cohen's research focuses on three areas: migration, development and nutrition. Since the early 1990s he has studied the impact, structure and outcome of migration from indigenous communities in Oaxaca, Mexico to the US with support from the National Science Foundation. He has also conducted comparative research on Mexican, Dominican and Turkish migration. His work on traditional foods, nutrition and migration was supported by the National Geographic Society. In addition to ongoing work in Oaxaca, he is currently studying the migration of Mexicans to Columbus. He is the co-editor of *Migration Letters* journal and serves on the editorial boards of several journals. His books include *Migration and Remittances during the Global Financial Crisis and Beyond* (World Bank, 2012 with I. Sirkeci and D. Ratha), and *Cultures of Migration, the global nature of contemporary mobility* (University of Texas Press, 2011 with I. Sirkeci) which was named 'Outstanding Academic Title' by the Choice magazine in the USA.

Karol P. Kaczorowski is a PhD candidate at the Institute of Sociology at Jagiellonian University in Cracow, Poland and is an associate of the Department of Sociology and Social Anthropology at the University of Science and Technology (AGH), Cracow. He is a graduate of sociology and religious studies. He works as a member of the Polish reaserch team studying Kurdish culture in a project titled "How to make a voice audible? Continuity and change of Kurdish culture and of social reality in postcolonial perspectives". Kaczorowski is the author of a book concerning opinions about the Arab Spring and the "Turkish model of democracy" in Turkey. He has published articles in the fields of sociology and cultural anthropology.

Souad Osseiran is a PhD candidate in the Anthropology department at Goldsmiths College, University of London. Souad undertook fieldwork with Syrian migrants/refugees living in Istanbul in 2012 and 2013. Her research focuses on Syrian migrants/refugees presence in Istanbul, the legal framework affecting their presence, migrants/refugees' waiting practices, and mobility towards Europe. Prior to joining the PhD program, Souad obtained an MSc in Social Anthropology from the University of Oxford.

Şevin Gülfer Sağnıç is a postgraduate student at Political Science and International Relations Department at Boğaziçi University. She holds an MA in International Relations with distinction from the University of Kent, UK. She has a BA in Political Science and International Relations from Marmara University, Istanbul. She worked and volunteered in organizations such as TESEV and Women's Voices Now.

Kristina Seidelsohn studied Sociology, Political Science and Cultural Studies in Cologne, Copenhagen and Berlin. During the period of 2008-2012, she was a research fellow funded by the German Research Foundation at the Training Group "Group focused enmity: Causes, phenomenology, consequences" based at Philipps-University Marburg and the University of Bielefeld and a PhD candidate at the Institute for Interdisciplinary Research on Conflict and Violence at the University of Bielefeld. Currently she is working as a research associate at the Disaster Research Unit (DRU), Department of Political and Social Sciences of the Free University Berlin. Her main research areas are urban development and social conflicts, residential segregation and environmental conditioning, security and safety in cities.

Ibrahim Sirkeci is Ria Professor of Transnational Studies and Marketing and the Director of the Regent's Centre for Transnational Studies (RCTS) at Regent's University London (UK). He holds a PhD in Geography from the University of Sheffield (UK) and a BA in Political Science and Public Administration from Bilkent University (Turkey). Prior to joining Regent's University London, Prof Sirkeci worked at the University of Bristol in the UK, Atilim, Hacettepe and Bilkent universities in Turkey. His main areas of expertise are Human Mobility, Transnational Marketing and Consumers, Marketing of Business Schools, Labour Markets, Remittances, and Segmentation. He is the editor of several journals including *Migration Letters, Remittances Review, Kurdish Studies,* and *Transnational Marketing Journal.* His books include *Turkish Migration Identity and Integration* (Transnational Press London, 2015), *Transnational Marketing and Transnational Consumers* (Springer, 2013), *Migration and Remittances during the Global Financial Crisis and Beyond* (World Bank, 2012), and *Cultures of Migration, the Global Nature of Contemporary Mobility* (University of Texas Press, 2011). He has been chairing the *Turkish Migration Conference* series since 2012.

Ulaş Sunata is Assistant Professor in the Department of Sociology at Bahçeşehir University, İstanbul, Turkey. Dr Sunata obtained her PhD in Sociology at the University of Osnabrück, Germany where she has worked as a Guest Fellow at the Institut für Migrationsforschung und Interkulturelle Studien (IMIS). She holds a Master of Science degree in Sociology and Bachelor of Arts in Statistics, both from Middle East Technical University (METU), Ankara, Turkey. Her research interests include information society, nationalism, migration and gender studies, on which she has published several articles and two books. She is the author of *Highly Skilled Labor Migration: The Case Study of ICT Specialists from Turkey in Germany.* Berlin, Münster: LIT Verlag (2011) and *Not a "Flight" from Home, But 'Potential Brain Drain'.* Saarbrücken: VDM Verlag (2010).

Therese Svensson was Research Assistant at Regent's Centre for Transnational Studies (RCTS), Regent's University London, UK. She is a graduate of Karstad University, Sweden, University of East London, and University College London, UK. She has worked at RCTS from September 2014 to April 2015.

Burcu Toğral-Koca is an Assistant Professor in the Department of Political Science and Public Administration at Eskişehir Osmangazi University, Turkey. She completed her undergraduate studies in International Relations and Sociology at the Middle East Technical University. She received her MA in European Studies and PhD in Political Science from the University of Hamburg, Germany. During her PhD studies, she was a visiting scholar at the University of Kent, Brussels, Belgium, and at the Fundacion Jose Ortega y Gasset, Madrid, Spain. She has also been involved in the work of the Hamburg Refugee Council for several years. Her fields of research interest are securitization of migration, Turkey's migration policy, biopolitcs of security and racism.

Ferhat Tekin is an Assistant Professor at Konya Necmettin Erbakan University. He graduated from Selcuk University's Sociology Department in 2001. In the same department, he completed his master's degree with a thesis titled "Political and Social Consequences of Tribe, Community and Kinship Patterns on the Process of Modernity and Rural Disintegration: The Case of Hakkari" in 2005 and his PhD thesis was titled "Border from a Sociological Aspect: The Case of Hakkari" submitted in 2012. Dr Ferhat Tekin has been working in Konya Necmettin Erbakan University's Faculty of the Social Sciences and Humanities as a lecturer since 2012. His main interest areas are border sociology, social change, alienation and modernization.

Pınar Yazgan is an Assistant Professor of Sociology at Sakarya University, Turkey. She received her BA, MA and PhD in Sociology, all from Sakarya University. Her dissertation focused on the sense of identity and belonging among migrants from Turkey residing in Denmark and was funded by The Scientific and Technological Research Council of Turkey (TUBITAK). She conducted field work in Denmark between 2007 and 2009. She also served as a visiting researcher at The Danish National Research Centre for Social Sciences in 2009. Her recent research projects focus on transnationalism, Turkish ethnic community in Norway, integration, identity, social belonging and ethnic media. She is the co-editor of *Göç Dergisi* and recently co-edited a special issue of the *Migration Letters* journal on Syrian crisis and migration.

Natalia Zotova is a PhD candidate at the Department of Anthropology, Ohio State University. She does research in the field of socio-cultural anthropology, investigating international migration from Central Asian countries to Russia and the USA. Natalia Zotova conducted fieldwork in different regions of the Russian Federation and Central Asia; organized and supervised surveys of Central Asian female migrants, their social vulnerability and sexual risks. The findings were published in peer-reviewed articles and presented at international conferences in Russia and the USA.

Chapter 1. Introduction

Ibrahim Sirkeci, Jeffrey H. Cohen, Pınar Yazgan, Natalia Zotova

Theories and models of contemporary migration often revolves around neofunctional models. They define migrants as rational actors who are focused on improving their economic, social, and political well-being which is enabled by access to opportunities that are not available in their origin communities and/or countries. Nevertheless, initiation of migration is largely driven by difficulties, discomfort, disagreements, tensions, and conflicts at the origin, while migration decision and destination choices are moderated by individual characteristics, cultural and social capital as well as by the local, national, and international context. In other words, people do not move when they are satisfied and comfortable with what they have and where they are. The number of movers around the world is relatively very small. The costs of migration and other moderating effects make international population movements an exception even today with an ever increasing mobility across the world.

While it is not difficult to find the economic benefits that accompany migration for nearly any mover; limiting our analysis of mobility to neofunctional possibilities masks other motivations that drive migration as well as the complex ways that migration decisions are made (Gallo, 2013; Levitt & Lamba-Nieves, 2013; Massey, 1990; Vianello, 2013). As the chapters in this book show, our ability to understand the conflicts and insecurities that surround migration is limited when we define mobility in neofunctional terms (and see Cohen & Sirkeci, 2011). After describing some of the central challenges to neofunctional models, we offer a dynamic framework that recognizes the complexities that confront movers and embraces the conflicts and insecurities that confound mobility.

Limits to neofunctional models

An emphasis on neofunctional models, economic wellbeing and rational decision-making by migrants errs in several important ways. First, the focus on individual movers limits our ability to understand the dynamic social milieu that surrounds migration decisions at points of origin and destination. While migrants are social agents who are actively engaged in decision-making, they are not independent actors. Even those movers who turn their backs on their families and communities of origin are making decisions that carry strong social ramifications (see for example the discussions in Ali, 2007; Lindstrom & Giorguli Saucedo, 2007). To better capture the dynamics of decision-making, chapters in this book define migrants as social actors who make decisions in response to a variety of different externalities. The externalities that influence migrant decision-making can include stay-at-homes, families and friends at points of origin; others at points of destination as well as more personal factors that include age, education, gender, self-identity and more. These may also be considered within human capital and social capital perspectives. Nevertheless, many of these factors—particularly those that represent the fixed and flexible resources available to movers—help movers to create frameworks that support mobility and build new networks around movement (Conway & Cohen, 2002). Defining the assets and externalities that support movers and characterize migration allows us to understand migration decision-making, outcomes of those decisions and the effects the decisions have on the households and communities that surround the mover (see Britton, 2013; Kindler & Szulecka, 2012; Triandafyllidou, 2009).

Second, neofunctional models of migration *focus on outcomes that are positive* and that are typically associated with finding comparatively better opportunities in destination communities. But the assumption that high wages alone define migration outcomes misses social factors that motivate mobility and that may have little to do with work. For many skilled and/or highly trained migrants, traveling to a new destination creates opportunities that do not rely on those skills (Hainmueller & Hiscox, 2010; Heyman, 2007). This is often quite apparent when undocumented movers with training must settle for work that does not build upon their skill set rather than risking that they may be discovered (often these are the migrants who fill low end, service jobs in restaurants or find temporary, semi-licensed or day labor).

Third, building further on the assumption that migrants seek jobs is the presumption that movers will select their destinations because there are jobs available. In fact, while we find that jobs are an important consideration, they are not the only thing migrants think about. Migrants may seek a destination where they will find fellow co-nationals living, and the may do this with little regard for the jobs that are available; they may also look toward the future or away from some past challenges as they decide on their destination (Lianos & Cavounidis, 2010).

Fourth, migration is a costly decision that can challenge the resources of a sending family (Pantea, 2012). Furthermore, the expenses associated with traveling across borders, resettling, learning new skills and languages and negotiating new life styles can come at a high price destabilizing a sending family's ability to maintain itself in the short term with only the promise of a long term gain. Long term gains are not guaranteed and remittance practices by movers while being critical nationally can play out quite differently for specific sending households.

Beyond neofunctionalism and the role of insecurity and conflict

While hope remains for a world in peace, we continue to witness a rising number of global and regional conflicts. In an ever globalising world, these conflicts vary both in intensity and cause and may stem from a multiplicity of reasons. Many questions arising from issues on conflict and security relate to mobility. Recent human influxes from war-torn Middle East also reflect global inequalities, which may be further heightened by foreign intervention in these conflicts. There is a clear need to take into account the role of conflicts and human insecurity in the analysis and conceptualisation of human mobility. We aim to lay another brick in this line of work.

Neofunctional models in migration emphasize economic wellbeing and the ways in which mobility satisfies a series of specific needs and provides the mover with a rational, secure path toward the future. Refocusing our work to look beyond neofunctionalist models in the study of migration does not reject the role movement can play in satisfying specific economic needs, producing higher wages and offering opportunities and securities unavailable at home. By looking beyond the neofunctional approach, we are able to explore the insecurities and conflicts that also characterize mobility (Cohen & Sirkeci, 2011).

The realities for most movers is that migration builds security and insecurity, and is based on well-practiced traditions as well as long-term conflicts that challenge and confront movers both in origin and destination communities (Bermudez, 2013; Nolin, 2002; Sirkeci, 2006). Migration is often built upon well-worn social networks and carries individuals to traditional destinations. But the traditions that characterize those networks and traditional destinations often repeat the logic of colonial relationships between the center and periphery (whether we describe the movement of Latin Americans, patterns in Central Asian and Russian migration or Turks in Europe as described by Menjívar & Abrego, 2012; Reeves, 2013; Sirkeci, Cohen, & Yazgan, 2012).

Unemployment and a lack of opportunities in origin communities push movers, while access to higher wages in destination communities pulls at migrants. Yet, migrant decision-making often reflects discrimination, exclusion and ill-treatment at points of origin and destination—higher wages at points of destination are perhaps best thought of in relative terms as those wages do not resolve the discrimination that typically welcomes non-native movers (Regamey, 2010; Trager, 2005). Even the familiar can become problematic and provoke both conflicts and insecurities for movers as they negotiate contrasting and conflicting cultural and linguistic environments at home and abroad.

Structural economic crisis, like those that gripped the globe in 2008 as well as those that played out on a more regional stage, and violence (from domestic to open warfare) shift the balance of opportunities for movers and non-movers alike. They can create new insecurities and lead to new decisions as well as new destinations (see Sirkeci et al., 2012). Many movers chose new destinations in response to xenophobia, discrimination, economic trouble and laws limiting employment. The destinations may include new forms of insecurity and new conflicts that can destabilize mobility as well as the outcomes of movement. The choice of destination is more than a move to satisfy a need or build toward a more secure future. The choice of a destination is part of the negotiation of security and insecurity, conflict and harmony that informs outcomes and builds upon past and present, ability and accommodation, the legal status, linguistic barriers and abilities, systems of social support, as well as jobs. All of the factors, externalities and assets bound the mover, the stay-at-home and the larger origin and destination communities, and potentially transform the perception of security, insecurity, conflict and harmony. The studies collected in this edited book offer evidence to our argument that migration does not provide an ultimate response to insecurities in the home countries or conflicts in traditional destinations; instead as hinted in some of the contributions, migration shifts the balance of power and security as insecurity and conflict are negotiated in the process of migration with particular reference to the Kurds and Kurdish migration.

Content of this book

In this edited volume, we have selected to include studies showing the conflict elements in migration experiences from Turkey. The next chapter takes us to the gang wars in Copenhagen as Yazgan and Svensson uncover discourses in relation to the groups defined as deviant or 'the minority group' within the framework of marginalisation, and their integration into 'criminal capital'. Souad Osseiran explores the social and political relations of Syrian and Turkish Kurds, who are living together in a neighbourhood in Istanbul. An interesting account of people who are kin but have been separated in the creation of two nation states. We continue with an analysis of the border and its impact on people as Ferhat Tekin looks into the case of Shemdinli (Shemdinan). His study was carried out in nine villages, all part of the Gerdi tribe with a focus on the perceptions of the border among the residents. The role of borders and border control is also the focus of Burcu Toğral Koca's chapter on Frontext and Turkish-Greek border. She tackles the issues with a Foucauldian approach on security, migration and development in a European context.

Chapter six focuses on the role of Kurdish Diaspora in Turkey's European Union accession process. Şevin Gülfer Sağnıç explores the diaspora activities with the accession question in mind. Manuela Freiheit and Kristina Seidelsohn, in the following chapter, help us to understand the role of city governance in this diaspora with a focus on Berlin-Neukölln, where along with Turks and Kurds more than 160 different nationalities reside.

Hanifi Barış, in chapter eight, takes us to an essential question: The Kurds and statelessness. After a detailed critique of Scot's work, he argues that forming alliances with states, remaining small in scale but choosing autonomy over subordination to one another, taking refuge in the mountains to escape state domination, crossing borders with little regard to their legitimacy when needed, and forming internal judiciary mechanisms are all strategies of keeping the state at a distance in Kurdish regions.

Returning home is a common myth among migrants. It is possibly an impossible undertaking for those who left their homes fleeing from violent conflicts or wars as many Syrians face today. Şemsa Özar offers rich narratives from Kurdish villagers who returned to their homes, where they were once evacuated from. She shares the views of people from Kavar village while questioning common misperceptions about the Kurdish issue. Karol Kaczorowski chased down those Kurdish people who left their homes and settled in Istanbul. Kaczorowski uses the conflict model of migration in understanding internal mobility of Kurds and discovers the ways in which young Kurdish migrants negotiating identity and coping with urban space where they face new insecurities. Imren Borsuk focuses on communal violence against Kurds in Turkey drawing upon media reported by *Özgur Gündem* and *Dicle Haber Ajansı (Dicle News Agency)* between 1999 and 2012. The last chapter in this edited book looks into the migration and military service nexus in Turkey qualitatively. Ulaş Sunata deals with the question of how the military service shapes civil men and their families' life courses.

Finally, we should acknowledge the contributions and efforts by many individuals and institutions in making this project a success. This edited volume took us nearly two years to complete as they are rather difficult to come about and the process requires input from so many parties. We would like to thank all our colleagues who have contributed to this volume, those who have participated at the Turkish Migration Conferences 2014 and 2015, as well as many others have volunteered to review the papers submitted to the conference and for the edited book. All these efforts combined made this book possible. We would like to thank our anonymous reviewers for their comments. We also thank Dr Welat Zeydanlioglu and Dr Anett Condick-Brough for their comments on the final draft. We also thank to institutions including Regent's University London and Ria Financial, and *Migration Letters* journal for their support. Finally, we thank our families and friends for their continuous support.

Chapter 2. Marginalisation and Copenhagen gang wars

Pınar Yazgan and Therese Svensson

In recent times, violent incidents have occurred between rival gangs in the so-called *'ghettos'* of Copenhagen (Politiken.dk, 2008). These turf wars have mostly taken place between the local Hell's Angels' gang and various other gangs. Discussions related to the gang wars in Copenhagen first appeared in the media in 2007-2008, between the local MC gang *'Hells Angels'* and the *'Black Cobra'* gang, which consists mainly of ethnic minority members (Schmidt, 2009, 2011: 605). Gang wars have taken place in *Nørrebro*, which is an area in the North of Copenhagen, where the concentration of immigrants is the highest in the city. The encounters between gangs have had disastrous effects with severe impacts upon the general impressions of foreigners in Denmark (Nasser, 2010). This paper proposes that gang wars in Denmark can be explained by various levels of marginalisation through negative social capital and grounded political discourses preventing integration as opposed to promoting it. Specifically, this chapter highlights discourses in relation to the groups defined as deviant or 'the minority group' within the framework of marginalisation, and their integration into criminal capital as the negative side of social capital.

The location where most of the gang violence and assaults have occurred is significant when considering the various factors involved in group categorization that may influence inter-group conflict. Throughout history, the area has been characterized by conflict not only in relation to gang wars but also to political conflict and demonstrations (Schmidt, 2011: 604). The area in Copenhagen, which is most commonly referred to by politicians and popular media discourses is an area in the North of Copenhagen referred to as *Nørrebro*. Approximately a 1/3 of the population in this area consists of migrants or their descendants (ibid: 605; Municipality of Copenhagen, 2009). Some of the representative minority groups in the area are Arabs, Turks, Somalians and Albanians (Skifter Andersen, 2006:13). The area itself is characterized as a poly-cultural society, mostly with immigrants of Middle Eastern origin (ibid). The main street is called *Nørrebrogarde* that runs through the area with a plethora of multi-ethnic restaurants and shops. Thus, the notion of space is an important one when considering conflict in the area. According to Massey (2005) space can be characterized as a relational concept that is created by individuals living together and their *'thrown-togetherness'*. Due to a series of events involving casualties and violent fights, Nørrebro has gone from notions of a positive poly-cultural society in the public mind to a springboard for political activism and identity represented by political manifestations in the area.

Marginalization and social exclusion

From a sociological standpoint, scientists have paid particular attention to how minorities are *'integrated'* into criminal or deviant behaviour due to their socio-economic position in society, which can be applied to the Copenhagen gang wars (e.g, Sampson & Wilson, 1995; Zick, 2001; Junger-Tas, 2001; Vazsonyi & Killias, 2001). Hassan (2010: 575) states that "*marginalisation fosters inter-generational transfer of disadvantage and may also contribute to their alienation from society and its values which makes them vulnerable to religious and non-religious radicalism*" in his work on socio-economic marginalization of Muslims in Australia. Furthermore, Alejandro Portes (2010) stated provocatively that Central American migrants assimilated very well into American society; assimilated into criminal gangs that is, due to persistent marginalization, lack of socio-economic possibilities and coping strategies. This can be described as 'segmented assimilation' (Portes & Zhou, 1993). When gangs are formed as a result of exclusion from society, the process can be seen as a negative form of social capital. The excluded individual may generally appeal to violence from time to time in order to make him/her accepted by the group and gain recognition. From this perspective, immigration does not cause crime and marginalization but immigrants may as Portes and colleagues (2005) suggested be brought into crime due to marginalization.

The concept of social capital has mostly been linked to positive values of groups. However, social capital may result in "*criminal capital*" when individuals become members of criminal groups (e.g, Mocan, Billups & Overland, 2005). If the values that hold society together are defined as social capital, then ethnic discrimination and exclusion may harm social integration and feelings of belonging to society. This is problematic for political discourses that may seem positive for the in-group (for the local group) whereas they may emerge as negative social capital for the out-group (ethnic minorities) (Karagül, 2005). Lin (2008: 8) referred to the concept of 'ethnic social capital', when referring to minority groups. Another term that has frequently been used to explain such a concept is the "*the dark side of social capital*" (e.g. Gargiulo, & Benassi, 1999; Schulman, & Anderson, 1999) in terms of inter-group relations, which may also imply the lack of social capital within the whole society as a consequence.

Discussions and majority rhetoric in the Danish media have been blamed as one potential factor involved in the processes of marginalization and escalation of violence in Copenhagen. As a result of several tragic events caused by gang violence, the political discourses have changed. In this way, theories of grounded politics can account for escalation of conflict, when considering marginalization hypotheses. Typically, the common discourses of 'Immigrants' and 'Muslim' have shifted to a focus on both simultaneously to stress the alleged incompatibility with inclusion of migrants into the Danish society and 'Danishness' in terms of values and beliefs held by the majority population (Schmidt, 2011). Thus, immigrants who want to integrate may be particularly prone to marginalization that in turn may increase their susceptibility to join violent gangs. Some studies indicates that social capital does not always have a positive influence on ethnic minority neighbourhoods and may also be the negative driving force for encouraging criminality and for involvement in deviant groups (e.g, Portes, 2000; Wright et al., 2001; Bayer et al., 2007). In this respect, social capital affects members of these groups not only positively.

Gang formation
Gang behavior has mostly been explained with reference to marginalization, group theory, racial studies or antisocial behavior analysis (Andersen & Morch, 2005). However, arguments have been put forward to suggest that youths in today's society are faced with pressures of individualization and identity formation as a lifelong challenge (Ziehe & Stubenrauch, 1982; Morch, 2010). This has occurred as a result of deinstitutionalization of post-modern societies in the Western hemisphere. Historically, a *'Bourgeois society'* structure formed young individuals' lives through standardised rules and prohibitions (Morch & Andersen, 2012). Family, school and institutions therefore, shaped youths' identities from early childhood to adulthood.

Modern society values self-determination and self-respect, which places the individual in the driver's seat. Thus, they appear to have endless opportunities as well as challenges. In this modern era, social support and peer friendships are necessary to help individuals build their own identities and career paths (Frønaes & Brusdal, 2000). Young people, therefore, may be particularly vulnerable, if they miss out on various opportunities offered them through education (Morch & Andersen, 2012). Because young people need the support that reproduces their gender, social and ethnic positions, young individuals' trajectories can revolve in such a way that they do not associate themselves with society, but with their immediate sense of group belonging. This is, unfortunately, true for young people who may come from a weak family with greater educational, cultural and socio-economic barriers. In this way, the immediate group memberships can provide gang members with the sense of self-direction that is valued in society, even though it represents negative social capital not for the individual, but for the society (Stafseng, 1996).

The media is involved in this process, by reinforcing the values of good education in society. Individuals who are not good in society are deemed losers. This in turn becomes problematic for the individuals involved because 'being a looser' or 'failing' may be individually interpreted as a personal attack, which reinforces the need to find different forms of success in life (Côté, 2000). In this scenario, education is of key importance in directing young individuals' lives, since it naturally marginalizes certain individuals by differentiating students. Thus, education systems contribute to the perception of difference in performance. By praising a 'winner', the system also creates a 'looser', which is problematic for integration into society (Morch & Andersen, 2012). For the individual who joins a gang, the membership itself may for them be perceived as 'top performance', for some students e.g. at difficulty in school. The school failed to bring them towards social inclusion, while instead the gang provides them with a valued identity and direction (Andersen & Morch, 2005).

For instance Portes and colleagues (2005: 1008) explained gang formation in their study in the following manner:

"The final external challenge confronting children of immigrants is that the social context they encounter, in American schools and neighbourhoods, may promote a set of undesirable outcomes inimical to successful integration such as dropping out of school, joining youth gangs, and using and selling drugs. This alternative path has been labelled downward assimilation because exposure to American society and entry into its social circles does not lead, in these cases, to upward mobility, but exactly to the opposite".

Marginalisation is a concept related to inequality and social exclusion (Marshall, 2003: 472). Social exclusion indicates the forms by which an individual is prevented from entirely integrating into society. For example, people who are surrounded by 'bad' schools and less job opportunities and live in 'ghetto areas' are deprived of the opportunities that would provide them with better positive social capital (Giddens, 2009: 402). Ghettos are typically characterised as socially discriminated areas where inhabitants experience socio-economic disadvantages, low levels of labour market attachment and higher crime rates. Historically, specific ethnic and religious groups characterised as minorities at the given point in time have populated these places. Today, such places can be urban areas with a high percentage of immigrants, unskilled labourers and individuals who have a low socio-economic status. At this point, inequalities emerge as a result of social exclusion. Exclusion can be considered a by-product of the global capital and the post-industrial social order (Byrne, 2001: 137).

An individuals' perception of their group membership largely influence their sense of inclusion or exclusion in society as identified by minority-majority group influences. Thus, ethnic minorities may encounter negative feelings or experiences associated with their minority status, due to difference in group membership. Members may or may not act upon such feelings, however, if they do, it might be due to motives initiated by *'upward social mobility'* and joining a criminal gang may provide a stronger sense of value and worth to the individual who feels marginalised. Excluded individuals who join criminal gangs gain protection from its members, positive identification and a sense of higher worth. In this respect, Hassan (2010: 575) claimed that: *"socioeconomic marginalisation and a sense of relative deprivation are often breeding grounds for religious and non-religious radicalisation"*.

Micro and macro analyses of social capital and resources available to immigrants convey that socio-economic policies in immigrant receiving countries can affect marginalisation and an individual's limited access to resources. Furthermore, Grossberg (1996) emphasized that studies of marginalization should include power relations to discuss differences between majority and minority groups. Instead, the focus of research has pertained to discussions on immigrants and inequality in Europe. At this point, the emphasis of existing research has extended to a combination of the classical inequality approach with the critical approach, citing group categorisation in policy and media rhetoric as the main villains (Andersson, 2003). Andersson (2003) conceptualized social inequality as a marginal position related to power relations and social space. Thus, the point that is being made is not that marginalisation is caused by social inequality, but rather that marginalization reveals the process involved that may lead to social inequality.

Overall, marginalisation increases from micro and macro levels when individuals of low socio-economic groups are transferred from one social structure to another by forces such as immigration. Their disadvantages are then added to the cultural, ethnic and religious differences within the new society (Giddens, 1997: 280). Marginal members of these types of groups perform an important function as members. Groups and leaders in particular find the opportunity to clarify the boundaries of the group through a defaming/excluding discourse against marginal members. If an individual or a group is marginalised, they are detached from the society in a way that conceptions of *'otherness'* might appear. These people are disconnected from dialogue, withdraw themselves, and live within the boundaries of their own sub-culture. The process of marginalisation is generally considered to involve self-defence mechanisms and behaviour that protects members from low or negative views of their own group identity (Warren, 2010: 133).

In the context of immigration, factors related to cultural and religious difference of immigrants is combined with the socio-economic structure within the new society such as the *Nørrebro* community in Copenhagen. For this reason, immigrants in Copenhagen might be perceived as the marginal group of the bigger society. The individual can thus be excluded in various ways, in the process of becoming marginal(ised). While Portes (1998) simply argues that exclusion of outsiders is one of the negative consequences of social capital, Lin (2000) emphasised inequality in social capital such as social economic achievements and quality of life. Dinessen and colleagues (2013: 163) suggests that marginalisation can be a product of the transformation of social capital into criminal capital (gang formation), which will be discussed in more detail in the last section in terms of ethnic groups and the negative consequences of social capital. Before that, the next section examines the term social capital in relation to inequality and discrimination.

Social capital as one potential source of inequality and discrimination

The concept of social capital can be traced back to ancient Greek philosophy, although, the expression itself first appeared in academic disputes during the 1980s. Robert Putnam's (2001) use of the concept has been adopted extensively, emphasizing networks and norms in his definition of social capital. Social capital can be considered a multi-faceted concept that includes factors such as citizenship, neighbourliness, trust, common values, group commitment, voluntariness, social bonds, civil and political participation. The benefits, indicators, and tendencies of these are controversial in that different social scientists have adopted different approaches (Faulkner, 2003: 287). The concept of social capital has been researched mostly using correlational designs, which has indicated links with networks and has been considered within the subjects of education, economics, health, welfare, crime and deviancy from the norm (e.g, Kawachi et al., 1999; Sampson & Laub, 1990; Messner et al., 2004). Field (2008) summarised his thesis on social capital succintly: connections are important. In this sense, he emphasised the importance of communicative networks. Membership with communicative networks and common values are also at the main part of the concept.

Dinesen and colleagues (2013) measured the relationship between social capital and violence on both a cognitive and structural level in relation to group conflict. On the other hand, Coleman (1995) and Putnam (1998) studied the social and political thought tradition in North America whereas Bourdieu (2011) rather focused on the continuity and inequality of social classes by focusing on traditional hierarchies. The outcome of group membership is comprised by the social information and connections that increase the reputation of people who have achieved their goals, which is referred to as social capital (Field, 2008: 18). Putnam (2002) divides social capital into two main types. The first is referred to as extroverted, inclusive, and bridging social capital, whereas the second type is introverted, exclusive, and bonding. Thus, social capital brings people together who experience social discrimination and who do not. Bonding social capital supports privileged identities and homogeneous groups. In addition, Van Oorschot and collegues (2010) argued that the level of ties have characterized the distinction between the different forms of social capital with weak ties at the one end and closed social capital with strong ties at the other end.

Social capital does not on its own signify social equality, inequality, or social commitment. On the contrary, the concept initially emphasized equal distribution of cultural resources and materials, while it was later considered within the context of social solidarity. One of the basic reasons as to why people join organizations might be the desire to gain recognition and connections (Mohan, 2002: 193). Thus, social capital may lead to inequality for the individuals who do not have a network and thus may face discrimination. Bourdieu focused on the explicit contribution of social capital to inequality (Field, 2008: 109). Additionally, Lin (2000: 787) stated, *"not all individuals or social groups acquire or receive expected returns from their social capital."* At this point, *"the dark side of the social capital"* becomes prominent and we can say that this side of social capital has largely remained unknown in research (ibid). Coleman emphasised the negative cooperation of social capital observed in criminal gangs. Social capital can cause negative consequences for most of the individuals and groups as well as for others (such as the victims of organized crimes). Field (2008) considers these negative consequences from two perspectives: firstly, consolidation of inequality by social capital, and secondly, consolidation of antisocial behaviour. At this point, Putnam argued whether there is an inconsistency between social capital, inequality and freedom to some extent, whereas Fukuyama focused on social capital's potential in arousing evil. Here, he points out hate groups as an example. Group solidarity among human communities is generally used against the minority individuals for the sake of hostility. Yet, he believes that the lack of social capital is much worse than minority discrimination.

Based on the above discussion with reference to existing literature; Field emphasized that there is an agreement between Bourdieu, Putnam, Coleman, and Fukuyama regarding the possibility that social capital may also have a dark side. Fukuyama stated that selfish lobbyists became engaged in group solidarity, while being hostile towards the individuals outside of the group. As stated by Bourdieu, people can create *"inequality"* by using social capital as the source of their reputation, rising status and privilege as powerful individuals by restricting resources of the powerless. Empirical studies have pointed out examples indicating the unfavorable impacts of social capital that tend to create inequality. The more homogeneous and restricted the networks were perceived as, the greater the discrimination against outsiders (Field, 2008: 100-113). Similarly, Adler and Kwon (2002) referred to the risks of social capital and explained that *"for the broader aggregate, the social capital of the focal group presents a real risk of negative externalities"*. One of the risks of social capital may be marginalisation as a result of the transformation of social capital into criminal capital (gang formation). The next section will cover gang formation in terms of ethnic groups and the negative consequences of social capital.

Gang formation as negative outcomes of social capital and gang wars in Denmark

Citizens of Turkish origin constitute the largest ethnic group in Denmark, followed by those of Iraqi, German, Bosnian and Pakistani origin. In Denmark, the total population consists of close to 10% immigrants and second-order migrants. The variety of immigrants is perceived as a challenging problem in terms of political culture based on homogeneity and solidarity. After the first group of refugees and guest workers brought their families together with them to Denmark through family reunification, the immigrant population of Denmark increased rapidly in the 1980s. Family reunification, which had been a disputed matter since 1983, became stricter in 1992. Thus, heterogeneous groups with different norms and social realities were formed in these new areas in Denmark. As a result of suspended bonds with the country of origin, immigrant communities started interacting with one other to protect their collective identities that were formed by their ethnic bonds (Yazgan, 2010: 49-50).

Denmark is organized as a welfare state based on the cultural similarity of its citizens, which is founded on a strong national identity and cultural homogeneity. The economic success of this model lies in its foundation of civil solidarity. The population of Denmark experienced negative growth rates despite increasing immigrant population with guest workers, refugees and family reunifications from the 1970s onwards. Living together with people from different ethnic backgrounds is unexpected for the society of Denmark, as it does not consider itself a country of immigration, which has brought about the challenge of dealing with difference for both the Danish society and politicians (Hedetoft, 2006: 1).

Recently, Denmark has faced problems in relation to gang wars. Such society-based problems have led to media discourses that problematize ethnic minorities. Problems related to these youth gangs are not only criminal, but also social problems. Marginalized individuals face discrimination in their educational and social life (Mørch & Andersen, 2012). An emphasis on homogeneity in the national 'Danish" identity along with discriminative discourses have caused tensions between ethnic minorities and the local population. In many situations, gunshots and murder have been involved, which are among the prominent social problems faced by the new generation. Exclusion and social tension affect the daily lives of immigrant youth and their everyday relations in society.

When considering social capital in relation to gang formation in Denmark, one of the prominent components has been social networks. The basic connection between these networks is similarity, weak and negative bonds that bring people from different social and cultural backgrounds together (Field, 2008: 93). This situation can be partly explained by unequal access to resources for immigrants who do not share similar social and cultural background with local citizens. Social capital is a resource used by its members to satisfy their benefits at some point, e.g. in finding a job, getting recognition, entering specific communities, finding a place to live. In this sense, resources vary depending on different types of social groups. In other words, social capital is also based on mutual benefits that require communication networks and commitment (Baker, 1990: 619).

Field (2008) made a clear distinction between productive social networks that aroused positive consequences for both members of the network and the entire community and bad networks that provide its members with positive benefits yet include negative consequences for the rest of the society. Organized crimes are examples of cases when criminal capital is an intended target of the communication network. However, in the example of gang wars in Copenhagen, or street gangs in Moscow that provide some sort of social protection to the marginal youth and Central

American gangs in California, another example of bad socialization is when members of minority groups join criminal gangs. In this sense, gangs of organized crime and illegal discrimination based on communication networks comprise *"the dark side of social capital"* (e.g. Portes 1998). Moreover, Reisig, Holtfreter, and Morash (2002) explain the relationship between women who are young, poor, and less educated and criminal behaviour. The researchers argued that women are less likely to develop human capital (e.g., education and job skills) necessary to overcome their adverse situations and more likely to rely on social resources that facilitate criminal behaviour (e.g., dealing drugs and prostitution). Thereby, this form of human capital has been coined *"negative human capital"* or *"criminal capital"* (Portes, 1998).

Putnam (1995) explains social capital by emphasizing bonds, norms, and the concept of trust. Social capital, social norms and communication networks contribute to the productivity of the individual within the group and this is based on trust among group members (Portes, 1998: 18). This distinction also emphasized the negative dimension of social capital, particularly by indicating the tendency of bonding social capital to support elite identities and sustain homogeneity as well as the exclusive character of elitist norms (Field, 2008: 45). For this reason, the outsiders will face discrimination and inequality. Helliwell and Putnam (2004: 1437) explained bonding social capital within the scope of gang formation as follows: *"we need to distinguish among different types of social capital, like the difference between 'bonding' social capital—these are links among people who are similar in ethnicity, age, social class, etc."*.

The negative dimension of social capital can be observed in violent criminal groups. Moving from Putnam's distinction of bridging and bonding social capital, we can say that criminal gang activities may emerge through the expansion of within group relations such as in the case of Copenhagen. In the context of immigration, bonding social capital generally protects homogeneity and supports privileged identities. When high bonding and low tolerance comes together, a regional gang community may emerge with bad intentions and emerging antisocial aims. In terms of gang formation, the marginalization process is related to an individual's encounter with discrimination due to his/her ethnic origin or socio-economic status. Many acts of crime can be related to inequality (Field, 2008: 86). In this sense, since bonding social capital is related to the risk of privilege, this may cause the negative consequences of inequality to emerge (Adler & Kwon, 2002: 22). Again, origin, economic status, and socio-cultural status may lead to spatial or social exclusion. And this may affect the equality of opportunity. As a result of discrimination and/or exclusion, the process of marginalization, which promotes criminal capital (criminal gangs and terrorists) may result from a lack of social capital.

There are several factors that might promote gang membership. Gang formation may be a result of or a contributing factor based on inequality and exclusion, within the context of ethnic minorities. From the point of view of the gang member, we should also consider the attractiveness of this gang within the context of the repulsiveness of discriminative attitudes and discourses. Gang membership may emerge in socially disorganized areas and in educationally unsuccessful individuals, when combined with problematic family structures of low socio-economic status. When it is conceptualized within the context of immigration, marginalization may bring about social exclusion and *'ghetto formation'*, thus criminal capital may emerge among immigrants. In order to understand individuals' gang activities and formations, understanding group dynamics is essential. Generally, members of specific gangs have different social backgrounds. Gang members may also hold memberships in different gangs simultaneously. Indicators of how different groups are in contact with each other can provide information on the nature of its members, what kind of violence they use and the structure of the group. Group membership is not merely based on ethnicity, language, and culture. It is also based on age, local similarities, and activities. In a way, family bonds, language, religious origin, common ways of behaviour and honour are all important influences that determine gang formation (White, 2008: 150). Whites (2008) conducted research on the youngest gang members in Australia and observed that different cultural identity and ethnicity can be influential at the centre of social relations as well as geography, age, connections, and neighbourhood. Members become part of groups through regional, educational, ethnic, religious and class-related backgrounds and friendships. Attractive factors are group activities, the size of the group, criminality, violence, music, drugs, affinity and show off. All values that hold the society together can be considered elements of social capital. However, any form of discrimination can be defined as negative capital (Karagül, 2005: 46).

Social capital can produce negative results, or the impact can be considered as the lack of social capital from another point of view. Something that is positive for the group may have a negative consequence for the society and this may influence discrimination and criminal behaviour, which can be stated as the lack of social capital across the entire society. As a negative form, the distrust and discrimination between ethnic minorities and the people of Denmark can be considered within this category. Danish identity construction and the feeling of "us" and "them" rhetoric may result in discrimination against the ethnic minorities left outside of this community and in the further alienation of them. In this case, gang formation is triggered as a negative consequence of social capital. Again, racism, discrimination and social disintegration are considered among the negative consequences of social capital. Warren (2010: 127) emphasised that contextual analyses are required rather than conceptual ones and focuses on the negative externalities produced by social capital. Regarding gang formation in Denmark, negative consequences of social capital are observed in many ways such as ethnic disintegration and criminalisation.

Concluding remarks

The study explored the relationship between the process of marginalisation and negative outcomes of social capital in the case of the *"Copenhagen Gang Wars"*. The theoretical literature on the subject of marginalisation has previously demonstrated links to the outcomes of social capital in terms of relations between members of the in-group and the out-group. Thus, some key questions within the discourse of gang wars in Denmark were discussed. First, how can gang formation be explained? This kind of formations in the context of migration often fall under integration, race and ethnicity studies. For this reason, this study approached the matter from the perspective of marginalisation to look closely at the production of inequalities and discrimination. The second question related to how social capital may emerge as the source of inequality and discrimination in terms of marginalisation of minority groups. To answer this question, we have reviewed the different terms attributed to social capital and its negative results. Finally, in this chapter we argued that gang wars in Denmark could be considered an outcome of the marginalisation process related to negative social capital. For this reason, excluded members of society might be involved in criminal networks for different reasons such as gaining a sense of belonging and recognition from such groups. However, in order to improve policy making and theory formation, further research is necessary in this line of research.

Chapter 3. Distance beyond the border: Kurds of Syria and Turkey in Istanbul[1]

Souad Osseiran

This chapter explores the social and political relations of Kurds from Syria and Turkey, who were living together in a neighbourhood in Istanbul. Kurds from Qamishli in Syria have relatives across the border in Turkey. They are kin who have been separated in the creation of the two nation states. The border did not deter continued ties, marriage, movement and exchange between them. As a consequence of the conflict in Syria, many Syrian nationals came to Istanbul to make their lives there. For many of those with family on the Turkish side of the border, they chose to settle in areas where their Turkish relative are living. For many, it is their first extended encounter with the Kurds of Turkey- their kin from across the border- while others have continuously come and gone to Istanbul for various reasons.

In this chapter, I use the term 'migrant/refugee' as Syrian nationals have been referred to by different statuses since the beginning of the influx into Turkey in 2011. Under the Regulation on Temporary Protection (Regulation no. 29153) released in October 2014, they are referred to as 'persons under temporary protection.' Prior to the release of the regulation they were referred to as 'guests' under the temporary protection of the Turkish state (AFAD, 2013)[2]. Yet Syrian nationals are in different position as some have no documents with them, some have obtained work permits and others are married to Turkish nationals[3]. Regardless of official categories or statuses, many Syrian nationals refer to themselves as refugees[4] while others refuse this identification seeing the term as pejorative. In an effort to maintain the ambiguity of the situation and the

---

[1] Research for this chapter was made possible through two student study grants provided by the British Institute at Ankara (BIAA). I would like to thank Professor Nicholas De Genova and Professor Frances Pine for their comments on previous versions of the chapter. I would also like to thank Rana Abdulfattah for her comments and thoughts on the chapter.

[2] AFAD is Afet ve Acil Durum Yönetimi Başkanlığı (Turkish Disaster and Emergency Management Presidency).

[3] Based on the Citizenship Law no 5901 (2009), obtaining a work permit or marrying a Turkish national are means of entering Turkish citizenship or obtaining permanent residence in Turkey.

[4] Lajā' لاجئ

tension between people's own modes of identification and official ones, migrant/refugee will be used in the chapter.

Syrian migrants/refugees are living in various neighbourhoods in Istanbul, but this chapter focuses on Kurds from Syria living in one neighbourhood amongst their relatives from the Turkish side of the border. My interlocutors used the terms Kurds of Syria or Syria's Kurds (A'krad Swryā) and Turkey's Kurds (A'krad Tarkyā) to distinguish whom they were talking about. Their mode of referencing will be followed in this chapter.

Many Kurds from Syria and Turkey, and in particular those from the border regions, are connected through kinship ties, trade and long standing cross-border relations. The Syrian Kurdish respondents who participated in the research however continuously criticised Turkey's Kurds. The dominant theme they repeated was 'they're different here' and people would either explain why they say this or just shrug indifferently. The complaints were similar to those made by other Syrian migrants/refugees about Turks. The similarity of the complaints highlighted that the tension between Turkey's and Syria's Kurds concerned something more than 'cultural difference'. It is possible to argue that the differences arise from distinct positions with respect to the Turkish state as citizens and non-citizens. In discussing 'difference' between Syria and Turkey's Kurds, the objective is to avoid presenting an account of the differences in such a way as to make them about 'culture' (cf. De Genova & Ramos-Zayas, 2003). I argue that differences, presented as cultural, mask political and economic inequalities. In recognizing the inequalities in citizenship and how they enter into relations, it is possible to evade the objectification of relations or reification of differences. Thus, the attempt is made to avoid approaching Turkey's and Syria's Kurds as "*culturally bounded*" groups.

I argue that the differences vocalized are tied to citizenship in Turkey and to the relationship of each with the Turkish state. The differences relate to a situation where Turkey's Kurds are citizens and Syrian migrants/refugees are outside citizenship (cf. De Genova & Ramos-Zayas, 2003). Turkey's Kurds, while citizens, have a complex relationship with the state as will be discussed. Syrian migrants/refugees' presence is conditional and depends on the Turkish state's continued offer of temporary protection (Regulation No. 29153). The different relationships with the state affect certain aspects of the relations between Turkey's

Kurds and Syria's Kurds living together in this one neighbourhood in Istanbul[5].

In the chapter, the inequalities between Syria's Kurds and Turkey's Kurds are explored, by focusing on the ways the inequalities born from their different positions with respect to the state play out in everyday life. Hence, it is necessary to examine the positions of each with respect to the state: Syrian migrants/refugees as 'persons' under temporary protection and Kurd's in Turkey as citizens who experience a conditional citizenship. I focus on the way the idea of Syrians as 'refugees' was constructed by Kurds in the area, and the way Syrian refugees problematized in this construction. I analyse comments made to Syrian refugees about their consumption practices and how Syrian refugees redirect the criticisms at Kurds in the area. Hospitality was another theme of censure directed at Kurds in the area. Consumption and hospitality are both means of countering the way Syrian migrants/refugees are located socially in the neighbourhood. The themes also provide a means of affirming certain values as socially important for Kurds of Turkey or Syria.

The chapter argues that the inequalities intrinsic to nation state politics of citizenship come into the everyday relations and interactions of Kurds from Syria and Turkey. The politics underpinning Syrian migrant/refugees presence in Turkey as 'persons' under temporary protection, formerly 'guests', enters into the ways Syrian migrants/refugees are being positioned in the social landscape. Underlying the criticisms directed towards their presence and practices is the politics of citizenship. Syria's Kurds, in turn redirect the criticism towards Turkey's Kurds living in the same neighbourhood. The redirection of criticism is an effort to challenge their precarious position in Istanbul. The examples used here are the product of particular historical circumstances where the encounter has come about due to the fighting in Syria and Syrians' migration to Istanbul. The circumstances of this encounter between Kurds from Syria and Turkey are crucial to understanding how relations have played out.

The chapter draws on ethnographic data gathered over the course of sixteen months of fieldwork with Syrian migrants/refugees living in Istanbul. The fieldwork extended from July 2012 until December 2013[6].

---

[5] The researcher cannot comment about other neighborhoods in Istanbul or other cities or provinces in Turkey as the research was restricted to Istanbul. Research conducted in the neighborhood of Aksaray did not raise similar issues.

[6] With Islamic State Fighters moving their fight to Kobanê in 2014 and engaging with Kurdish forces controlling that area, Turkey's Kurds in many areas and cities came out in support of the Kurdish forces in Kobanê (cf. Pérouse, 2014). The events must have affected relations between Syria's and Turkey's Kurds in Istanbul, but further research is necessary to understand the effect of these events.

My research examines Syrian migrants/refugees' presence in Istanbul, their activities, and the ways they mark or make time. During the fieldwork, I spent nine months engaging in participant observation with Syrian migrants/refugees from the city of Qamishli living in the 'Jezera' neighbourhood in Istanbul[7]. The data presented here emerged inadvertently rather than being the main focus of the research. Everyday encounters and events in the area prompted respondents to speak about 'differences' between Turkey and Syria's Kurds. The data was gathered through unstructured interviews undertaken over the course of the nine months. The interviews were held in respondents' homes or in the local park. The interviews were conducted in Arabic as all the respondents speak both Kurdish and Arabic.

Some theoretical considerations
Citizenship and non-citizenship statuses

For the purposes of the chapter, it is useful to begin by thinking about citizenship and non-citizenship as state defined legal statuses (cf. Goldring & Landolt, 2013: 3). As legal statuses each is characterized by rights (cf. Goldring & Landolt, 2013: 3). Non-citizenship statuses are various whether forms of temporary authorization, temporary worker programmes, permanent residence, asylum seeker status, or 'illegal' status to mention a few. Non-citizenship statuses entail different rights and varying degrees of access to them (Goldring & Landolt, 2013; Rajkumar et al., 2012). The rights associated with citizenship or non-citizenship can be political, civil, cultural and social amongst others. The rights change over time, expanding to include some people or contracting and expelling others (Goldring & Landolt, 2013, p. 5). At the same time, rights are no longer necessarily tied to nation states as supra-national bodies such as the EU assign rights to the citizens of all member states (Yeğen, 2004: 51-52).

The section explores the ways Kurds in Turkey have been approached as citizens and the particularities of the form of non-citizenship which Syrian migrants/refugees have under temporary protection. Despite the rights associated with citizenship status, citizenship can be hierarchical and exclusionary. Not all citizens can access their rights in the same way (cf. De Genova & Zayas, 2003). At the same time, many migrants holding different forms of non-citizen status perform citizenship in certain ways and at particular moments (cf. Goldring & Landolt, 2013; Bosniak, 2000).

---

[7] It is necessary to highlight that Syrian migrants/refugees from other provinces such as Aleppo or Damascus were also living in the neighborhood. The data presented here does not incorporate the comments or perspective of Turkey's Kurds due to the time limits of the research. Further research is necessary to situate their perspectives on Syrian migrant/refugees presence beyond the comments mentioned here.

Citizenship and non-citizenship form a spectrum of legal statuses and people move between them officially and unofficially. Regardless of these forms of adoption or movement, the statuses affect the lives of the people holding them in practical and existential ways (cf. Mountz et al., 2002; cf. Young, 2013).

Kurds in Turkey and citizenship

In the early days of the republic, the state emphasised the 'Turkish-ness' of citizens and those applying to become Turkish citizens as part of its efforts to create a homogenous nation. A condition for entering Turkish citizenship was proof of "Turkish descent and culture" (Kirişçi, 2000, p. 4)[8]. The citizenship law changed in 2009, but of interest here is the emphasis on Turkish descent and culture as conditions for membership. These conditions extended beyond persons seeking to become citizens to the ways citizenship was defined (cf. Yeğen, 2004). Yeğen (2004: 55-56) explains that Turkish citizenship appeared to follow a "political/territorial" conception of membership, but closer examination of practices and various official documents shows the ways ethnicity underlies the conception of citizenship. Various ideas of 'Turkish-ness' and being a citizen co-existed (Yeğen, 2004). The emphasis on 'Turkish-ness' and these variations in conception to citizenship, gave rise to exclusionary and assimilationist policies and practices (Yeğen, 2009).

Kurds in Turkey are citizens, but their position as citizens has been complicated by the state approach to citizenship. Yeğen (2009: 607-608) explained how Turkish citizenship as it was formulated in 1924 was two tiered. The model recognized that some people were considered Turkish and others, namely non-Muslim populations in Turkey, were *"Turkish through citizenship"* (Yeğen, 2009: 607-608; 2004: 59-61). Kurds were then positioned as potentially Turkish through assimilation (Yeğen, 2009). They were presented as 'backward' and 'traditional', making them the 'objects' of nationalist modernization projects (Zeydanlioğlu, 2008: 7-10). State policies aimed at 'Turkifying' the Kurdish population (Zeydanlioğlu, 2008: 10-11). The state relied on violence, forcefully moving people westwards, restricting the use of the Kurdish language, targeted educational policies and other processes to transform Kurds into Turks (cf. Yeğen, 2009; cf. Zeydanlioğlu, 2008).

From the 1990s onwards, policies shifted to some extent moving away from forced assimilation. The responses shifted as forced assimilation had not succeeded (Yeğen, 2009). Kurds' position as *"prospective Turks"* has not disappeared entirely but is largely unsettled. The persistence of a sense

---

[8] Alongside Turkish descent and culture, religion was a key consideration (Kirişçi, 2000).

of 'Kurdish-ness', active demands for justice for past acts of state violence, political rights, calls for changes to be made to the definition of citizenship, and demands for language recognition all alter Kurds' position with respect to citizenship. The shift from *"prospective Turks"* has brought into question Kurds' loyalty to the Turkish state (Yeğen, 2009: 610-615).

In 2013, the government made some constitutional 'reforms' that allowed the teaching of Kurdish in private schools and the formation of Kurdish political parties (ICG, 2013). The reforms did not cover many other important issues such as the redefinition of Turkish citizenship, changes to Turkey's anti-terrorism laws or the electoral systems, which were part of Kurdish demands (ICG, 2013: 18-22). Without a redefinition of citizenship within the constitution, Kurds are citizens who unsettle the concept of citizenship in Turkey in its current formulation.

Temporary protected status

Non-citizenship in the case of Syrian migrants/refugees is a situation of conditional presence. With the start of the influx of Syrian nationals into Turkey in April 2011, the state granted those entering 'guest', misafir, status. Soon after, the state announced that Syrian refugees entering Turkey are under the temporary protection of the Turkish state. Temporary protection is an international concept used elsewhere, in the US (Mountz et al., 20002) and EU states (Koser & Black 1999), in cases of mass refugee influx. The state declared the temporary protection, but did not release the regulation to clarify Syrian refugees' rights or obligations (Yinanç, 2013). At the same time, Syrian migrants/refugees continued to be referred to as 'guests' (Yinanç, 2013; AFAD 2013). 'Guest' status, without an announcement of the terms of the temporary protection, made their presence contingent on the state's continued benevolence (cf. Kirişçi, 2000: 12; cf. Özden, 2013: 5; cf. Yinanç, 2013).

The Regulation on Temporary Protection was released in October 2014. It outlines the rights and duties of those to whom it is applied[9]. Based on the regulation, Syrian nationals are referred to as 'persons under temporary protection' (Regulation no. 29153, art. 3(1- f, g)). The Regulation explains that the Council of Ministers have the authority to decide the duration of the temporary protection, the regions or areas within Turkey to which it will be applied, and the extent of the access to services such as healthcare or education (Regulation no. 29153, art. 9, (1); art. 10, (1); art. 11; İneli-Ciğer 2014). The time migrants/refugee spend in Turkey under temporary

---

[9] Law No. 6458 on Foreigners and International Protection released in April 2013 mentions temporary protection. It explained that further legislation was required to clarify various points of the temporary protection. The Regulation fulfills this aim though some issues remain unclear (cf. İneli-Ciğer 2014).

protection does not count towards citizenship (Regulation no. 29153, art. 25, (1)). According to the regulation, Temporary protection is expected to end with the return of migrants/refugees, but the Regulation articulates the possibilities of their remaining under different statuses (art. 11; art. 14). Temporary protection sets up Syrian migrants/refugees presence as a conditional presence contingent on the state (cf. Mountz et al., 2002). Future presence under a different status is possible, but still dependent on the government in power at that time.

Citizenship and non-citizenship statuses give rise to inequalities. In the case of Turkey's Kurds and Syrian migrants/refugees, the inequalities are experienced in distinct ways. The relationship with the state generates substantive inequalities between Kurds from Syria and Turkey. The inequalities emerge in the current context where Kurds from Syria and Turkey are living together. As part of the encounter and sharing of spaces, the inequalities are constructed as 'cultural' terms of difference and enter into the everyday lives of Syrian migrants/ refugees and Kurds in Turkey.

Ethnographic considerations

Various ethnographies highlight the ways differences stemming from positions of inequality emerge in interlocutors' discourses about close 'others'. Green (1998) undertaking fieldwork in Northern Greece, in the Epirots region, found that many interlocutors had relatives across the border in Albanian. The Epirots region was divided by the forming of the two states. Relations continued between kin living across the border despite the border. In the early 1990s, many of those kin from Albanian crossed the border into Greece. While originally aided by their relatives in Greece, with the growing numbers coming into the area Green's (1998: 97-98) Greek interlocutors' discourse about their relatives changed. Many interlocutors' discourses shifted from highlighting the kinship ties with their relatives across the border to downplaying those ties on the basis the Greek speaking migrants' from Albanian had become Albanian. They shifted from an ethnic discourse to a nationalist one due to the intensified encounter. Green (1998) explains that the migrants arriving posed a threat as labour power and their reliance on local resources to survive. Similarly, Pilkington (1998) explores the relationship between Russian speaking migrants and refugees returning to Russia from former Soviet Republics and the local communities the migrants and refugees moved to. Pilkington (1998) explains how Russian speaking migrants and refugees returning to these areas in Russia enacted cultural and social boundaries distinguishing themselves from the local communities. Drawing from the engagement of various actors, she outlines the ways the boundaries between the migrant/refugee 'we' and the local 'them' is enacted. In the context of

Turkey, Parla (2007), examines the ways Bulgarian Turks migrating to Istanbul after 1990 to work were approached differently by Turkish citizens and the state than Bulgarian Turks who came to Turkey in 1989 and were given citizenship as political refugees. She argues that those who came in 1989 were approached as "ethnic kin" who were returning to the homeland whereas those entering after 1990 were evaluated in terms of their labour and deemed temporarily present. The differentiation and designation of Bulgarian Turks coming in the post-1990 period as 'other' was due to the reasons underlying their presence in Turkey and the potential temporariness of their presence occurred despite ethnic, linguistic, and religious commonality. Due to the differentiation, the post-1990 migrants Parla (2007: 169) conducted fieldwork with assigned their belonging as elsewhere in Bulgaria rather than in Turkey as part of the 'Turkish' nation. Alternately, De Genova and Ramos Zayas (2003) rely on their distinct fieldworks to examine and problematize the ways the term 'Latino' is applied to a multitude of persons in the US. They analysed the ways two groups: Mexican migrants and their US born children, and Puerto Ricans and their US born children engage and their discourses about each other. Their research criticizes the ways 'Latino' is applied as a homogenizing category by exploring the tensions in the relations between Mexican migrants and Puerto Ricans living in Chicago. They argue that the engagement takes particular forms and certain boundaries are evoked due to the relationship of each migrants and Puerto Ricans to the US state. De Genova and Ramos Zayas (2003), situate the engagement of the two groups with each other in terms of citizenship rather than social or cultural differences. The various research highlight that identification with a particular ethnic category or marker is not only contingent and contextual, but also lacks the possibility for homogenization. In many instances, boundaries are evoked with close others and distant kin. Examining the underlying relations whether to the state or as labour complicates the distinctions evoked and moves the argument from one of social or cultural difference to the political and economic.

In this context, Kurds from Syria's criticisms to their kin from Turkey hinged around the construction of Syrian migrants/refugees as 'refugees', disputes about consumption practices, class performance and hospitality.

Being in need
The figure of the refugee and what it means to be a refugee is complex and problematic. Who is a refugee? Who is in exile? When does one stop being a refugee? What are the ways in which it is enacted? The image of refugees conjures the expectation of being 'in need'. However, refugees are not identical, as class, race, and religion all affect individuals'

experiences of being 'refugees' (Malkki, 1995). The image developed by the state and media in Turkey is that of a refugee population[10]. In the following, I focus on the ways refugee-ness as a state of being in need was problematized by Syrian migrants/refugees.

They contested discourses they were facing from Turkey's Kurds that constructed them as 'taking' or 'being in need' (Malkki, 1995: 159). The stories and criticisms would have been shared in any case, but some were purposefully recounted due to my capacity as an anthropologist researching the situation and conditions of Syrian migrant/refugee presence in Istanbul. Migrants/refugees sought to show how they do not fulfill the idea of refugee-ness as it is formed for them. In clarifying their position, they challenge their position of inequality in Turkey. In countering the claims of being in need and asserting their dignity they also, in a way, criticised my project and presence.

I returned to Turkey in August 2013 after traveling and went to see Amira. Amira is a woman in her early 40s from Qamishli. She had been living in Istanbul with her husband and children from prior to the uprising in Syria. Her family came to Turkey to seek asylum, because her husband had faced problems with the intelligence apparatus in Syria. At the time they moved to the neighbourhood, there were only a few other families from Syria living there. Amira witnessed the neighbourhood slowly change as more families from Syria began arriving from 2011 onwards. I asked her about the other families I know in the area to catch up on events. Some of the Kora family members, a family both of us know, had a huge fight with some Kurds in the area on a street close to where the Kora family were living. There was an exchange of insults in the street and it erupted into violence. The police and local municipal authorities intervened to end it as did the Kora family's Turkish relatives. Amira had complained many times before about how Kurds 'here' treated Syrian migrants/refugees, but it had not escalated into violence until that point. Amira explained that Kurds were complaining about Syrian

---

[10] Images of Syrians as 'refugees' in need are disseminated to the Turkish public through media coverage and images of people crossing the border from Syria. Images and reports about the refugee camps inside Turkey and the situation of Syrian migrants/refugees in different Turkish cities adds to general understanding of Syrian's situation in Turkey. Some government and politicians' comments and statements also evoke the image of Syrian nationals in Turkey 'refugees' in need or alternately as 'migrants' who are taking from Turkish nationals. Billboard advertisements asking for donations for aid operations in Syria are visible in Istanbul both at street level and in certain banks. These images also promote the conceptualization of Syrian migrants/refugees as being 'in need'. These images counter other discourses within Turkey that questions the state support for Syrian refugees and the revolution in Syria; however covering all of these issues are beyond the scope of the chapter.

migrants/refugees crowding the neighbourhood, competing for jobs, and raising the cost of goods and rent (cf. Green 96). She addressed the complaints arguing that Syrian presence was neither taking from Turkey's Kurds nor affecting them badly.

"They have profited too here, they speak as if the Syrians are receiving assistance or something. They are not. They are living out of their own work. They are paying their rent here out of their own work and effort. They are putting their money into the country.... The state wants people to come here. They do... They want them registered (in the camp) and then they can go where ever. If the state didn't want people to come here it wouldn't let people move around. They complain like in the Pazar[11], as you know when it is close to the evening everyone goes shopping for vegetables because they bring the prices down. The women might come out in the day and buy clothes or eggs for instance but the vegetables most people wait till the evening. Now you can hear the women complaining in the evening of the Pazar, 'ouff we can't walk there are so many people since the Syrians came'. A friend of ours when the fight happened he heard an old lady from here saying in front of him, 'what are these Syrians? When they came we went around and begged for a carpet and a mattress for them.' He told her, 'excuse me we do not usually talk out of politeness but you should not be saying that. It is not appropriate. How many Syrian families did you beg things for? We ask each other, we never ask you for help.'"

Amira's response is a refusal of the position assigned to her and other Syrians within the local social landscape. Amira contested it by evoking migrants/refugees' labour and contribution as indicators of their independence. Additionally, she drew on the image of a community that assists its own disputing the idea that Syrian migrants/refugees are burdensome. Interestingly, in other instances Amira complained about Syrian migrants/refugees in the area for various reasons such as their refusal to share information about access to resources. However, in that moment when she was talking about the claims of Kurds in the area and the fight, countering those claims was more important than addressing her issues with other Syrian migrants/refugees.

The issue of need appeared as a theme for critique with other respondents. Oum Jamal is a widower in her 60s from the city of Qamishli. She had been living in Damascus for several years before the uprising began as well as keeping a house in Qamishli. She left Damascus in the summer of 2012 and went to Qamishli before travelling to Istanbul. Her

---

[11] The Pazar is the weekly market which takes place in the area. It takes place in neighbourhoods all over the city on different days of the week.

youngest son had been working in Lebanon for many years and he provided for her and his unmarried sister who lived with her. She is considered an important figure in her extended family with family members asking for her advice on different matters. She complained about how Kurds in the area spoke about Syrians. In particular if they used their flight from Syria as a reason for pity. Oum Jamal found such discourse undignified. In June 2013, she recounted with anger,

"*The Turks here think we are wealthy. Yesterday in the Pazar I was buying tomatoes with Aliaa and I asked the man for only 2 lira, he told me no, you say you have no money, but look at the gold bracelets on your hand, you say you have no money but you have! I told him these bracelets are not from your father! Give me back my money I will not buy from you! The Turks act as if we have come here to beg[12]. We were not like this in Syria. When people came in from Deir or Raqa we did not do this, we knew these people came from houses not from the street[13]. They had a house before they fled. In Syria no one lives on the street. We would not have done this.*"

In his response to Oum Jamal, the tomato seller equated being a 'refugee' with 'being in need'. A particular idea of Syrians as refugees and in need steps in for all Syrian migrants/refugees. In the process, individuals' histories and socio-economic differences are glossed over. The category of 'refugee' here homogenizes the people it is assigned to and levels out inequalities or differences such as social status or class. Oum Jamal with her gold bracelets confused the idea of being 'in need' and by extension her position as a potential refugee. She raised the suspicion that she was not a proper 'refugee' because she displayed signs of wealth. She rejected the homogenization of Syrians as one kind of refugee, which constructed them as equally in need. The construction raised questions of deservedness when Syrian migrants/refugees complicated the category.

Oum Jamal's understanding of being a 'refugee' was more complex accounting for class and material wealth. Oum Jamal compared the way Syrian migrants/refugees were being constituted as 'refugees' in Istanbul with the ways people in Qamishli categorized Syrians coming to the area fleeing the fighting in their areas. Through the comparison, Oum Jamal criticized the treatment she had received in Turkey. She explained that people in Qamishli dealt with those who came to the city based on an understanding of social class and status in Syria. Despite their displacement those who fled were not homogenized. Even though people

---

[12] الاتراك بيتصرفوا كأن نحن جاين نشحد Alatrak bytṣrfwā ka'n nhn jayn nishḥd
[13] Deir ez Zor and Raqa are two provinces close to Qamishli province.

fleeing might be strangers to Qamishli[14], their social status and class has more relevance and was easier to read, than it does in the context of Istanbul. Her response brings up the issue of social relations and position in Syria which are undermined by the move to Istanbul. Oum Jamal also began her complaint with the words, 'The Turks' and then spoke about the tomato seller, but Oum Jamal did not speak Turkish. She speaks Kurdish and Arabic, and when I went with her to the Pazar she spoke to the vendors in Kurdish. In her comment, she collapsed differences between Kurds and Turks, distancing Kurds in Turkey from Syria's Kurds in their practices and attitudes (cf. Green, 1998).

Nadia is a friend of Amira's who is in her early thirties, and the mother of three children. She had visited this part of Istanbul many times as her mother and siblings, who have Turkish nationality, live there. Her husband had sustained a work related leg injury in 2010 and was unable to work, so they decided to move from Qamishli to Istanbul. Nadia has been sorting out her claim to become a Turkish citizen in a bid to help her family settle in Turkey.

In the summer of 2013, I visited her after the family moved to a new apartment in a different part of Jezera neighbourhood. It was a basement apartment in a newly constructed building. They stayed there only a few months as the landlord gave them problems prompting them to move out. It was the basement apartment and there was a vent, 1.5 by 1.5 metres, which all the kitchen windows of the above apartments opened onto. During one visit as we sat talking in the kitchen, I heard her neighbours talking in an above kitchen. She laughed when I pointed it out, *"Yeah! See we can hear everything! In the hall or in the corridor if I say hello none of them respond, they just walk past. They think they are in Europe! Köy means village in Turkey and this is part of ---köy, they are living in a village not Europe!!"*

Her ability to tune into her neighbours fights and conversations- their personal lives- was contrasted to the way they performed neighbourly relations. She interpreted their performance as imitating ideas of relations in Europe. Europe is known for neighbours being unfamiliar with each other despite living in close proximity. Nadia used the area's name, an indicator of its status as a former village, to criticise their performance.

---

[14] Kenan, Amira's husband, had explained to me that many Kurds from Qamishli sold their properties there in the early 2000s and moved to Damascus or Aleppo. The move happened following draught in the Northern provinces. Following the start of the uprising in 2010, some Kurds from Qamishli living in Damascus moved back to Qamishli, but faced difficulties as they no longer had a base there. Some decided to move on to Turkey from Qamishli.

The family moved out of that flat a few months later and moved into another basement apartment a few streets away. I visited her in the winter of 2014, and she met me at the top of the road to guide me to their house. She explained that the street was 'mushrshḥ[15]', but the people kinder and more helpful than the ones living in the other building. She then reflected on the difference and related it to the socio-economic situation of her current and former neighbours. Nadia originally explained her former neighbours' performance as trying to be European, but then considered that it might be because of their socio-economic situation. By ignoring Nadia in the hall, her neighbours situated their middle class status in contrast to her socio-economic status. Nadia's family's situation as not quite middle class might have served as a reminder of something her neighbours wanted to forget- a reminder of their migration to Istanbul or attempts to change their socio-economic statuses.

Consumption

Interlocutors used food to discuss consumption and hospitality. Consumption was a theme through which the inequalities were articulated. Syria's Kurds' consumption was noticed and commented on by their neighbours. Various respondents recounted how Kurds in the neighbourhood made judgements about them due to their consumption. They then redirected the criticism back at Turkey's Kurds. In directing the censure back at Turkey's Kurds, respondents sought to readdress their unequal footing in the social landscape. Some migrants/refugees' consumption practices confused the ways they are constructed as 'refugees' who are in need. The consumption practices raised questions about deservedness. It raised the question of how some of Syria's Kurds who have come as 'refugees' can engage in conspicuous consumption?

Amira's relative, Abu Ahmed, came to Jezera in the summer of 2013 as two of his sons were going to be drafted for mandatory military service. His household in Istanbul comprised between seven and nine people. A greengrocer in Syria, his family would have been considered working class. In Istanbul, his adult children are working to maintain the family. They lived in a ground floor apartment that summer and became acquainted with their neighbours as a result. Neighbours in the building next door to them, mainly elderly and middle aged ladies, would sit outside their building on the steps working and socializing in the afternoons and early evenings. They watched their children play as they worked on fleece for household bedding or other chores. Sitting outside was partly a way to observe their neighbours', comment on them and

---

[15] مشرشح Unkempt and can be used to refer to poor.

socialize with them. The family never commented about any of their neighbours, especially as some had helped them, but rather made general complaints. Abu Ahmed explained that his neighbours' eyes would grow big when they saw how much fruit and vegetable he brought home from the Pazar. He recounted a neighbour's comment on his family's consumption,

"They tell me you Syrians work to eat, you like your stomachs (he patted his belly as he said it) Here they are not like this. The other day they saw how much bread I brought and the neighbour asked me, 'is all this for your family?' I of course told her no we have guests coming. They buy their bread once and they buy a small amount."

The family's consumption, a visible practice, made them vulnerable to censure. The comment highlighted that modest consumption is socially valued (De Genova & Ramos Zayas, 2003). At the same time, the comment indicated that the family's consumption belied the idea that they are in need. Their consumption practices confuse the construction of 'refugee'. It raises questions about how some Syrians as migrants/refugees are able to consume in this manner.

Underlying the comment is also an issue of division between citizens and non-citizens. In saying that Syrians work to eat- consume the fruit of their labour- the context behind their presence in Turkey is highlighted. Families or individuals seeking to settle in Istanbul would use their money differently, perhaps saving it for a long term investment. These respondents were neither saving their money to spend it elsewhere nor were they spending it in a way which would indicate their intention to settle in Turkey. The fact they were in Turkey temporarily with the hope of return meant what is produced here can also be consumed here. It fosters no ties or links to an elsewhere. It situates them as both temporarily present, with a forecasted future elsewhere, in Syria or a third country, which is deferred or unclear at present.

Hospitality

Hospitality is another practice where Turkey's Kurds were designated as culturally different. Hospitality entails being open to others, kin or strangers, and willingly providing them with shelter and sustenance. Kenan, Amira's husband, used hospitality as an example of how Turkey's Kurds are different. Hospitality as a valued social performance emerges as important for Kurds from Syria especially as an obligation they have not received in Turkey. Kenan had agreed to take me to meet some families from Qamishli living in the area when I first began coming there towards the end of 2012. He knew many of the families from Qamishli living in the area and had good ties with them. He directed families to the various

NGOs in Istanbul, because he had been living in the city for longer and knew the different NGOs that offer assistance to migrants and refugees. Having lived in Turkey for longer, he was also better acquainted with Kurds in the area. We set off one evening in January 2013 after having dinner with his family, and he spoke about Turkey's Kurds as we walked.

"Yes (they are relatives) but they are different[16]. The Kurds in Syria they will sell a child to make their guest feel welcome. The Kurds here, they only follow money. They will not let you stay more than a few days with them..."

In downplaying Turkey's Kurds' hospitality, Kenan touched on Syrian migrants/refugees' position as persons who have been forced to seek refuge. Kurds from Syria have come to the area as refugees and guests. They are dependent in some instances on extended family for shelter and sustenance until they rent an apartment. They experience their relatives' hospitality from a position of need which affects how the hospitality is received.

Amira's cousin was visiting her family when I came by one day. He is a Kurd from Syria in his mid-forties who had been living in Mardin for several years. He owned a super-market there, but had decided to move on to Europe. He had been unable to get Turkish citizenship, even though his mother was born in Turkey and he had applied for citizenship. He believed that the process was taking a long time because he is Kurdish. He was staying with his maternal aunt and her family while he was in Istanbul. That day Amira was convincing him to spend the night at her house as she knew he was uncomfortable in his aunt's house. He said of his relatives,

"I love my aunt but I can't stand her children. Even though they are wealthy, I am wealthier in hospitality[17]. When I want to eat, I cook and then whomever is around I call them into my supermarket. The Turks they hide their food under the table if they see their brother coming into the store. They are always amazed at me..."

Hospitality is a desirable and valued quality and part of social practices. His generosity is contrasted to his relatives' perceived material wealth. He recognized that having something of value, but insisted that the immaterial quality of hospitality was superior. It is an attempt to mitigate the existent inequality between him and his relatives where they are citizens and he is not. He moves from the personal to a generalization making his relative's behaviour, their lack of hospitality, common across Turkey. While criticising his relatives or Turks in general, he explains how hospitality is a quality valued by Kurds in Syria. He describes his performance as a means

---

[16] I had asked him, 'But aren't the Kurds here and the ones in Syria relatives?'

[17] ولو هني اغنيا بس انا اغنى بالضيافة wlw hny āghnya bas ana aghnai bldyafa.

of substantiating the claim that Kurds from Syria are hospitable. The comments are both a critique and serve as reminders for Syria's Kurds of desirable qualities. Syrians regardless of the region or locality they come from can explain or cite stereotypes and jokes about their region and other regions. For instance, people from some areas or cities are known for their stinginess and others for their generosity. In this case, his comment is directed at Turks and Kurds in Turkey. The differences in Syria are irrelevant, where what is at stake is shifting his position of inequality with respect to Turkish citizens.

Conclusion

In this chapter, I explored how citizenship enters into the daily interactions and relations of Kurds from Syria and Turkey in Istanbul. I argued that the differences cited by my interlocutors arise from the inequalities of citizenship rather than as a matter of 'culture'. The inequalities emerge in both obvious and nuanced ways in everyday life whether as criticisms or comments about consumption or hospitality or being 'in need'. In analysing the criticisms, comments, and circumstances in which they arise, it is possible to examine the underlying politics of citizenship that affects Syria's and Turkey's Kurds in relationship with each other. The differences stem from political inequalities, as opposed to culture. The exchanges and interactions are avenues that serve to mitigate the inequalities experienced due to their positions. Syria's Kurds, officially temporarily protected by the state, attempt to distinguish themselves from Kurds in the area to contest the temporary nature of their presence in Turkey. The exchanges are a means of alleviating their position of disadvantage. They challenge ideas constructed of them as being 'in need' because of the war in Syria and their migration to Istanbul. Similarly, consumption and hospitality are practices used to highlight their moral superiority to Turkey's Kurds. The comments made by some of Turkey's Kurds' to the Syrian respondents mentioned in the chapter, situate Syrian migrants/refugees within the local social landscape; they are approached as competition for jobs and resources. Supposed differences in culture, thus strategically mask political and economic inequalities. The inequalities are established by the state in its policy of ambiguity, regarding Syrian migrant/refugee presence, as well as its continual downplaying of Turkey's Kurds' who demand more inclusive citizenship.

Chapter 4. Border people's border perception: The case of Shemdinli (Shemdinan)

Ferhat Tekin

Whether it is territorial or sociopolitical, the border is a sociological factor that gains its significance and function from the people it divides. In other words, it functions as the main instrument for all types of categorizations (social, political, ideological etc.). There is no doubt that demarcating has been an act since the early history of humankind. Individuals, groups, societies or political entities marked borders in almost all periods in order to determine themselves. However, the determination of borders based on soil is completely a modern fact and the rigid and sharp lines are also unique to the modern nation-state.

Based on the idea of the nation-state, territorial borders were handled from a statist, positivist and macro perspective for a very long period (almost throughout the 20th Century). As Donnan and Wilson point out, international borders were considered as spaces reflecting the physical borders of state power and at the same time special expressions of territorial divisions and political organization of states (2002: 83). Furthermore, Özgen stresses that traditional studies carried out on borders are related to *"humanless spaces and that these are based on macro and geophysical levels"* (2004: 6). However, with globalization and the spread of post-modern theory, the rich interdisciplinary researches in the 1990's led to the perception of borders as social formations possessing both material and symbolic appearance instead of determining them as signs reflecting the rigid and absolute lines of the state (Diener and Hagen, 2010: 9). During this period, a wider international community of border scholars in contrast to their predecessors developed new perspectives theorizing the political, economic, social, psychological, and cultural meanings of borders (Paasi, 2009: 218).

Therefore, this chapter focuses on borders, people and their border perception, inspired by post-modern, micro, anti-deterministic and anti-positivist approaches to borders. In this context, it centres upon the perception of the border, how the border people live with it, what relationship they have with the people of other side of the border who are members of the Gerdi tribe living in the Turkey-Iraq border region (Şemdinli-Derecik). The study was carried out in 9 villages tied to the

Gerdi tribe.[1] Attention was paid to provide a heterogeneous group in terms of age, marital status, gender, and profession. Thus, the interviews were maintained with various people such as old, middle-aged and young; male and female; married, single and divorced; working as a village guard, artisan, smuggler, farmer and housewife. In this framework, interviews were carried out with a total of 62 participants of whom 42 were men and 20 women.

Here, I would like to summarize the methodology of the research. The study was completely qualitative. Therefore, this fieldwork made use of techniques such as case studies, focus group discussions, semi-structured questionnaires and dialogues based on observations and listening to life stories.

Nation-State borders and border people

Edward Soja states in his work *The Political Organization of Space* (1971) that the nation-state is the most common organizational structure in human history and expresses that the territorial characteristic of this socio-political organization is extremely visible. In pre-modern social organizations, there was *"a social definition of the territory rather than a territorial definition a society"* (Soja, 1971: 13). However, as Soja puts it, the arrangement of space in that sense has changed in the modern era. Thus, the central state of the pre-modern and especially the Western nation-state system needed a dynamic, functional organisation drawn clearly and rigidly, in which society is within the defined borders in order to provide coordination, integration and the stability of administration (Soja, 1971: 15). In other words, *"the political society was defined in terms of territory with the appearance of especially Western nationalism, and there was a transition (a move) from jus sanguinis to jus solis"* (Soja, 1971: 15).

Borders are the aspects determining the territorial limits of state hegemony, in other words drawing the framework of national spaces in terms of the nation-state. In consequence, they point to the realm of state authority and to the nationality of the space. In this context, as put by Gupta and Ferguson, territory, space and culture are considered isomorphic since in the eyes of the state territorial borders were related equally to both national and cultural borders (1992:7). However, this consideration is problematic in many aspects because people, groups or societies located in the periphery of the territory or the border region are not seen as having

---

[1]Villages in which the study was conducted: Aralık (Perave), Beşikağaç (Nıhava), Derecik (Rubarok), Dereboyu (Çemekürk), Gökçetaş (Müseka), Kırca (Begor), Koryürek (Begıjne), Samanlı (Mava), Yeşilova (İsya).

social networks with the other side of the border. In fact, many border societies have social, cultural, economic, etc. ties with the other side of the border. It is possible to come across this fact in many parts of the world, but the Middle-Eastern geography including Turkey might be the region with the highest rate. For instance, in almost all borders of Turkey in the south (Syria), east (Iraq, Iran) and north-east (Georgia) have socio-cultural and economic relations with the other side, which they continue in official and unofficial ways.

The modern territorial state often drew a line ignoring human relations (or relatives). Consequently, many parts of the world and especially the everyday life was disrupted. Thus, as Ahmed states:

The foundation of states in Africa and Asia meant a separation considered cruel by the members of tribes since it divided their villages and tribes. A significant example are the Pathans who are separated between Afghanistan and Pakistan ... another example valid today is the case of the Kurds who have a noble but tragic fate and deep roots, and are divided among half a dozen nations. Muslim tribes are right in blaming Western forces for attempting to draw down and dirty borders (Ahmed, 1995: 156).

Actually, no matter how the border attempts to separate people of the same ethnicity, society or community and to impose on them a different identity and culture, it usually has not been successful. In Horsman and Marshall's words, *"there always has been a tension between the stagnant, enduring and rigid requirements of national borders, and the changing, temporary and flexible requirements of humans. If the basic fiction of the nation-state is ethnic, racial, linguistic and cultural homogeneity; these borders keep denying this structure"* (Donnan & Wilson, 2002: 11).

In general, if the culture of the region connects the two sides of the border, it challenges the border functioning as a hindrance and this weakens its "border effect" (Brunet-Jailly & Dupeyron, 2007: 6). Therefore, if the culture of border societies can be observed on the other side, that is, if language, religion, ethnicity and socio-economic indicators are prevalent on the other side of the border, it can be said that these international borders are challenged (2007: 6). This perspective on the border culture can be observed in the South-eastern borders of Turkey. Especially, Şemdinli, which is the subject of study here, is one of the regions where such a border culture can clearly be seen since the same cultural characteristics are present on both sides of the border. Thus, the "border effect" is quite weak here.

Perception of border among the residents of Şemdinli (the Gerdi Tribe)

Usually, there are huge differences in terms of border perceptions among the border societies or border people and those looking into the matter from a nation-state or official perspective. For the former group, the border means a divisional line enforced and unfairly applied in their social spaces; whereas, for the latter, border and culture are isomorphic and border means a wall of "difference" and "security" separating "us" from the "foreigner". However, border communities do not perceive it as imposed by the central authority, on the contrary, they perceive the border as something dividing their life space (territorial space) and dividing them from each other. It is possible to say that this perception is dominant in the border regions in the South, East and Northeast of Turkey. For instance, the border perception in Ceylanpınar, Nusaybin, Silopi, Uludere, Çukurca, Şemdinli, Saray, Posof, Borçka and Hopa exactly oppose to the official/central perception.

In this context, as Migdal underlines *"mental maps may challenge official maps or school maps"* when it comes to borders (2004:7) because this is one of the most natural aspects of the socio-cultural and economic past/history of people from both sides. To put it another way, the history of the mentioned border people is much older than that of the border. Therefore, the strength of the spatial-social memory relation here reinforces the perception of the border as an artificial and imposed phenomenon (Tekin, 2013: 62). In this regard, stories, memories, pains, reunions, happy moments in the minds of the border community take an important place. However, this memory is a wounded one because the hampering role of the border is the cause for this wound. Therefore, if it is looked upon from the perspective of the border community, the border is always a hurtful phenomenon due to its permanent prohibition and disruptiveness. Their minds or mental maps perceive the border in relation to negative experience instead of the mental map of nation-state.

Especially, since the 1990's, the relations of border people in Turkey to the Turkey-Iraq border (Şemdinli, Çukurca, Uludere etc.) with the other side can be seen in two ways. In fact, socio-cultural and economic ties between the tribes separated by the border have been continued until the 1980's and 1990's – though interrupted occasionally. However, with the intensifying struggle between the PKK and the Turkish state in the late 1980's and early 1990's, these relations were seriously affected. Nevertheless, it is obvious that border villages accepting the "village guardianship" in those years continued their relations with the other side due to this guardianship. On the other hand, some groups who lived in the border region but had not accepted the guardianship and thus had moved to inner regions weakened their ties with their relatives on the other side of the border. As a consequence, as Özgen and Birgün put it, *"since the uprisings of the PKK, being a border citizen is determined by whether or not to accept bribe given by the state in order to prevent the support of the organization. If you live on the border line, you accept the guardianship and make sure of smuggling continues"* (Özgen, Birgün, 2013). Otherwise, you leave your home and are deprived from the social and economic revenue of the border.

The economic activities with the other side of the border improved the living standards of the Gerdi tribe. People of the region express that their material wealth has increased especially since the 1990's and mention that two major factors played a role: the permission of the state to smuggle and the autonomy of the Kurds on the other side. Thus, after the Iraqi Kurds obtained a regional administrative identity, their material conditions changed positively and this change influenced this side of the border.

One border citizen implies that the border trade intensified from the 1990's on and gained an unofficial legitimacy due to several reasons (guardianship and financial difficulties):

The border trade gained importance especially since 1992-1993. Most of the people in the region make their living through the trade. Horticulture has weakened to a great extent. In fact, the wages from village guardianship is not sufficient to make ends meet. What is left is only the border trade. The officials here are also aware of it. They know about the ties (relatives, tribe) we have with the other side. Therefore, we are able to do free trade (Koryürek, male, aged 45).

Despite the fact that the Gerdis benefit from the revenues of the border, they feel insecure and anxious. The reason for this is the probability that they might face a similar experience like in Roboski (Uludere). As seen in the case of Roboski, there is no legitimacy of their relationship with the other side although they have tribal and family relations with them. Consequently, the thing that worries them most is that they might any moment face an official view saying "they are violating the border" and what might happen afterwards. Therefore, as Özgen states:

"Today you may cross but tomorrow you may not, today you may smuggle but tomorrow you may be killed; now, you might be considered legal, an hour later you might be evaluated otherwise. However, those living on the border are aware of all the lies. They also know how hurtful it is to be exposed to lies. They are aware of the pain caused by being the subject of lies, and the fury of being the object of lies" (2013: 2).

A woman (aged 55) living in the village Aralık (Pareve) and whose one son and brother live on the other side (Diyana) expressed that they were not much affected; neither from the social nor from the cultural aspect when the two states separated the land. Actually, what this woman stated, as shown below, reflects in general terms the views of the people from the border region (Rubarok/Derecik). In other words, the border is perceived from a geographical aspect. The physical appearance (wires, mines, towers) is quite insignificant when compared to the Turkish-Syrian border. There is a border but it is not that concrete to invade people's minds.

The border here is Rabar (stream Hacıbekir). This side is in Turkey, the other side is in Iraq. However, this has never affected our relations with the other side of the border. We come and go whenever we want. It does no matter if we go to Besüsen (Ortaklar) or to Beşiley (aged 55, female).[2]

As can be understood from these statements, the Gerdi tribe uses the names of the places (villages and towns) when referring to the "other side of the border". For example, they prefer to say "this or that in Diyana" or "this or that relative in Bermize" (Kurdish) instead of saying "those on the other side of the border" or "Iraqi Kurds" when they speak of their relatives there. But if moved further inland like Hakkari (Colemerg) centre or Yüksekova (Gewer), they prefer to use "Iraqi Kurds" for the people on the other side. No doubt that this difference is related to their kinship with the other side and the type of relationship they have. As stated above, the border divided the Gerdi tribe into two. However, this never led to the perception of being member of two nation states. To put it in another way, although the border divided them spatially, there is no such border in their minds. Their connection from the psycho-social and socio-cultural perspective reflects this fact. Consequently, they continue their tribal and relative connections intensively. They keep on visiting each other and have mixed marriages. As Baud and Schendel put it, "borders separate people on both sides who have social and cultural historical ties, but at the same time unite them since they both are bounded to the border. This paradox character of the border should be kept in mind as a metaphor of the blurriness of nation building" (1997: 243).

Rural dissolution in the east and southeast where Kurds are mainly located and the weakening dissolution of tribal and family ties along with urbanization are quite visible. Tribal and family ties, on the other hand, are stronger in rural societies. This fact can be seen in the Gerdi tribe. Moreover, the strength of relations and tribal ideology among the Gerdi is not restricted to this side of the border.

---

[2] Beşiley is a village of the Gerdi tribe on the other side of the border.

A member of the Gerdi (aged 70) who was interviewed in Derecik, states the hardship of keeping their relations with their families on the other side implying the tribal ideology:

First of all, both members from this side and the other side are the same. We are cousins (pismam).³ Being related means being together in all cases. Even if there is a border between us, this does not weaken our family relationships. We share our pains and joys often by visiting each other. We further enforce our relations with mixed marriages.

In addition, an inhabitant of Kırca (Begor) speaks of their closeness with them in reference to the Gerdi region on the other side of the border:

I do not think that there is a difference between us and them because everything is the same, from our customs to our lifestyles and the way we talk. However, there is a great difference between us and Colemerg (Hakkari) and Gewer (Yüksekova) in many ways. It is not just us who say this; those coming from there (Hakkari, Yüksekova) also state that we are different in many ways (male, aged 52).

On the other hand, an old man from the town Derecik (Rübarok) said the following implying the situation prior to the border:

"We are family with the people from the other side; we are of the same tribe. 80-90 years ago, there was no such thing as a border. The English came and divided us according to their interests. Some of us were left here (Turkey) and some of us on the other side (Iraq). But we did not break away, we kept on visiting each other and we still do it. First of all, we are related to those on the other side, share the same customs, traditions and conventions. We have mixed marriages and trade with each other. Therefore, we certainly feel closer to the other side in contrast to Hakkari and Yüksekova".

As can be understood from the statements above, tribal and family relations tightly connected the Gerdi on both sides of the border. In other words, the Gerdi tribe responded to the border dividing its territory into two with tribal and family ties, but did not attempt to challenge the border itself. Instead, they caused the transformation of the border, to which they were imposed for 90 years, with various applications during various periods. Thus, they adapted the border with their social capital based on family connections to their socio-cultural spatial structure. Consequently, a culture unique to the border emerged.

---

³ In the tribal ideology, the term cousin (pısmam) has a much wider meaning. For a member everyone coming from the same ancestor is a cousin. This term is so wide-reaching that it is even used for people whom they have never met. In other words, it can be seen as an "imagined community".

Conclusion

One of the significant outcomes of this study is that the border people perceive the border in their own way, which is in contrast with the official or state-centred perspective. As it can be seen in the Şemdinli sample, the border does not indicate the same meaning for border people as it does for the state. For people living on the border, it bears a detaching meaning dividing a social, cultural and economic spatial whole; whereas for the statist or official perspective, it is a sign of sovereignty and security and a line sharply separating "us" from the "stranger".

Another point which needs to be highlighted is that the socio-cultural structure of the border region has reached a cross-border dimension. This fact is obvious in the Gerdi tribe study. The Gerdi tribe, located on both sides of the border, hardly present any differences in social, cultural and economic terms and have a mutual "us" conception. The density of relationships "the two sides" have with each other is a clear indicator. The tribal ideology and culture in the Gerdi region has reached a cross-border dimension and made it insignificant. In other words, the border lost its meaning to a great extent and so to speak has gone through a symbolic transformation. The strength of the "us" conception and the density of social relationships between "both sides" leads the Gerdi to say "there is actually no border".

Chapter 5. Development, security and the role of Frontex on the Turkish-Greek border

Burcu Toğral Koca

Parallel to the intensification of the EU integration process, the discourses and practices governing the migration issue have significantly changed in Europe.[1] Previously seen as an innocent economic activity, blessed with a vital role in the construction of European economies after World War Two, welcomed and encouraged by European states, dealt with through economic and humanitarian discourses, migration has been transformed into a security matter in that it 'constitutes' a threat to European societies. It has been increasingly linked to criminality, socio-economic problems, 'cultural deprivation', and lately to terrorism. This transformation started mainly in the mid-1970s, but accelerated with the redefinition of security in the wake of the Cold War. To be more precise, the traditional security thinking of the Cold War years, which confined itself to state-centric and military-oriented conceptualizations, has shifted to include various issues ranging from environment and poverty to population movement. This widening of the security agenda to different areas and utilization of security language for non-military issues have had important repercussions for migration. In this transformation of security, migration has come to be increasingly framed, analyzed and governed through security lenses. In other words, migration has been securitized and this securitization[2] process has increasingly appeared in public discourses and academic research.

On the other hand, the securitization of migration is closely linked to another discourse. Again being on the rise since the 1990s, this discourse has constructed a link between security and development and fed on the

---

[1] See for a detailed analysis, Toğral (2011).
[2] The concept of securitization was, first, introduced by the so-called Copenhagen School of Security Studies. Waever, one of the protagonist of this School, states that securitization is the successful construction of an issue as an 'existential threat' to the designated referent object through 'speech acts' of securitizing actors, which justifies extraordinary security policies - e.g. using conscription, secrecy, and other means only legitimate when dealing with 'security matters' (Waever, 2000). Later, the concept of securitization has gained a theoretical status and been revised and reinterpreted. For example, those following a Foucauldian approach, such as Bigo from the Paris School of Security Studies, Huysmans and Balzacq have applied a sociological understanding and focused on the role of practices rather than 'speech acts' in the process of securitization. Similarly, this study also takes the securitization as a process developing through practices.

notion of 'there can be no development without security and no security without development' (see UN, 2005). Even though such reasoning can be defined as conservative, rigid and superficial, it has been accepted by certain political and academic circles without being discussed in depth.[3] More importantly, this link has structured policies of states, international and non-governmental organizations. As stated by Wilson:

"[T]he notion of 'development' increasingly appeared in public pronouncements in the context of military intervention, combating terrorism, preventing migration and securing populations in the global North, a set of linkages which were to crystallise in the development/security paradigm, according to which, as Tony Blair put it, 'the yearning is for order and stability and if it doesn't exist elsewhere, it is unlikely to exist here" (Wilson, 2012: 3).

However, there have also emerged critical voices against this link and its impact on the issue of migration. One of them analyses the nexus between security and development in the context of a biopolitical distinction between 'developed' and 'underdeveloped' species-life (Duffield, 2007). Following Foucault, this biopolitical distinction enables the administration of life at the aggregate level of population and entails a regularity power (see Foucault 1991: 2003).

"This biopolitical governance comprises devices, techniques used to ensure the spatial distribution of individual bodies (their separation, their alignment, their serialization, and their surveillance) and the organization around those individuals, of a whole field of visibility. They were also techniques that could take control over bodies' and populations" (Foucault, 2004: 242).

When it comes to the relationship among development, security and migration, this biopolitical governance points to the technology of control/security addressing the underdeveloped 'surplus' population. In such a context:

"Rather than development being concerned with reducing the economic gap between rich and poor countries, or extending to the latter the levels of social protection existing in the former, as a technology of security it functions to contain and manage underdevelopment's destabilizing effects, especially its circulatory epiphenomena such as undocumented migrants, asylum seekers, transborder shadow economies or criminal networks" (Duffield, 2007: ix).

As in case of this excerpt, this chapter deals with the development and migration nexus not in the classical and traditional sense, which mainly focuses on the positive or negative impact of migration on receiving and

---

[3] See for a detailed analysis, Bilgen (2014) and Wilson (2012).

sending countries and considers development 'as a benign act of helping others' (ibid.: viii) or as 'a neutral, technical field' (Wilson, 2012: 6). Rather, it analyses how this nexus functions as part of a broader biopolitical governance at the practical and discursive level. In particular, it is based on the idea that 'development as a regime of biopolitical governance' acts as a strategy to ensure security of the 'developed' West. In analysing this security architecture, a vast amount of literature has provided significant insights. In particular, this literature explores the logic and dynamics of the securitization of migration in the EU. To put it differently, how migration is administered as a security issue through discourses and practices is the main concern of these studies.[4] By dwelling upon existing literature and combining it with a Foucauldian approach on biopolitics, the following pages attempt to shed light on this new security architecture and the interconnection between security, migration and development in a European context. Then, through drawing on archival analysis of governmental/non-governmental and legal sources, these conceptual and analytical discussions will be made more tangible with a specific focus on Frontex and its role on the Turkish-Greek border. At the same time, implications for human rights of biopolitical governance will be also delineated.

The security-development nexus in the EU's migration regime

As stated above, migration has been increasingly transformed into a security question in Europe. In effect, it is widely asserted that this securitization process has developed parallel to the intensification of the EU integration process[5]. Especially, following the establishment of the Single Market and Schengen Regime, which resulted in the abolition of internal border controls, it is contended that migration has turned into a security issue. This is linked to the assumption that removal of internal borders would result in a "security deficit", since a Europe without internal borders could be abused and become "a haven for criminals and illegal immigrants" (Karanja, 2000: 217). The September 11 attacks and subsequent acts of terrorism in Europe have added new dimensions to these ongoing developments and prompted the political discourses and academic interests regarding this securitization process.

However, these developments do not mean that migration as a whole has been securitized or that all types of mobility is considered a threat. Undeniably, today, nationals of some privileged countries belonging to the 'developed' West enjoy the freedom of movement without much of an

---

[4] See among others, Bigo (2000) and (2002); Huysmans 2006; van Munster (2009); Baldaccini and Guild (2007); and Balzacq (2008).

[5] See Huysmans (2006); Bigo (2002); and Karanja (2006).

interruption and without being imprisoned within any kind of borders (either territorial or non-territorial) (Toğral, 2011: 219). Rich tourists and highly skilled/semi-skilled labour force meeting market demands have still been welcomed by the EU/member states. The securitized group of migrants are likely to be asylum seekers, refugees and undocumented immigrants or to come from poor and Muslim countries. They are the 'human surpluses'. In other words, they constitute the "volume of humans made redundant by capitalism's global triumph... [they are] the superfluous, supernumerary and redundant population – the excess of the rejects of the labour market, and the refuse of the market-targeted economy, over the capacity of recycling arrangements" (Bauman, 2007: 28-29). They are designated as a threat to cultural identity, the welfare state and internal security of the EU and/or 'developed' West (see Huysmans, 2006). Therefore, they came to be dealt with harsh measures of biopolitics. These measures refer to the technologies of controlling and containing excessive freedom employed with the aim of regulating the 'human surplus' 'threatening others' (ibid.: 32).

In this context, development as a regime of biopolitics has also been a securitized strategy separating 'wanted' individuals/groups/states from the 'unwanted', 'dangerous' ones. To put it differently, this securitization of development is closely linked to the securitization of migration as both of these processes strive to contain and exclude 'dangerous' others in order to "secure the Western way of life" (Duffield, 2007: 2)[6]. In case of migration, this security architecture and biopolitical governance function through:

"The creation of a continuum of threats and general unease in which many different actors exchange their fears and beliefs in the process of making a risky and dangerous society. The professionals in charge of the management of risk and fear especially transfer the legitimacy they gain from struggles against terrorism, criminals, spies, and counterfeiters toward other targets, most notably transnational political activists, people crossing borders, or people born in the country but with foreign parents" (Bigo, 2002: 63).

Under this security architecture, certain group of migrants - integrated into such a continuum - are reduced to "pliable bodies that could be improved, shaped and regimented, but also exterminated if deemed unnecessary or dangerous" (Hansen and Stepputat, 2005: 17). In other words, 'irregular' and poor immigrants, asylum seekers, refugees and migrants with different cultural traits by definition have to be rehabilitated and/or kept away from the 'developed' West. As eloquently stated by Buur

---

[6] As Duffield further depicts "the opposite of containment is the unsecured circulation of surplus population that external poverty, instability and associated social breakdown continually threaten" (Duffield, 2007: 184).

et al. in their analysis of the security-development nexus, those groups of migrants are securitized and criminalized and at the same time "demonized as border crossers in a world where national borders are perceived as leaking. Hence border controls are being replaced by different designs of "spatial control" (Buur *et al.*, 2007: 26). They further argue that, in such a context, "programmes and discourses of development are deliberately used for the purposes of security" (ibid.: 29). As will be detailed in the following pages, a more 'humanitarian' discourse, such as saving and improving lives of migrants, is also invoked in order to mask the very political and securitarian character of this development-security nexus informing the biopolitical governance. Again as argued by Buur *et al.*,

"This combination of discourse and practice exploits an image of the responsible and caring state that is nonetheless able to assert its sovereignty fully and exclude from development those it considers a threat or defines as enemies of the state. Where violent state practices have in some cases both increased and become visible, in other cases criminalization and securitization have become invisible by being embedded in ordinary development projects" (ibid.: 33).

If one has a closer look at the EU and member states' migration practices, it is clearly seen that they are endowed with security and policing aspects aiming at controlling, sometimes, excluding and containing certain group of migrants. In particular, surveillance and risk analysis constitute corner stones of these migration practices in differentiating 'risky' bodies from the 'un-risky' ones. Current visa policies with their discriminatory and exclusionary approach towards certain group of migrants, detention and deportation practices, which clash with basic human rights, reflect this approach. Furthermore, various databases, biometric technologies, electronic fences, sophisticated radar systems or military-like devices exemplify that border control practices are culminated by high-technological devices, which were previously used for military purposes.

An increasing role granted to police as well as the use of para-military bodies, intelligence services or security experts demonstrate how security logic prevails in the field of migration. Following the September 11 attacks, convergence of migration practices with anti-terrorist measures represents another sign of this biopolitical governance aiming at controlling and filtering populations. Last but not least, integration practices cemented by culturalist and racialized discourses and operating through mandatory programmes, are likely to deal with migrants as 'threatening others' that should be rehabilitated, tamed and normalized to be included into the 'developed' world. In short, these techniques or measures are seeking to regulate and control migrants both inside and outside 'borders' dividing "not land, but populations" (ibid.: 6). They separate the 'developed' world from the 'underdeveloped' one. In short, as part of biopolitical governance, all these techniques and measures aim to "render visible, categorize, discipline, contain, and exclude the transgressive and mobile other" (Vasquez, 2012: 82).

Of those techniques and measures, the European Agency for the Management of Operational Cooperation at the External Borders of the Member States of the European Union, titled under the acronym Frontex (hereafter also referred to as the Agency) provides a suitable laboratory framework to illustrate the functioning of this security architecture. Having been established on 26 October 2004, operating since May 2005, the Agency, indeed, institutionalized the European border management regime. Its origin is found in the counter-terrorism policy framework, but it has later turned into one of the main bodies in the fight against 'irregular' immigration. Its budget and human resources have grown rapidly.[7] The following sections will scrutinize Frontex and its functioning and operational settings to explain how this body reflects the nexus between security, migration and development as an agent of biopolitical governance.

Frontex as an agent of biopolitical governance

The Agency's institutional and operational settings signify a clear securitization of migration and include main facets of the biopolitical governance.

First, in all its pursuits, the main task of the Agency is to control and contain 'unwanted' border crossings that have been undertaken by 'irregular' immigrants, asylum seekers and refugees on sea, land and air borders; thereby to ensure the internal security of the EU.[8] In doing this, the Agency has been conducting joint operations in cooperation with member states as well as with the source or transit countries for 'irregular' migrants and asylum seekers. These joint operations, which include

---

[7] For example, while Frontex got 89, 2 million euros in 2014, the European Asylum Support Office (EASO) received only 15, 6 million euros for the same year (UAÖ, 2014: 17).

[8] Article 2 of the Founding Regulation of the Agency outlined its main tasks as follows: 1) Risk analysis on the irregular movements targeting member states; 2) Coordination of operational cooperation between member states on the basis of this risk analysis and proposing joint operations at the Union's external land, sea and air borders; 3) Training of the border guard authorities of member states; 4) Facilitating the attainment of research and development goals; 5) Providing a rapid crisis-response capability available to all member states; 6) Assisting member states in joint return operations (see Council of the European Union, 2004). As it is not possible to detail all these tasks in the scope of this paper, a more general overview will be given in order to show the role of the Agency in the biopolitical governance. Indeed, all these tasks are closely related to each other.

apprehension, disembarkation, deportation practices and transfer of 'irregular' migrants into detention centres, have clear securitarian character.[9] Such sort of cooperative actions among states, especially those conducted at sea borders, "have been traditionally deployed to address more traditional security issues, such as military attacks from a third state, piracy or drug trafficking" (Leonard, 2010: 240).

Besides, involvement of actors with para-military status from member states in these joint operations reveals how militarization and securitization of migration controls are intensified by the practices and institutional structure of the Frontex. Similarly, the Agency is in charge of assisting member states through technical and operational means in cases where a rapid crisis-response is required. This assistance can be provided either by establishing a cooperation between two or more member states or through involvement of experts from the Agency to help member states tackle these 'crisis' situations. This framework has become much more sophisticated with the changes laid down by the Regulation 863/2007 amending the Agency's founding Regulation. The most significant 'novelty' introduced with this amendment is the establishment of the Rapid Borders Intervention Teams (RABITs) "for the purposes of providing rapid operational assistance [...] to a requesting State facing a situation of urgent and exceptional pressure, especially the arrivals of the external borders of large numbers of third-country nationals trying to enter the territory of the Member State illegally" (European Parliament and Council of the European Union, 2007). It is stated that member states "may ask for the support of the RABITs under particular *threat* from illegal migration" (ibid., emphasis added). It is further important to note that with the 863/2007 Regulation, members of the team were allowed to carry arms and use force with the authorization of the host member state (Article 6 (6)).

Against this backdrop, the framework, which utilizes the wording of 'threat' and 'crisis', mandatory character of the participation as well as the composition of the team equipped with military-devices represent another securitarian sign of Frontex. Furthermore, Frontex came to work in close cooperation with the security and intelligence-based bodies, such as EUROPOL, the European Anti-Fraud Office (OLAF), EUROJUST, the Union Satellite Centre (EUSC), the EU's intelligence body Joint Situation Centre (JSC), the Police Chief's Task Force and Interpol. More importantly, as in case of other operational activities, the Agency expands this structure into transit and source countries by establishing cooperation

---

[9] See for a detailed analysis, Leonard (2010) and Lutterbeck (2006).

with their intelligence services. Javier Quesada, head of the Risk Analysis Unit, made this clear with the following words:

"We started creating intelligence communities in third countries in the Western Balkans, at the eastern borders of the EU member states and now in Africa. And we intend to continue developing these communities" (Frontex, 2010: 65).

The Agency, indeed, represents itself as an intelligence-based body to control and manage 'risks' and 'threats' in its official statements. Keeping in mind that the concept of 'intelligence' has traditionally pointed to the information gathered in the face of threats to national security (Gill and Phytian 2006: 1), "the use of this concept, rather than more neutral concepts such as *'data'* or *'information'*, already contributes to securitizing asylum and migration in the EU" (Leonard 2010: 242). Besides, the rationale structuring its risk analysis model represents a preventive approach. Laitinen, the head of the Agency, reveals this very well as follows:

"We assess what is the likely threat that threatens the external borders, border security, and EU citizens from outside. In other words, criminal pressure, in terms of illegal migration, human trafficking, and so on, not disregarding other types of organized crime and fighting international terrorism" (Neal, 2009: 348-349).

This discourse represents a clear security continuum established among different phenomenon, such as crime, 'irregular' immigration, human trafficking and terrorism and, thereby, provoking criminalization of 'irregular' immigration under a risk assessment model. Further, it fits well with what Bigo describes as "a proactive logic which anticipates the risks and the threats, locating the potential adversaries even before they have consciousness of being a threat to others" (Bigo, 2005: 86).

Another contentious issue is that this intelligence-based risk analysis is built upon the necessity of ensuring secrecy of operations. The Decision of the Management Board of 21 September 2006 maintains that:

"In order to safeguard the ability to carry out its tasks, special attention should be paid to the specific requirements of Frontex as a specialized body tasked with improving the integrated management of the external borders of the member states of the EU. Therefore, full account of the sensitive nature of tasks carried out by Frontex, in particular in relation to operations at borders and border related data should be taken" (Frontex, 2006).

At this juncture, the justification follows from the argument that collected data, details of operations and sources of information should be kept in secrecy in order to secure the success of operations (Carrera, 2007: 14). However, this secrecy impedes not only principles of transparency and democratic accountability, but also prevents the public from taking an active stance against possible breach of fundamental rights and rule of law. As contended eloquently by Carrera "by applying the secrecy rule the very source of legitimizing the operation cannot be at all contested, reviewed and in the end made democratically accountable" (ibid.: 14). This lack of transparency and democratic accountability is augmented by the limited role granted to the European Parliament (EP) both in negotiation process of the Draft Regulation establishing Frontex and later in scrutinizing its activities, though, recently, its role was extended to control the budget allocated to the Agency. Furthermore, this operational setting and the practices of the Agency, particularly joint operations, are also controversial from a legal point of view.[10] To be more precise, Frontex operations are likely to prevent asylum seekers from lodging their claims in European countries. As in case of readmission agreements, those seeking protection are indiscriminately treated as part of 'irregular' and 'economic' immigrants or the so-called 'mix flows'. Turning migrants back across the borders without taking into account their possible claims for asylum, impedes the principle of *non-refoulement*. This is mainly because, as put forward by the United Nations High Commissioner for Refugees (UNCHR), the *non-refoulement* principle, also requires "non-rejection at the border" meaning that persons cannot be sent back to a country where there is a possibility of persecution, torture and other forms of ill-treatments (Debenedetti, 2006: 23). In a similar vein, Papastavridis contends that "the application of the [principle of *non-refoulement*] appears to be especially problematic in the majority of [joint operations conducted by the Frontex] since it is very likely that the persons on board the intercepted vessels would be forced to return to their countries of origin, where they may be subject to torture or inhuman or degrading treatments" (Papastavridis, 2010: 75).

Despite these problems, the Agency's operations have been justified with a reference to the 'moral obligation' of the EU to "prevent, not least to end the suffering and dying on the high seas" (w2eu, 2014). The Agency is framed as a significant technical tool to manage 'irregular' immigration in a 'humanitarian way' in various official statements and documents (see Toğral Koca, 2013:163). However, this line of argument masks the role of securitarian border controls in these tragedies. Migrants have to resort to dangerous routes to enter the EU in response to the intensified control and surveillance measures. At the same time, these human tragedies especially on the sea are likely to be utilized to:

---

[10] See Guild and Bigo (2010); Baldaccini (2010); and Gil-Bazo (2006).

"Justify the militarization of the borders and the widening of the activities of a Europeanized border management system. At the same time it enables the EU to turn on its head the old call to 'fight what causes people to become refugees, not the refugees' and integrate border management into a larger concept of a policy of 'migration and development', which legitimizes broad-based socio-technical intervention in the countries of origin and transit" (w2eu, 2014).

To conclude this section, Frontex has become one of the most important agents in the biopolitical governance that securitize, categorize, and filter 'surplus' population deemed to be a threat to European security.

Frontex on the Turkish-Greek border

The Turkish-Greek border has witnessed significant changes in recent years due to its geographic position at the EU's external border. One of them is that the border has become the main entry point for 'irregular' movements into the EU. Unprecedented numbers of 'irregular' migrants, including mainly Afghans, Iraqis, Palestinians, Eritreans, Sudanese, Somalis and recently Syrians are trying to cross the border through relying on human smugglers and traffickers.In fleeing persecution, social, political and economic problems experienced in their 'home' countries, they are risking their future in quest for a better life in Europe. There are several reasons behind this change. First, intensified surveillance and control measures around Spain and Italy have led to shifts in the routes of 'irregular' movements towards the Eastern Mediterranean.[11] Second, the war in Afghanistan, political instabilities in Iraq and more recently the Syrian war[12] have forced thousands of people to migrate to Europe via Turkey. In this context, both Greece and Turkey have turned into countries of transit as well as destination for 'irregular' migrants, asylum seekers and refugees. This is confirmed by Frontex as well:

---

[11] However, it should be also noted that following the uprisings in the Middle East and "Arab Spring" in 2011, Italy (also Malta) has again witnessed the arrival of an important number of "irregular" migrants especially on the island of Lampedusa. Human rights violation and mistreatment of migrants within and around the island have attracted considerable public attention and criticism. More recently, on 3 October 2013, more than 350 people, most of them Eritreans, died when the boat carrying them sank close to the island. An in-depth analysis of the EP's Directorate-General for External Policies confirmed that this tragedy "put trans-Mediterranean migration back on top of the political agenda" (Manrique Gil et al., 2014: 4). This tragedy has also led to enormous increase in funding of Frontex operations (EUR 7.9 million for 2013) conducted in the Mediterranean (ibid.: 9).

[12] Since the Syrian crisis, Syrians have been the major nationality detected on the Eastern Mediterranean route in general and on the Turkish-Greek border in particular (Gil et al, 2014: 7).

"Following decreased departures from Libya and Western Africa, Turkey has now become the most important transit country for illegal migration...As a corollary to the sharp decreases registered in Italy and Spain, the number of detections of illegal border crossings in Greece rose from 50% of the total EU detections to 75% of the total" (Frontex, 2010a: 3-6).

In response to these changes, Greece has taken steps of its own, with the help of EU funding, in order to tackle these 'irregular' border crossings. In particular, through technological means, such as watchtowers, thermal vision cameras and other night vision devices, border surveillance has been strengthened. More strikingly, a 10.5 km-long and 4 meter high, barbed-wire fence that cost more than 3 million euros was constructed along its border with Turkey. Besides, Greek authorities have increased the number of patrol agents on the border. On the other hand, as all these surveillance measures have remained limited to keep migrants away from the border, Greece has increasingly relied on Frontex. The first operation by the Agency was conducted in 2006 "in the framework of the joint operation Poseidon, which includes activities at land, sea and air borders" (Kasparek & Wagner, 2012: 185). During this operation, Frontex provided Greece with surveillance technology, such as helicopters, ships and infrared cameras and its technical expertise in interception and deportation processes. Following this, other significant assistance came with the operation Attica, "a so-called pilot project to establish and extend the deportation capabilities of the Greek state as well as the project that led to a first regional Frontex office in October 2010" (ibid.). This first specialized regional branch of Frontex, called Frontex Operational Office, in Piraeus targets the whole Eastern Mediterranean. Another significant operation is the deployment of the RABITs, for the first time, in the region of Orestiada from November 2010 to March 2011 following an urgent call from the Greek government because of an "exceptional mass of inflow of *'irregular'* immigrants" (Carrera and Guild, 2010: 1). This call was framed legitimate by the EU with a reference to the 'humanitarian' and 'moral' obligation of the EU/member states vis-à-vis migrants dying and risking their lives while crossing the border. This is made clear in the following statement by former Home Affairs Commissioner Cecilia Malmström:

"The situation at the Greek land border with Turkey is increasingly worrying. The flows of people crossing the border irregularly have reached alarming proportions and Greece is manifestly not able to face this situation alone. I am very concerned about the humanitarian situation. I trust that proper assistance will be given to all persons crossing the border and that the request for international protection will be considered

in full compliance with the EU and international standards" (European Commission, 2010).

Accordingly, 175 border control specialists on the Greek region of Orestiada and neighbouring areas were deployed initially for a period of two months with the aim of strengthening external border security and preventing 'irregular' migrants (Carrera & Guild, 2010: 1). The operation was welcomed, as it was believed to have led to reductions in the number of detections (House of Commons, 2011: 24).[13] Yet, the necessity to keep on policing was emphasized by Frontex due to the ongoing and 'high risk' of 'irregular' border crossings (see Frontex, 2010b). Right after the end of the RABIT operation, the land operation Poseidon was made permanent in early March 2011 and later, expanded to the Bulgarian-Turkish border. All these operations, especially the deployment of the RABITs, were highly criticized and defined as a failure on two grounds[14]:

"First, the deployment is merely of an emergency, temporary and (in)security (police)-driven nature; and second, the strengthening of the common EU external border between Greece and Turkey may further increase the tensions by enlarging the distance between the external border control practices and Europe's commitment to the rights and freedom of asylum-seekers and refugees" (Carrera and Guild, 2010, preface).

To put it differently, first, the role of the Agency seems to be based on a "reactive logic where the response only follows after the unwanted travellers have rendered themselves visible by continually arriving at a particular physical border section" (Hobolth, 2006: 18). Second, under the operations asylum seekers and refugees can be deported to places where there is a risk of persecution; therefore *non-refoulement* principle is not respected. Indeed, people seeking protection do not need to be deported to their countries of origin to be subjected to inhuman treatments, since neither Turkey nor Greece provide them with a genuine refugee protection and asylum system. As criticized and reported by various non-governmental and governmental organizations, in Greece, migrants are put into detention centres, where the conditions are worrying[15]. In these

---

[13] It was stated that 'Since the deployment of the RABIT operation, the numbers of irregular crossings have dropped by approximately 75 %' (European Commission, 2011).

[14] For a comprehensive analysis and critique of the RABIT operation, see Human Rights Watch (2011).

[15] In M.S.S. v. Belgium case, the ECHR determined that the detention practices of Greece infringe upon Article 3 of the European Convention on Human Rights prohibiting torture, inhuman and degrading treatments. Besides, the ECHR also concluded in a January 2011 review of reports from various organizations, "All the centers visited by bodies and organizations that produced the reports...describe a similar situation to varying degrees of gravity: Overcrowding, dirt, lack of ventilation, little or no possibility of taking a walk, no

centres, they do not have access to fair and effective asylum procedures and cannot enjoy their procedural safeguards in full sense. Furthermore, they are exposed to degrading, cruel practices, and violence both in detention centres and during deportation processes.[16] Regarding these problems in Greece, a Report from the Parliamentary Assembly of the Council of Europe stated that:

"Human rights of migrants, asylum seekers and refugees are being violated due to the system of automatic detention in substandard conditions, and a lack of access to asylum and basic provisions. This situation affects the human dignity of these people, but also increases the risk of refoulement" (Strik, 2013: 3).

More strikingly, in recent years, numerous incidents resulting in death and lost bodies show that Greek authorities have been conducting illegal and violent push-back operations rather than saving lives in the Mediterranean[17]. Frontex has also been blamed for these violations. The forceful returns of migrants to countries, where there is a risk of persecution and other ill-treatments, and Frontex's role in these violations were also denounced by the European Court of Justice in its 2012 judgment in the *Hirsi v Italy* case (Peers, 2014).

On the other hand, Turkey is also being criticized as maintaining the geographical reservation to the 1951 Geneva Convention relating to the status of refugees. Under this system, Turkey does not grant refugee status to non-Europeans. Hence, despite Turkey's transformation into a country of destination and transit for thousands of asylum seekers especially following the Syrian crisis, a large amount of people is excluded from an effective asylum system. Besides, inhuman detention practices and centres have been highly condemned as failing to meet international human rights standards.[18]

Despite these problems and controversies, the role of Frontex on the Turkish-Greek border has become much more visible. This role is not only

---

place to relax, insufficient mattresses, no free access to toilets, inadequate sanitary facilities, no privacy, limited access to care. Many of the people interviewed also complained of insults, particularly racist insults, proffered by staff and the use of physical violence by guards" (Human Rights Watch, 2011, p. 3). See for further analysis, Human Rights Watch (2011) and (2008); Amnesty International (2013); and UNHCR (2010).

[16] It should also be noted that Frontex is here seen as responsible for exposing migrants to inhuman and degrading conditions in detention centers in Greece by knowingly transferring them into these centers (Human Rights Watch, 2011).

[17] See BBC, 2014 and Manrique Gil et al., 2014.

[18] Turkish NGOs working in the field of asylum issue are very critical of the situation in detention or the so-called receptions centers. They argue that not only poor and inhuman reception conditions but also strict security regulations in these places similar to those in prisons run counter the genuine refugee protection regime (See for a detailed analysis, Çetin (2011) and Amnesty International (2009)).

structured by the intensified cooperation between Greece and Frontex but also with the integration of Turkey into this security framework focusing on control and containment. In fact, it can be said that the EU/Greece and Frontex cooperation seem to make Turkey a 'buffer zone' in order to protect 'Europe' against the 'destabilizing effects' of 'underdeveloped' regions. This approach is well confirmed by Klaus Roesler, the director of Frontex's Operations Division, stating in one of his interviews that the Agency

"Is expecting to conclude a working agreement soon. The first would be to integrate Turkey into the border regime (similar to the case of Libya). On an institutional level, Frontex is trying to connect with the Turkish coast guard and to involve them in joint maneuvers" (Deliso, 2011).

Following this, the cooperation between the Agency and Turkey became more formal with the signature of the Memorandum of Understanding on Cooperation between the parties on 28 May 2012. This memorandum identifies the "main areas of the practical cooperation to be developed in the field of preventing "*irregular*" migration" (MFA, 2012). With the *Roadmap towards a Visa-Free Regime with Turkey* of 16 December 2013, implementing this Memorandum in an effective manner through developing joint cooperation initiatives and exchanging data and risk analysis were set as requirements to be fulfilled by Turkey for visa-free travel. On the other hand, according to Frontex, visa liberalization agreements between the EU and non-EU countries carry the risk of "abuse of new legal channels to enter and subsequent stay in the EU" and "increased facilitation of secondary movements of illegal stayers in the EU" (Frontex, 2013: 20-21). Given this, the EU not only urges Turkey to have close cooperation with Frontex; but also to tighten its visa regime.

Last but not least, official statements of the EU and Frontex claim that all these joint operations and cooperation with Turkey have been reducing the number of 'irregular' crossings. However, there are counter arguments saying that "neither the strategy towards Turkey nor the improved border surveillance seems to have made a significant contribution to stopping or minimizing flows" (Kasparek and Wagner, 2012: 187). On the contrary, in the face of the Syrian civil war, 'irregular' crossings have increased tremendously. Against this background, Kasparek and Wagner argue that Frontex and Greece seem to follow a new strategy – that is internalization of the border (ibid.). One of the most visible examples of this strategy is the establishment of the so-called screening centres within and around Greek borders. It is argued that these centres serve to differentiate "legitimate travellers" from "illegitimate" ones thereby allowing for a "differential treatment" (ibid.). In other words, those deemed to be 'risky' or in most of the cases, 'economic migrants' are to be deported after being checked within these places.

Concluding remarks

In this chapter we discussed the development-security nexus as a reflection of the biopolitical governance, how this nexus has informed the EU migration regime and the impact of resultant practices on human rights of migrants. It is seen that the EU's migration practices in general and Frontex operations in particular are likely to integrate certain groups of migrants into a security framework emphasizing policing and defence. In other words, by utilizing outward-directed, securitarian practices, the EU has been trying to separate "'good' circulation – such as finance, investment, trade, information, skilled labour, tourism, - from 'bad' circulation associated with underdevelopment: Refugees, asylum seekers, unskilled migrants, shadow economies, trafficking drugs and terrorism" (Duffield, 2007: 30). Despite the attempts to justify this securitization process with a reference to 'moral' and 'humanitarian' obligations of the EU vis-à-vis 'irregular' immigrants, asylum seekers and refugees, the current developments show just the opposite. Migrants' rights and dignity have been at stake under this migration regime. People resort to more dangerous routes in response to intensified surveillance and militarization practices around EU's external borders. Their lives are endangered and asylum seekers are prevented from lodging their claims in the European territory. They are seen as mere 'bodies' dying and being perish during their journeys; some of them find their ways into statistics. Yet, most of them are invisible in this biopolitical governance. All these do not imply that the EU and member states have the sole responsibility in this securitization process. Third-countries, such as Turkey, have also been in the process of replicating similar securitarian practices.

However, it should also be noted that, in recent years, there have been changes to legal and policy frameworks of this security architecture in order to address shortfalls. For example, the Agency endorsed a Fundamental Rights Strategy in March 2011 and a Code of Conduct in June 2011 for joint return operations coordinated by Frontex. More recently, new rules governing maritime surveillance operations were adopted in April 2014. Even though these documents underlined the fact that all Frontex operations have to be in conformity with fundamental rights and brought forward some improvements with respect to search, rescue, interception and disembarkation issues, crucial loopholes about *non-refoulement*, procedural rights of migrants, accountability and transparency of Frontex remain intact.[19] Similarly, Greece adopted the Greek Action Plan on Asylum and Migration Management to reform its migration practices in line with human rights principles in August 2010. Yet, the Plan put emphasis, again, on surveillance and security measures, rather than on improving the conditions for migrants within and around the borders[20]. On the other hand, Turkey passed the new Law on Foreigners and International Protection (LFIP) in April 2014. This new law has been welcomed by various sectors due to the legal and institutional frameworks provided principally for asylum seekers and refugees. Nevertheless, the LFIP continues to maintain the geographical reservation and even integrates some of the securitarian measures of the EU, such as 'first country of asylum' and 'safe third country' principles, long detention periods and accelerated procedures for asylum claims. Furthermore, recently, in the light of massive arrivals of Syrian refugees in Europe after crossing the Aegean Sea from Turkey, Angela Merkel held talks with Turkey's President R. T. Erdogan and his Prime Minister A. Davutoglu on 18 October 2015. Accordingly, Merkel has sought Turkey's help in controlling and containing Syrian refugees through increasing border controls in return for financial aid, "acceleration of EU membership talks and for concessions on liberalized visa requirements" (Arslan, 2015). This picture illustrates that on the one hand, the EU and the respective states are invoking a humanitarian discourse to justify their security-oriented practices, on the other hand they are prioritizing "more security (Frontex) and not going at the heart of the issue, which is that of human rights protection of refugees" as well as of 'irregular' immigrants (Carrera and Guild, 2010: 15). In fact, as stated by Reid-Henry, "the extent to which these [practices] facilitate an on-the-ground praxis that takes full advantage of ambiguities in international law while maintaining a façade of respect for human rights, is increasingly becoming a law" (Reid-Henry, 2013: 208).

Against this backdrop, it is fundamental to ask what kind of migration regime the EU, Greece and Turkey are promoting. Is the emerging biopolitical governance favouring the dominant class and 'securitizing' those who are coming from poor regions of the world? Is it a neo-liberal regime sustaining and enhancing the free movement of capital, rich people as well as of 'qualified' labour force and disregarding the rights of migrants forced to immigrate to the West in quest for a better life? There is a need for a critical reflection on these questions in order to challenge,

---

[19] For a critical overview of these changes, see Babická (2013), Peers (2014) and Keller (2014).
[20] See the Reports prepared by Strik (2013) and Amnesty International (2011).

deconstruct, and problematize the 'legitimacy' of borders and the 'securitarian' practices capturing our political thinking.

Acknowledgement
Earlier version already published in Turkish in the journal, *Göç Dergisi* (www.gocdergisi.com): Koca, B. (2014). Biyopolitika, güvenlik ve Frontex'in Türkiye-Yunanistan sınırındaki rolü. *Göç Dergisi*, 1(1): 57-76. http://tplondon.com/dergi/index.php/gd/ article/view/4.

Chapter 6. Contributor or barrier: The role of Kurdish Diaspora in Turkey's European Union accession process

Şevin Gülfer Sağnıç

Introduction
Castles and Miller explain the character of the international as a part of a "transnational revolution that is reshaping societies and politics around the globe" (1998: 5). Diaspora communities which form as the direct result of the international migration process constitute a driving force for restructuring world politics. Transnational activities of diaspora members change the meaning of local and global; and conflicts no longer stay in their national border but reach the international arena.

One of the frequently studied diaspora communities is the Kurdish diaspora in Europe, mainly comprised of guest workers[1], and political refugees from Turkey. The Kurdish diaspora's activities in Europe were instrumental to Kurdish identity formation (Sirkeci, 2003: 241). Television channels served as a tool for increasing national awareness; non-political Kurds in Europe were politicised and the relatively liberal circumstances in Europe compared to those in Turkey had served to improve the Kurdish literature and history writing. Arrival of Kurdish migrants also brought the Kurdish question into Europe. The Kurdish question which arose due to mass killings, forced evacuations and displacement of Kurds in Turkey was no longer limited to the domestic politics of Turkey. Kurdish diaspora organizations, through violent and non-violent means, promoted their cause in Europe and forced European governments and the European Union (EU) to become a party in this conflict. Meanwhile, Turkey has been trying to become a member of the EU. The negotiations for accession take longer than expected. After 40 years of efforts, in 2004, Turkey finally achieved candidacy status. However, the accession process is open-ended with many barriers including the Kurdish issue. In the annual progress reports of the EU on Turkey's accession process, the volume and emphasis on the Kurdish issue are increasing with the effect of the diaspora activities in Europe.

---

[1] The "guest worker", as a policy and as a concept had been heavily criticised. In this paper, I use the term to refer those who went as a part of the guest worker policy and I use it in order to underline the differences between the migration waves.

The main question of this chapter is "What is the role of diaspora activities in considering Turkey's accession to the EU?" The answer to this question is important for general international migration literature. Secondly, as indicated by Wahlbeck (2002:221), diaspora studies are helpful in closing the gap between before- and after-migration analysis and understanding the transnational reality in which refugees live and thus showing the continuity in the migration phenomenon. Thirdly, it is important to understand what refugees can do or achieve in their host societies. While the Kurdish diaspora in Europe has been studied sociologically and politically, there is a lack of studies investigating the relationship between the transnational actors of the Kurdish question in Turkey and its effect on Turkey's EU accession process.

This study argues that the Kurdish diaspora in Europe utilized Turkey's EU accession process to gain more democratic rights in Turkey, which has had a negative influence on Turkey's chances for joining the EU. The diaspora is both a barrier and a contributor for the accession process. It wants Turkey to join the EU and makes effort on the continuation of the process but it does not want Turkey to join without solving the Kurdish question in a democratic way and so blocks the process in terms of pressuring the EU not to accept Turkey's membership without a peaceful solution to the Kurdish question. The chapter analyses the role of the Kurdish diaspora and its activities in relation to Turkey's European Union accession process with a focus on the importation of the Kurdish question into Europe through Kurdish migration. The main objective is revealing the consequences of the diaspora activities in this context.

The correlation between the changes in the attitude of the EU and the advancement of the diaspora is a key focus of this chapter. The increasing influential capacity and change in the means and opportunities expose the advancement of the Kurdish diaspora in transnational political context. In order to study this relationship, the Human Rights and Protection of Minorities chapters in the progress reports before (1998, 1999, 2000) and after (2011, 2012, 2013) the advancement of the Kurdish diaspora is analysed. The correlation between changes and improvements in the reports and the diaspora activities constitute an important indicator for the influential strength. Consequently discussions demonstrate how the process had been affected by the diaspora activities. Interviews with the representatives of the Brussels Kurdish Institute, The Kurdish Bureau and the Nûçe TV are used to analyse the motivations and expectations of the Kurdish diaspora organizations. These diaspora institutions were selected among those with activities that would affect the EU-Turkey relations.

Evolution of the diaspora activities and its advancement

Kurds in Europe

The Kurdish diaspora is not homogenous. Different political, economic and sociological conditions created different migration waves and thus different profiles within the diaspora. The nature of diaspora activities has also changed over time and so did their effectiveness.

There are approximately 1 million Kurds in Europe. Two-thirds of all Turkish Kurds in Europe live in Germany, approximately 500,000 to 700,000 (Eccarius-Kelly, 2008: 15). In the 1950s, due to the bilateral agreements with Western European countries, workers from Turkey started to migrate to Europe (Bruinessen, 1998: 45). In this group of, so called, Gastarbiter (guest workers) there were many individuals of Kurdish origin, many of whom discovered their identities for the first time in their host countries (Bruinessen, 1998: 45). Despite this self-discovery process, the next twenty years, following the first wave of the migration, did not bring a high level of political activism to the Kurdish migrant workers. According to Bruinessen, until the late 1970s Kurds were very reluctant to emphasize their Kurdish identity or become involved with politics (Bruinessen, 1998: 45). The appropriate background for such politicization was finally created by the development of satellite TV stations (Khayati, 2008:85).

After the 1980 military coup in Turkey political refugees arrived in Europe (Sirkeci and Esipova, 2013: 4). These political refugees strengthened the context for politicization that had been created by self-discovery and the satellite stations. This migration wave that continued through the 1990s and brought the conflict in Turkey to Europe (Ayata, 2011: 145). Formerly politicized Kurds urged to mobilize those who had arrived in Europe during the earlier migration waves with the motive for creating a second base for the Kurdish struggle (Ayata, 2011: 145). According to Vera Eccarius-Kelly, these Kurds "transferred clandestine political resistance networks to Europe, and thereby changed the composition of the respective diasporas from predominantly apolitical guest worker communities to networked and homeland-oriented political activist organizations" (Eccarius-Kelly, 2002: 92). The importance of these migration waves is two-fold. First of all, the Kurdish diaspora in Europe played a key role in the advancement of Kurdish identity and nationalism. Secondly, as Barkey and Fuller put it, the Kurdish problem had been exported to Europe via the migration of over one million Kurdish residents. Political activities that led to domestic disruption and violence between Turkish and Kurdish communities in the Kurdish diaspora subsequently forced the EU to take a position (Barkey & Fuller, 1998:

165); the Kurdish question became a domestic issue for the European states.

Despite the fact that there are different Kurdish organizations in Europe such as Rizgari or Kawa, PKK was the major organization that shaped the diaspora (Başer, 2011: 15). In the 1980s and 1990s the PKK's ideology consisted of a combination of Marxism and Kurdish nationalism. The PKK defined as a militarist separatist group by European states (Eccarius-Kelly, 2014: 65). Its activities in Europe by the exiled cadres were in line with its ideology and tactics in Turkey (Eccarius-Kelly, 2014: 65). The PKK conducted activities as organising petitions and campaigns, violent and non-violent mass demonstrations and protests, sit-ins, highway blockades, hunger strikes and self-immolation (Başer, 2011: 15). But the violent activities were placed on the front burner. In the late 1980s in Western Europe, twenty people died due to the conflict among Turkish-born Kurds; according to the police the PKK was responsible for these deaths (Gunter, 1991: 13). Because of the killings in Sweden between 1984 and 1985, nine Kurds were held under "commune arrest" for several years (Gunter, 1991: 13). Consequently, the PKK was added to the terrorist organization list in Sweden in 1984 and the PKK leader Abdullah Öcalan's entry into the country was refused (Gunter, 1991: 13). When Swedish Prime Minister Olof Palme was assassinated on 28 February 1986, officials including Stockholm Chief of Police Hans Holmer were convinced that the PKK was responsible for the murder (Gunter, 1991: 13). The police forces were breaking into every Kurdish apartment, not only in Sweden but throughout Europe (Lelyveld, 1986). Another assassination in 1988 led once again to accusations against the PKK. Siegfried Wielsputz, the West German consular affairs attaché was killed in Paris. For a long time these violent activities associated with the PKK barriered the diaspora's ability to make the EU take a stance against Turkey on the Kurdish issue. It even made a reverse effect.

When the Kurdish question became a domestic problem in Europe, European countries offered financial aid and political asylum in exchange for pacification of the PKK (Gunter, 1991: 16). As a reaction to Europe's negative attitude and pacification attempts towards PKK the Kurdish movement adopted a more hostile attitude. Öcalan argued that European countries are no different from the Turkish state, both of whom try to assimilate Kurds and corrupt the PKK. The "Brussels circle", by which he means the institutions and members of the EU, was a fellow NATO member and its aim was to protect Turkish territorial integrity. Kurds should have had party and military training in the "war zone" and join to the struggle against Turkey in order to avoid European trap (Gunter, 1991: 16).

In the meantime, Kurdish intellectuals continued to mobilize the Kurdish migrants, get institutionalized and politicize the guest worker organizations. The Paris Kurdish Institute, the Kurdish Parliament in Exile (*Parlamana Kurdîstane Lî Derveyî Welat*- PKDW), the Kurdistan National Congress (*Kongreya Neteweyî ya Kurdistanê*- KNK), and the television channel MED TV can be listed as the main bodies created by the diaspora in this migration period.

The arrest of the PKK leader Abdullah Öcalan in February 1999 became a turning point for Kurds. In his defence, Öcalan explained the PKK's objective as obtaining political and cultural rights for Kurds instead of an independent Kurdish state (Turkey vs. Abdullah Öcalan, 1999). It was an ideological shift for the PKK. The new political reality made structural and strategic adjustments unavoidable. The European diaspora was affected deeply by the ideological shift; subsequently they started to adopt the discourse of national minority rights instead of independence (Khayati, 2008: 87). Eccarius-Kelly explains the new agenda of the Kurds in Europe as "diaspora Kurdish protesters shifted away from separatist articulations to more culturally based grievances such as the right to study and speak their ethnic language, to select Kurdish names for their children, to operate Kurdish TV and radio programs, and to openly perform regional cultural practices" (Eccarius-Kelly, 2014: 7). The change in the agenda resulted in the transformation of the structure of the diaspora political organizations in favour of transnational social movement organizations (Eccarius-Kelly, 2014: 8). The aggressive protests were mostly replaced by non-violent social movement activities. In terms of considering themselves legitimate representatives of the Kurds, publicly presenting a unified front, pushing for the recognition of their agenda, developing connections with allied actors and seeking new political opportunities for achieving acceptance, the Kurdish diaspora assumed the role of a typical transnational social movement (Khayati, 2008: 87). The early claims of the Kurdish diaspora, such as independence and socialism, had low receptivity at the EU level. Negative attitudes towards Europe as well as legitimacy problems for its institutions and violent activities were the main internal propensities that decreased the diaspora's access to EU institutions. The changes in ideology and activities of the Kurdish intellectuals increased its access to EU institutions mainly by defending human rights in Turkey, an issue that has very high receptivity in the EU. The Kurdish approach renounced violence and embraced peaceful activities resulting in increased legitimacy, power and effectiveness. Slowly after this consolidation the diaspora's effect became visible in the EU-Turkey relations. But before moving to its effects the current position of the diaspora should be discussed.

The Kurdish standpoint

The Kurdish movement is generally regarded as a trap for Turkey's EU accession process. Yet the reality is far from this belief. Instead of putting an end to Turkey's integration dream, the Kurdish movements generally approach this process as an opportunity for democratization in Turkey. In other words, they are instrumentalizing the process in order to empower their struggle for more rights. Additionally, Kurds generally see Europe as the third party responsible for the conflict. Derviş Ferho, the head of the Brussels Kurdish Institute, says "it is the European states who drew borders in the middle of the Kurdistan" (Ferho, 2014). Amed Dicle, a well-known journalist from the Kurdish television channel Nûçe, adds "the current situation of Kurdistan is the result of European policies. This is the main reason that the powerful decision-making mechanisms in Europe refuse to do anything to change the status-quo" (Dicle, 2014). The founder of the Brussels-based organization the Kurdish Bureau for Liaison and Information (*Buroya Kurdî*), Pervîn Jamîl says, "I want Turkey to be member of the EU because it will mean that Turkey has fulfilled the criteria, and then by being a part of the Union it will have to protect democracy" (Jamîl, 2014). There is also fear among diaspora members: "If Turkey enters the EU without solving the Kurdish problem, it will also use European power to supress Kurds, and actually this is what Turkey hopes" (Dicle, 2014). This concern explains the Kurdish desire to put the Kurdish issue on the top of the accession agenda. These motivations do not stay on the discursive level. For example in 2004 a leading Kurdish diaspora organization, The Paris Kurdish Institute prepared an announcement which was signed by 200 Kurdish intellectuals living in Europe and Turkey just before the EU summit in which they explained their support and expectations from the process (BIA News Center, 2004). As addition to this letter, Leyla Zana's letter to EU officials such as then President of the EC Romano Prodi and the EU term president Anders Rasmussen to demand a negotiation calendar for Turkey proves that the support of the Kurds for the process is not only rhetorical but also active.

The Kurdish organizations desire Turkish membership once Turkey meets the criteria. In sum, currently Kurds do not want to halt the accession process, instead they want it to continue. But they want to reach their objectives at the end of the process, and in order to do so they are trying to be an actor in the EU-Turkey negotiations. They also see Europe as a natural actor in the Kurdish issue, so they want European governments to pay more attention to the region. The activities of the Kurdish diaspora should be analysed from this angle.

Activities, opportunities and capabilities of the Diaspora

The evolution of the Kurdish diaspora from a terrorism-related violent group into a human rights-oriented social movement increased opportunities for it in the European context. In the EU, the language for negotiation is provided by the discourse on human rights (Ostergaard-Nielsen, 2001: 15). This also became the case for the Kurds a discursive shift to human rights created support for the Kurdish diaspora from the human rights organizations as well as from some members of the European Parliament. Consequently, the new attitude of the diaspora was given an indirect voice in the EU; libertarian bloc parties signalled willingness to discuss the Kurdish question within the debates over Turkey's EU accession (Eccarius-Kelly, 2002: 8). Besides, some conservative governments such as those of Greece and Germany, who were opposed to Turkey's EU membership supported the Kurdish diaspora's activities to stifle negotiations (Eccarius-Kelly, 2002: 8).

The structure of the European Union provides multiple channels of entry to the decision-making mechanism. The Kurdish diaspora in Europe uses these channels to put pressure on Turkey for political reforms affecting the European Union to do the same. Despite the fact that the European Court of Human Rights (ECtHR) has no direct connection with the EU, its decisions play a role in the accession process. Firstly, the public hearing method and detailed press releases for the decisions legitimizes the Kurdish minority's political stance and assists Kurds' attempts to mobilize support among European allies (Eccarius-Kelly, 2002: 111). Secondly, the court and the EU share the same values, so the decisions of the court easily find a place in the progress reports. Kurds are aware of the role of the court for the EU. There are organizations that support Kurdish applications to the court such as the London-based Kurdish Human Rights Project (KHRP). Since its foundation in 1992 until 2011, it has brought 500 cases to the United Nations committees and European Court of Human Rights (Gruber Foundation, 2011). Thanks to the results of the cases brought to the court by the KHRP, Turkey has been forced to allow oral courtroom testimony to be given in Kurdish (1996). In 2003 during the abolition of capital punishment, KHRP's arguments were the landmark for judgement. Finally in 2007 rape committed by state actors was classified as torture (Gruber Foundation, 2011). The organization also publishes handbooks on application to the ECHR in several languages (Gruber Foundation, 2011). The scope of its activities includes "anyone who has been the victim of a human rights violation in the Kurdish regions" (KHRP). With the cooperation of Turkey based organizations such as the Human Rights Association [İnsan Hakları Derneği – IHD] that provides support and information for application to ECtHR, many cases were brought to the court (İnsan Hakları Derneği). All these efforts put Turkey at the top of the list of ECtHR for a long time. Until 2012[2] Turkey was following Russia on the list of countries with the highest number of applications. In 2404 cases between 1959 and 2011, the court ruled that Turkey violated at least one article of the European Convention on Human Rights. Consequently, among the 47 states Turkey was at the top of the violation list (BİA Haber Merkezi, 2012).

European Kurds are less successful in their cooperation with the European Commission and European Council, the main EU bodies that deal with accession. Eccarius-Kelly points to structural and organizational problems as the reason. First of all due to the fact that Turkey is not a member state, nor did it sign the 1997 Amsterdam Treaty, the commission has limited powers over Turkey. Secondly, the Kurdish diaspora in Europe lacks insider knowledge and expertise. Additionally, the diaspora has neither political unity nor highly educated members among its leadership to sustain such large-scale insider lobbying (Eccarius-Kelly, 2002: 111-112). According to Casier, the "European Commission has always maintained its own policy regarding the way in which it addresses issues related to the Kurdish question with the Turkish government and its administration" (Casier, 2011: 29). Yet the power of ethnic Kurds holding EU citizenship should not be underestimated. They are able to join political parties and elections and also pressure their host states through lobbying and protests.

The European Parliament, the only directly elected EU institution, provides better political opportunities for Kurds than the European Commission. Kurds in Europe benefit from the power of the Parliament in several ways. Kurdish EU citizens are being elected to the parliament, through which they attempt to influence Turkey's EU accession process. Feleknas Uca, a Kurdish-German MP, is one well-known example. She was part of the Confederal Group of European United Left/Nordic Green Left (GUE/NGL) from 1999 to 2009 (The European Parliament). During this time she worked in the Delegation on the EU-Turkey Joint Parliamentary Committee (European Parliament). As indicated by Eccarius-Kelly, she contributed to the dissemination of the human rights situation in Turkey and also the Kurdish question and she is regarded as pro-Kurdish (Eccarius-Kelly, 2002: 112).

The Kurdish-origin voters in Europe also force European politicians to take Kurdish demands into consideration. There is a sizeable Kurdish

---

[2] In 2012 a new legislated law allowed individual application to the Constitutional Court in Turkey in order to reduce the applications to ECtHR. To gauge the effectiveness of the Constitutional Court ECtHR decided to not accept applications from Turkey for two years period (Özçınar, 2012).

population in Europe with increasing numbers and so does the number of the voters. In order to target these voters the European politicians deal with the Kurdish issue and cooperate with the Kurdish institutions occasionally (Ferho, 2014). Consequently, it is not surprising that before the parliamentary elections in 2014, candidates frequently stressed the importance of the Kurdish question for Turkey's accession (Serinci, 2014).

Providing information is another effective tool for Kurds. During an interview for this study the Brussels-based Kurdish Bureau's representative Pervîn Jamîl explained that their monthly newsletter is being sent to more than 2000 European Parliament members (MPs). The newsletter has been described as practical information sources by these MPs (Jamîl, 2014). Institutions such as KHRP organise speeches in the Parliament on the human rights situation in Turkey and on the use of Kurdish language in Turkey (KHRP). Additionally, the parliament's structure offers consultation to the NGOs (Eccarius-Kelly, 2002:112). The Kurds in Europe clearly use this chance to promote their cause to the parliamentarians. Derviş Ferho says that the Brussels Kurdish Institute regularly provides briefings to the members of the Parliament (Ferho, 2014).

The European Union Turkey Civic Commission (EUTCC) which is formed by the Rafto Foundation (Norway), Kurdish Human Rights Project (United Kingdom), and Medico International (Germany) is cooperating with the Bar Human Rights Committee of England and Wales. The EUTCC is in favour of Turkey's membership but only after fulfilling the Copenhagen Criteria. It is monitoring the situation in Turkey with particular focus on minority rights and the Kurdish question (EUTCC). The EUTCC annually organizes conferences titled "Turkey, EU and the Kurds" in the European Parliament. These conferences are held just before the annual progress report when the Parliament is preparing its draft resolution. Casier underlines the importance of timing and argues that the aim is to affect the opinions of the MPs (Casier, 2011: 22).

In addition to the activities in the Parliament, indirect pressure on the Commission and a high number of applications to the ECtHR, the structural conditions in Europe provide the essential background for awareness raising campaigns. Freedom of speech, freedom of assembly, and subsidies for non-governmental organizations all offer a chance to get institutionalized and conduct peaceful protests. This is obvious in the three interviewed diaspora organizations in Brussels. The Brussels Kurdish Institute is ranked 72nd among the most successful non-governmental institutions in Belgium. It publishes books mostly in Flemish and French as well as a monthly magazine; institute staff give guest lectures on Kurds at universities and high schools; they have regular contact with the

European media and they provide archival sources to the Flemish Regional Archive. The Institute is in contact with all Belgian political parties (Ferho, 2014).

Nûçe TV has weekly broadcasts in English. They also provide consultation and information to European NGOs and the media (Dicle, 2014). The Kurdish Bureau organizes several conferences every month. The newsletter prepared by the Bureau reaches more than 5000 recipients providing information and organizing cultural events (Jamîl, 2014).

Kurdish diaspora seemingly uses every channel to influence European decision making mechanisms. The political opportunities in Europe have increased for Kurds. Currently Kurdish diaspora provides new networks and links essential for all social movements. Additionally, the diaspora institutions are advancing strategically. According to Ruşen Çakır, a Turkish journalist who is a specialist on the Kurdish issue, the Kurdish movement has put down roots in Europe for two main reasons: (1) The Kurdish movement, especially the PKK, invested in Europe by founding lots of institutions and the cadres in these institutions are very professional; (2) Political migrants vastly politicized other migrants, which also strengthened the Turkish - Kurdish separation (Çakır, 2010). Therefore it would not be easy to wipe the Kurdish movement off the map in Europe. Ibrahim Sirkeci explains importance of political activities of the Kurdish diaspora as: "politically, the Kurdish cause gained respect among Western populations only with the help of demonstrations and informal diplomacy of immigrant populations in the European capitals" (Sirkeci, 2003: 242). Furthermore, as Andreas Blätte put "the Kurdish diaspora's activities are directed at European institutions" (Eccarius-Kelly, 2014: 4). According to Eccarius-Kelly these activities are successful thanks to the intersecting interests among national representatives of the EU member states and the Kurdish diaspora activists. Despite the belief that non-citizen migrants are excluded from the EU channels Kurds became a quasi-insider group in the EU with the help of their constant access to the Parliament (Eccarius-Kelly, 2014: 3). Currently the diaspora activists are contributors to the reports on Turkey and regular consultants on the situation of the minorities in Turkey (Eccarius-Kelly, 2014: 9). Consequently, the diaspora activists are in a position to inform the EU policy making and instrumentalize the process to gain ethno-political rights in Turkey.

Progress reports and the Kurdish issue

Although the European Union started to release reports on Turkey starting from 1998, the human rights situation in Turkey has been under the monitoring procedure of the Council of Europe since 1996 (European Commission, 1998: 14). Progress reports constitute the main documents about the accession process. They also provide a good illustration of the EU's stance on particular issues such as the Kurdish issue.

In the first report in 1998, there was limited reference to the Kurdish issue and Kurds; the Kurdish issue was seen to be bounded with terrorism and the PKK. EU's support for Turkey in combating terrorism was underlined several times. The report makes reference to a 1997 Presidency statement beginning with an allowance to Turkey: "While aware of the extent of the problem Turkey is facing in the south-east...." Then it reminds Turkey her international human rights obligations: "the Union nevertheless stresses that the fight against terrorism must be conducted with due respect for human rights and the rule of law, and calls for a political solution" (European Commission, 1998: 10). The report criticizes regular disappearances, torture and extra-judicial executions, but also states that these abuses had mostly occurred in the army's and government's responses to the problems in southeast Turkey. Despite the EU's sensitivity on human rights, this emphasis reflects a rather a state security-centred approach. The Kurds' demands and problems did not get a direct mention in the report, but the problems were briefly explained in the description of the general situation in Turkey with a limited reference to Kurds (European Commission, 1998: 10).

The year after the first report, European countries more directly felt the Kurdish issue. The report in 1999 has a special importance since Öcalan, the Kurdish leader, was captured on 15th February 1999. Widespread Kurdish protests took place in more than 20 European and Western cities featuring self-immolation and hostage taking (Claffey, Bugua, & Sisk, 1999). Such events brought the Kurdish issue into European agenda. Despite the fact that protests in Europe proved that Kurdish diaspora has a capacity to challenge European states and increase awareness of the Kurdish issue in Turkey. Nevertheless violence in these protests created a backlash for Kurds in Europe. On 22 February 1999, the General Affairs Council released a declaration which was also quoted in the regular report in 1999. The declaration condemned all forms of terrorism, but more importantly, there was open criticism of Turkey. The EU was calling Turkey to respect human rights, the rule of law and the democratic norms as before. However unlike the 1998 report, the EU threatened Turkey: "Turkey's efforts in dealing with these problems in this spirit cannot but affect EU-Turkey relations positively" (European Commission, 1998: 6). The declaration also gave first signals of the EU attitude towards Kurds as suggesting Turkey to separate the fight against terrorism and the search for political solutions, and also promising Turkey to support it politically and financially to reach reconciliation (European Commission, 1998: 6). Another important difference between the 1998 and the 1999 report is the elaboration of the problem. The 1998 report was portraying the Kurdish question in Turkey as a regional problem, recommending a non-military solution to the issues in the southeast region. Yet in the conclusion section, the 1999 report requested Turkey to extend the scope of democratic reforms to include Kurds. This was an early sign that the EU was beginning to see the Kurdish issue as something more than a regional phenomenon of terrorism.

The following progress report in 2000 again dealt with the Kurdish issue under the general context of rights. The tension decreased between PKK and Turkey due to postponement of the death sentence of Öcalan and the PKK's ceasefire. Consequently the size of the 2000 progress report was smaller but it still kept repeating the EU's stance on death penalty (European Commission, 1998: 14). Emphasis on cultural rights of Kurds (i.e. education and language), civil and political issues (i.e. torture, disappearances, prison conditions, freedom of expression and political participation) continued and expanded. In the section on minority rights and protection of minorities, the tone of criticism towards Turkey was stronger compared to previous reports. The 2000 report went further than just stating the situation in Turkey and listing the articles in the Treaty of Lausanne, but it actually challenged the articles of the treaty and underlined that Muslim ethnic groups (e.g. Kurds) are to be treated as minorities and they are also in need of protection: "Regardless of whether or not Turkey is not willing to consider any ethnic groups with a cultural identity and common traditions as 'national minorities', members of such groups are clearly still denied certain basic rights" (European Commission, 1998: 19).

The next ten years saw important changes. Kurdish political groups distanced themselves from the armed struggle and started to focus on politics while also building links with the EU[3]. According to Eccarius-Kelly, 1995-2005 was a period of maturing for the Kurdish diaspora. Lobbying activities gained an important position and the diaspora became a quasi-insider group in this period. Since the mid-1990s, the Kurdish diaspora sought new opportunities for Kurds. "Under the leadership of Kurdish diaspora members in Europe, Kurdish activists engaged in aggressive campaigns of transnational lobbying instead of orchestrated campaign of terror" (Eccarius- Kelly, 2014: 7). The rise of activities right after the arrest of Öcalan showed the power of the Kurds in Europe.

In the 2011 report, there was a specific section on the Kurdish issue titled "the situation in the east and the south-east". It should also be noted

---

[3] After this thesis completed in 2014, important changes had occurred due to the war against ISIS and the PKK/ PYD's role in this fight. There is need for further research and discussion regarding the changes in the EU- Kurdish relations after the war against ISIS.

that the scope of analysis also included the eastern provinces which are relatively less problematic as compared to the south-east. Another symbolic change had been made to the part about *Newroz;* it had been written in Kurdish (European Commission, 1998: 27). This was important because when the commission published this report, the letters "q, x, w" were forbidden in Turkey (to prevent writing in Kurdish).

Additionally, the focus on the Kurdish issue shifted away from state security concerns and terrorist activities to democratic rights of Kurdish population. However, the EU condemnation of the PKK's activities in the region remained. Human rights violations were not mentioned as 'unintended' but rather as 'avoidable consequences'. This is a sign of understanding the essence of the Kurdish question. Police and security forces' attitudes towards demonstrators and legal proceedings on charges of terrorist propaganda were criticized while also portraying protests and protestors as part of the civil society and human rights agenda instead of activities of the PKK (European Commission, 1998: 27).

In 2012, the European Commission defined the Kurdish issue as a key challenge for Turkey (European Commission, 1998: 7) and explained the components of the Kurdish issue as "citizenship, use of mother tongue, and decentralization" (European Commission, 1998: 8). It was important because the report defined the Kurdish issue as separate from the terrorist characteristics and did not use the state centred security approach. State security were mentioned in the reports in 1998, 1999 and relatively less so in 2000, indicating the EU's understanding of Turkish concerns. However, the 2012 report adopted the Kurdish politicians' view in defining the Kurdish issue (Ilıcak, 2012). This report made suggestions consistent with the Kurdish demands such as increasing decentralization and allowing the use of languages other than Turkish (European Commission, 1998: 11). In the 2012 report, there was one more Kurdish word in addition to *Newroz* which entered the report in 2011. The report gave the Kurdish name of a city in parenthesis.[4] It was symbolically important indication of the EU's changing stance towards the Kurdish language. This report was considered by the Turkish government as the worst EU report on Turkey (Anadolu Ajansı, 2012). Chair of the Turkish Grand National Assembly's constitution committee, a well-known politician from the government, threw the progress report in a rubbish bin at a press conference (Gazeteciler online, 2012). The government published its own - alternative - progress report for 2012, in January 2013 to explain the reforms Turkey had implemented (T.C. Avrupa Birliği Bakanlığı, 2012).

---

[4] Before 1980s, names of the 23 cities and 12.000 villages had been changed due to different reasons. One of the main aims of these changes was replacing the Kurdish names with Turkish names (Nişanyan, 2011: 14).

The sixteenth progress report of the European Union was released in 2013. The situation in the east and the south-east dealt with similar issues as the 2012 report. The report also emphasized the hunger strike of the Kurdish prisoners (European Commission, 1998: 15) which also had been widely supported by the Kurds in Europe (Çetin, 2012). One of the most important points of the report was the more overtly pursued stance towards arrest due to the PKK/KCK membership. The report defined the arrested people as journalists, academicians, students, and human rights defenders (European Commission, 1998: 15) rather than members of an armed group.[5] The last reports offered some solutions for local governance, education in the mother tongue, the KCK arrests, and the concept of citizenship. These issues actually constitute the main demands of the Kurds in Turkey (Al Jazeera, 2013). The indirect general recommendations were replaced by direct criticisms, and solutions were recommended in the latest reports right after the Kurdish diaspora settled its institutions and activities. Some Turkish commentators and think tanks such as Bilgesam pointed to *alternative information sources* of the commission as the main reason of this pro-Kurdish attitude, claiming that the EU was not being informed objectively (Dede & Kaya, 2013; emphasis added by the author). Similarly, in his press release on the 2013 progress report, the minister of EU affairs, Mevlüt Çavuşoğlu, stated that there are efforts to instrumentalise the EU-Turkey relations and that the EU was supporting these efforts (Çavuşoğlu, 2014). Casier says that without the activities of the Kurdish diaspora there would not have been such an emphasis on the Kurdish issue (Casier, 2011:11).

In short, the emphasis on the Kurdish issue increased over time and the attitude of the EU towards the issue changed. Özsöz states that in earlier reports the Kurdish issue was seen rather as part of politics of terrorism and referred to within the armed conflict framework, but in later years, economic, social and cultural aspects of the issue have also been highlighted (Özsöz, 2012: 11). Thus the Kurdish issue was separated from the context of terrorism and mentioned in different chapters of the report. Kurdish issue has been defined separately from terrorism, while also some Kurdish words were used in these later reports. Even some demands of the Kurdish political movement were included in policy proposals in addressing the Kurdish question, reflecting all these changes took place between 2000 and 2012.

---

[5] These arrested people charged as the members of an armed group, on the base of the Turkish Criminal Code Article 314 (European Commission, 2013: 15).

Conclusion

In this chapter, the role of the Kurdish diaspora activities in transnational politics in relation to Turkey's EU accession process is explored. The Kurdish movement seemingly have aimed at instrumentalizing the EU accession process rather than blocking Turkey's accession. The diaspora changed its means and focus by employing an insider group strategy in the EU.

Kurdish diaspora in Europe distanced itself from allegedly being a 'separatist terrorist' organization and positioned as a social and political movement. The human rights discourse has empowered its institutions. Activities and the scope of the activities widened to include publishing reports, preparing monthly newsletters, organizing conferences in the EU parliament and other main stream venues, and lobbying. As discussed in this chapter, there is also a shift in the EU's approach towards the Kurdish issue in Turkey. Alongside the Diaspora's influence, it is acknowledged that other factors such as newly opened chapters in accession process, growing relations between Turkey and the EU, the accession negotiations since 2005 have played a role in this shift, which led to a steady increase in the scope and space allocated to the issue in these reports over time. The shift was not only a technical growth of pages and words, but also the emphasis have shifted too. This represents a change in mentality and shift to a more understanding position in favour of the Kurds. This can be at least partly credited to the the diaspora's pro-EU strategy in Turkey's accession process.

"Diasporas powerfully embody broader trends in the changing nature of nation-states" says Vertovec (2005). Diasporas are creating new political realities and they are influential actors in transnational politics. This is what Kurdish diaspora has seemed to be doing in the context of the EU-Turkey accession process.

Acknowledgement

I am grateful to Dr. Amanda Klekowski von Koppenfels for her aspiring guidance and constructive comments and to Dr. Elise Féron for her support and enlightening comments.

Chapter 7. Perspectives on conflicts and potentials in a changing neighbourhood: Berlin-Neukölln and the role of urban governance

Manuela Freiheit and Kristina Seidelsohn

Cities operate more and more like enterprises as they are confronted with an increasing global competition for investments, business locations, fairs and tourism, as well as scientific and creative excellence. On the other hand, economic, political and social changes since the late 1960s have caused mounting social and urban fragmentation which has led to upward revaluation or devaluation of some inner-city districts. Those neighbourhoods are characterized by a concentration of developmental, ecological, infrastructural and socio-economic problems as well as ethnic-cultural diversity (cf. Franke et al., 2000:244ff.). Based on the assumption that the process taking place in these areas reinforce themselves continuously, many American and European cities developed political programs in the early 1990s to counteract the 'downward spiral' by bringing different sectors of local government and civil society together. This paradigm-shift from physical urban development to social issues represents a new, integrative approach of governmental action in local contexts and tries to overcome conventional town planning measures. One example of such a method is the program 'Districts with Special Development Needs - The Socially Integrative City' (in short: *Soziale Stadt*) initiated by the national government and the governments of the federal states of Germany in 1999.[1] The program is corporately financed by the EU, the German federal government, its *Länder* and the affected German municipalities. Comparably, such social and urban development policies can be found in many OECD countries (FN). They are regarded as appropriate tools to prevent further drifts and to improve the local living and housing conditions in those neighbourhoods (cf. e.g. Häußermann, 2004; Böhme et al., 2008). Central elements of the program are therefore the concentration of resources and cooperation, a coordination of formerly separated departments and hierarchical levels, participation and decision-making competencies for the citizenry, business and industry, the formulation of 'Integrated Action Plans' and the establishment of new

---

[1] If not indicated otherwise, the information on the *Socially Integrative City* program can be found on the *Soziale Stadt* web page http://www.sozialestadt.de/ available on: 20.10.2015.

management structures on the neighbourhood level (cf. e.g. Becker & Löhr, 2000; Franke et al., 2000; Alisch, 2002; Güntner, 2007). To realize these complex tasks a *neighbourhood management system* was implemented as a key instrument. In general, a neighbourhood management (in short: NM) functions as an administrative coordinator in project-funding and -implementation. It is intended to integrate strategies and players in neighbourhood development, link up economic and social development projects, and strengthen the scope and capacity of residents to take action, especially groups that have been difficult or impossible to reach so far.

Critics, however, point out that not the social causes of disadvantaged neighbourhoods, but merely their symptoms are tackled, and evaluate the effects of the integrated neighbourhood approach as highly ambivalent (cf. e.g. Walther & Güntner, 2007:355). On the one hand, neighbourhood management seems to be more flexible and adaptable to specific local characteristics. On the other hand, neighbourhood management itself could not solve the manifold and complex problems determined on the supra-regional level. Rather, it would fragment urban development policy in many short-term projects and fade out the causes of ongoing pauperization and social inequality which comes along with a pro-competitive policy. Also the claim of the program to enhance citizen's participation and activation in terms of empowerment and to help people to help themselves has been variously criticized and interpreted as an expressionand transfer of neoliberal strategies to the level of the districts (cf. e.g. Elwood, 2002; Savitch & Vogel, 2005; Künkel, 2008; Lanz, 2009).

Against this background the question arises whether the revitalization of multi-ethnic and disadvantaged neighbourhoods could be understood as a social and urban policy that is suited to counteract the diverse and wide range of social problems. Besides the improvement of the local living and housing conditions, the overriding aim of the *Soziale Stadt* program is the enhancement of community cohesion and the social and cultural integration of the neighbourhoods' inhabitants. If neighbourhood policy, however, could be regarded as an expression of a pro-competitive and neoliberal urban policy, this would mean that the measures generate ambivalent effects and they primarily support existing power-constellations, although the interests and needs of the disadvantaged population groups are the actual objectives of the *Soziale Stadt* program.

By means of the changing neighbourhood *Reuterquartier* in the northern part of Berlin-Neukölln this question shall be further analysed and evaluated empirically how pro-competitive and neoliberal conceptions and practices like privatization, deregulation and flexibility influence the implementation of programs like the *Soziale Stadt* program and which effects on the social cohesion within the neighbourhood can be observed.[2] Hence, three different fields of urban policy intervention are analysed in this chapter: inhabitant participation and political activation, economic revitalization and employment as well as the housing-policy through neighbourhood management at local level.

Social mixing vs. gentrification

The ideal of 'social mixing' as a major component of neighbourhood improvement policies has been variously criticized. It is based on the assumption that in socially mixed neighbourhoods the chances increase to overcome poverty and promote social capital within the neighbourhood (cf. Nieszery, 2008). For example, the interim evaluations of the *Soziale Stadt* program states: "If the situation has to be changed, the context has to be modified by a change of the appearance of the neighbourhood and the social situation or rather the social milieus." (IfS, 2004: 37) But mostly that would mean: 'moving middle-income people into low-income inner-city neighbourhoods' (Lees, 2008: 2451) which often trigger gentrification processes and the displacement of lower income residents. Furthermore, there is no empirical evidence so far, as Loretta Lees points out (ibid.), that 'social mixing' shows the expected positive area effects. Neil Smith (1996) goes one step further. He does not only suggest that the myth of social mixing has failed, but also interprets the idea of social mixing as an expression of a 'revanchist urban policy' (ibid.) since the mix would be considered almost exclusively as the recapture of working-class areas by the middle class and rarely the other way round. Especially Smith's argumentation that gentrification could be understood as a global *governance* strategy of a neoliberal urbanism is trendsetting (cf. Smith, 2002; Slater, 2006: 75). A characteristic dimension of this governance change is the involvement of private actors and non-profit organizations in municipal administration tasks and projects of urban planning and economic growth (cf. ibid.). These public-private partnerships are highlighted and analysed in areas such as social work or public safety, but

---

[2] Data collection was conducted by a combination of document analysis (e.g. official statistics and reports regarding the *Soziale Stadt* program) and qualitative interviews with local authorities and representatives of the municipality and neighborhood organizations (such as neighborhood manager, the head of the division of the *Soziale Stadt* program, private developer agencies, as well as educators and teachers, street and social workers) between January 2009 and September 2010 in Berlin-Neukölln as part of the authors' PhD thesis at the Institute for Interdisciplinary Research on Conflict and Violence (IKG). In total we carried out 22 expert interviews and 15 group discussions with long-term residents and newcomers. However, the present article is mainly based on the interviews with the experts and the various documents.

also in areas like environmental protection or water supply (cf. e.g. Hackworth, 2007; Rosen & Razin, 2009; Blakeley, 2010).

At the same time, the withdrawal of governmental engagement in public housing construction and the ongoing privatization of real estate have led to a market-controlled housing sector since the late 1980s. "Between 1999 and 2008", for example, "municipalities, federal and state governments lost 553,000 units from its holdings and thus lost property rights, while private parties, including many foreign investors, recorded a gain of 627,000 residential units" (Siebel, 2010: 29). In doing so, the number of flats reserved for low-income households has halved throughout Germany since the early 1980s while the number of households dependent on transfer payments has increased sharply. Indeed, recent developments in Berlins' housing policy show a stronger commitment for social housing construction and the question of affordable housing[3], but it seems to be highly questionable if the demand can be covered in the foreseeable future.

Moreover, many studies emphasize the authoritarian character of 'neoliberal gentrification' which is documented in terms of *zero tolerance policies* and comes along with stigmatization, criminalization and displacement or exclusion of marginalized groups like immigrants, homosexuals or homeless people (cf. Swanson, 2007; Aalbers, 2010). Accordingly, one can say, the neoliberal city 'is a city that is typically characterized by the declining significance of public housing and public spaces, and the rise of entrepreneurial privatized landscapes of gentrification, downtown redevelopment, mega projects and other forms of uneven development' (Rosen & Razin, 2009:1703).

With regards to the investigation area, the changing neighbourhood *Reuterquartier* in Berlin-Neukölln, the following questions gain importance: Which developments should be initiated by public institutions? In which relationship framework, they should work together? How institutionalized networks influence inclusion and exclusion of different social groups within the neighbourhood?

Berlin-Neukölln and the role of urban governance

The neighbourhood of *Neukölln-Reuterquartier*, an area with approximately 19,441 residents in the northern part of Berlin-Neukölln, was classified as one of the "Districts with Special Development Needs". With a population of approximately 306,000 residents, Neukölln is home to about 9% of all Berliners and people from more than 160 different nationalities. Besides the ethnic and cultural diversity the *Reuterquartier* –

---

[3] See the web page of the *Senate Department for Urban Development and the Environment*: http://www.stadtentwicklung.berlin.de/index_en.shtml.

as other neighbourhoods in the densely populated northern part of Neukölln with about 160,000 residents – is characterized by social marginality and spatial disadvantages like the lack of green areas and open space, a great need for renovation and modernization, insufficient social and cultural infrastructure, in particular inadequate leisure facilities for children and teenagers, the loss of small businesses, trade and services, as well as declining or inadequate jobs and training opportunities. Moreover, the neighbourhood is characterized by long-term unemployment and above-average dependence on state benefits, poverty, an over proportionate influx of underprivileged households and migrants, a high proportion of one-parent families (mainly single mothers), as well as conflicts between different population segments, vandalism and crime, school problems among children and teenagers, drug and alcohol abuse, and a negative image in the eyes of both residents and outsiders. For example, in 2012, 24% of the inhabitants in the *Reuterquartier* received social security benefits (cf. Quartiermanagement Reuterplatz, 2013). The unemployment rate was 10-14% (ibid.) and exceeded the city-wide average (9.4%). Compared to the whole northern part of Berlin-Neukölln, 56-65% of children and juveniles living in the investigation area are affected by poverty (cf. Difu, 2013). 44.2% of the inhabitants have a migration background (cf. Quartiermanagement Reuterplatz, 2013) and the majority are of Turkish and Arabic origin. More than 95% of the children are non-German native speakers, therefore better-off households and education-oriented families with German or with migration background often leave the area as soon as their children reach the compulsory school age (ibid.).

In order to address these social challenges, a neighbourhood management and the provision of neighbourhood funds as main components of the whole *Soziale Stadt* program was implemented in 2003 by a private development agency who was introduced by *the Senate Department of Urban Development and the Environment* and the *District Office Neukölln*. Overall, 34 neighbourhood management offices were opened in Berlin selected on the basis of socio-demographic indicators like unemployment, dependence on social welfare, the percentage of migrants, increasing vacancy and the economic situation in the neighbourhoods. On the one hand, all available funds are applied to structural modernization and maintenance of neglected buildings, public parks and infrastructures. On the other hand, the implemented offices cooperate with inhabitants and local advisory boards in developing social projects and actions against the low level of education, language barriers and unemployment in order to solve the problems of criminality and violence. Accordingly, the neighbourhood management of the investigation area, Neukölln-Reuterquartier, acts in the sphere of local economy as well as traffic planning or dog excrement, social infrastructure or topics like physical health and violence prevention. The main focus, however, is on issues like education, integration and participation in terms of a neighbourhood council, working groups or own (small) projects. As the head of division of Berlin's *Senate Department of Urban Development and the Environment* pointed out, the involvement of the inhabitants should foster identification as well as a 'new sense of responsibility' which 'roughly means that you feel responsible for your neighbour' and at its best strengthen public spirit and community cohesion. Thereby, the neighbourhood management address multiplicators on the meta-level rather than individuals and is responsible for administration like reporting, control of available funds, assessment, as well as project monitoring, but is not engaged in any social work. The head of the division argues that 50% of its success will depend upon cross-departmental communication and networking as well as public participation. Numerous projects were realized through the *Soziale Stadt* program during the previous years, including language courses, after-school care, sports programs, as well as art projects and cultural events (for an overview of funded projects during the period of 2002-2013 see http://www.reuter-quartier.de/Projekte.27.0.html). Therefore, various horizontal networks of multiple stakeholders emerged and strengthened the cooperation within the neighbourhood and beyond.

In the following, three different fields of political action at the neighbourhood-level should be analysed. These are resident activities and political participation, economic revitalization and employment as well as the housing market.

Inhabitant activation and political participation

On the one hand, the *Soziale Stadt* program and project funding is characterized by diversification, decentralized management and flexibility in respect to different local contexts. On the contrary, the apportionment of funds is marked by the neighbourhood management as too complicated for the draw on inhabitant-participation. Therefore, the decision-making process is not governed by inhabitants but by means of active actors, which have to tackle a large number of projects. At the same time, the NM-staff noticed strong regulation and control in terms of top-down policies and mentioned, "they observe and control us intensively, and especially the EU has sharp eyes on everything". Moreover, the district exchange is reviewing the NM`s economic efficiency constantly in cooperation with an external and private test centre. The funding by the

'European-Social-Fond' (ESF) is proved by the district exchange, which makes use of an external private inspection authority as well. "Actually, every single rubber is checked five times, this is really cruel". The respondents marked the EU-funding-law as difficult to explain to local inhabitants. Although many small-scale projects are described as uncomplicated and manageable, a lot of projects suffer from inadequate counselling compared to more complex and/or expensive ones. Due to labour shortages, mentoring and consulting was deferred and became less intense. During the period of inquiry, only two persons were responsible for the neighbourhood management *Reuterquartier* with 20,000 residents, comparable to the size of a small German town.

On behalf of the neighbourhood management, a study about inhabitant-participation concludes, as the respondents of the neighbourhood management point out, "that the procedure of project funding reduces the involvement of the inhabitants by trend" and discourages potentially interested persons (cf. Straßburger & Wurtzbacher, 2009). Furthermore, the local advisory boards are filled with academics and middle-class-people, which do not represent the NM's target audience. "There is a certain clientele of course, which remain excluded. For example, it is difficult for migrants to understand the procedures, and we notice constantly that migrants stay away". The major barrier for the increase of participation is a lack of verbal skills because German as well as 'academic language' are foreign languages for many.

However, the neighbourhood management perceived difficulties in collaboration with cultural- and migrant-associations as well. The respondents described these associations as underfunded, nonprofessional, paternalistic and rarely locally oriented. They are characterized by staffing shortage and act mainly as a substitute for the 'culture of the country of origin'. Activities by migrant-associations are hardly attended by German inhabitants and vice-versa. NM-staff have noticed "how blatantly separated they are and how little contact they have with each other. [...] Many, especially the younger population are left-winged, open-minded and tolerant, but one has to say clearly, they still have nothing to do with each other".

Besides these negative evaluations of the inter-group relations, positive examples of the political participation of female residents with migration background can be observed. The head of division of the *Soziale Stadt* program in Berlin describes the success of the program on the basis of a self-organization against substance abuse "between women with migration background who noticed that they have to fight for themselves [...]. At this point, the NM comes into play and says yes, you are right, we support you in the process of self-organization [...]". The 'help for self-help' strategy shows that the ability of urban governance for regulation is not simply disappearing, but shifting from formal to informal types of government. The management capacity should be transmitted from public institutions to individuals or small and independently acting units. However, the implementation of the strategy is dependent on necessary capital for individual responsibility and self-monitoring, which many socially weak households and migrants are missing.

In addition, the political participation of migrants within the established political parties and the municipality is still lacking. The commissioner for integration and migration in Neukölln criticizes, for example, that the local council ('Bezirksverordnetenversammlung') holds "52 people and only three of them have a migration background [...]. One person of the SPD [Social Democratic Party], one of the 'Linke' [Left-wing Party] and one of the CDU [Christian Democratic Party]. Unfortunately, none of them has its seeds in Arabic countries and this is just not enough in proportion to 40% of residents with migration background". Therefore, the elected government of the municipality rarely represents the population of Neukölln and its ethnic-cultural diversity. Quite often devaluation and prejudice like the assumed lack of willingness to integrate and participate, especially against Muslims, form the basis of justification and spatial separation by political stakeholders and in many cases exceed the 'political correctness'. At the same time, the spatial structures visualize the political power relations of the borough, as the commissioner for integration and migration in Neukölln continues, since most of the better-off households and current members of the local council are living in the southern part of Neukölln: "It is blatant how North- and South-Neukölln diverge. [...] Migrants are invisible in South-Neukölln, because they are 'Bildungsbuerger', they got houses and company's and middle-class jobs". Hence, contact-segregation between different ethnic-cultural groups and social classes within the neighbourhood is framed by residential segregation within the whole borough Neukölln; the North is represented by the poor and socially weak households whereas the southern part gives home to the (German) middle class.

In summary, the empirical data shows on the one hand that low threshold projects as in the case of the association of the female residents with migration background work well but generate a short-term and unclear situation unable to counteract the social problems in the long term. Large-scale projects on the other hand often fail due to the complex and complicated procedure of project funding which discourage local and less educated residents as well as inhabitants with a lack of verbal skills to apply. Moreover, one can say, that decentralization and the ongoing transition to flexible structures of decision-making and procedures within the framework of urban development policy debilitate the inhabitant participation of socially weak groups and/or migrants and mainly benefit and support the residents in upper social positions and therefore present local power constellations rather than to change them.

Economic revitalization and employment

Besides these ethnic and social separations, the physical as well as the economic structure within the area of investigation were characterized by an obvious 'broken-windows'-situation up to recent years. Thus vacant shops should be replaced and rented out temporarily or even better, permanently, to stabilize the district in the long term. Therefore the neighbourhood management launched in 2005 the private developer agency *Zwischennutzungsagentur* ('agency for interim use') with a term of three years – an agency for urban planning focusing on sustainable urban development, landscaping and real estate industry. The *Zwischennutzungsagentur* provides (local) networking possibilities at no charge and selects room-seekers and landlords beforehand. After an initial consultation of interested parties the agency calls for a short concept about business ideas and land use, because, as an interviewee of the agency pointed out, "the more likeable and interesting a business idea, the more you get a good deal with the landlord, it's as simple as that". Thereby, the settling of newcomers irrespective of industrial location is detached from selection criteria by the *Soziale Stadt* program and therefore dependent on the agency networks as well as the networks of the newcomers themselves. The consultation between neighbourhood management and the 'agency for interim use' can be described as loose rather than well-coordinated. In most cases, interested persons pre-selected by the agency are available beforehand and they 'just want the space', 'only some came from the NM, so we ask them from time to time what we are allowed to do'. A lively discussion is conducted with the local promotion of economic development and limited to the newcomers. Working mostly in the field of creative industries the new inhabitants are allowed to suggest preferred neighbours or specific companies. The settling is carried out by the agency through the creation of so called 'micro locations' instead of a 'watering-can principle', because the latter is less effective and visible than concentrated grouping. During the project run time (2005-2008) 56 business-units were reactivated and 16 of these were used as co-working spaces or joint ventures. In this process of industrial location around 200 employment opportunities emerged, 66% of these within the sector of Creative Industries, with health- and social-services making up the remaining majority. Around 30% of the new enterprises and joint ventures have a non-German background, and half are autochthonous inhabitants (cf. Brammer, 2008).

Despite this trend and independently of this development, the unemployment rate among young people and residents with a migration background is still increasing (cf. Quartiersmanagement Reuterplatz, 2013). The opening of new stores and cafés, art galleries and studios, as well as cultural events does not really open up new job perspectives for them. These groups rarely get in contact with the *Zwischennutzungsagentur*, working mainly as tradesmen and self-employed workers along radial highways which represent the administrative borders of the *Soziale Stadt* program. Although these areas have a special need for advisory services due to the high level of fluctuation, the market is self-regulated at the spatial borders. A large number of residents receiving social welfare suffer from insufficient and short-time consulting by the public *Job Centre* and declare bankruptcy after few months, as the respondent of the *Zwischennutzungsagentur* illustrates. Mainly affected by these developments are residents with a low level of education and with migration background. By contrast, the 'agency for interim use' pursues the efficient strategy of 'inspection-tours' for newcomers in small groups. This networking-strategy enables the immediate experience by the landlords that 'only young people' are coming which are "totally different than company's founders in former times" and is much more effective compared to counselling-strategies by public institutions.

Housing market

At the same time and comparable to similar gentrification processes in other inner cities, well-educated and young middle class people, often with a German or another Western background, have moved to the *Reuterquartier*. Most of them are students, academics, artists and designers, who generally have a rather low or precarious income, but are characterized in contrast to the long-term residents by factors such as having a high formal education and a high level of professional prestige. These changes in neighbourhood character and population structure encourage the purchase of real estate as investment property by big enterprises and large-scale investors. Furthermore, the increasing privatization of public spaces and former state-controlled policy areas like security in local traffic or in schools can be observed in North-Neukölln and the *Reuterquartier*. Also the regional and national media picked up the topic 'Gentrification and North-Neukölln' with heightened interest since 2007, which has slightly improved the public perception of the neighbourhood, although the stereotype of the 'Ghetto North-Neukölln' is still prevalent. While in 2010 the small-scale social analyses of the spatial monitoring have shown little shifts in the population structure of the area thus far, a current study shows that 'within the neighbourhood Reuterplatz the gentrification-process is obvious in recent years' (TOPOS Stadtforschung, 2011:49). This development is rarely opposed by state-control and urban development policies because sufficient social housing is not available (cf. Quartiersmanagement Reuterplatz, 2011). The NM faces the increasing fear of rising rents via presentations in cooperation with the tenants union about 'Rent index, running costs, rent and Hartz IV (Social Security Benefits)', but the core of the problem, adequate supply of affordable housing, cannot be solved so far.

As a consequence of this process, the *Zwischennutzung project* funding was stopped. However, a follow up project in cooperation with the district exchange and the 'House- and landlord- association Neukölln' began (2009-2011), which aimed to stabilize the residing enterprises and projects, to link local landlords and to sensitize them about the difficulties of socially deprived long-term residents. While the younger generation of landlords shows positive reactions regarding these sensitizing-strategies, hedge funds and long-term landlords in old age, in many cases, refuse cooperation with the agency. The ongoing sale of property is mainly caused by an increasing interest in profits and goes along with little relatedness to the neighbourhood, which leads to rising rents and includes the stealthy displacement of poorer long-term residents. Hence, one can see less 'social mixing', but instead the recapturing of particular inner-city neighbourhoods by the middle class, in which migrants are still underrepresented.

Currently the *Zwischennutzungsagentur* is working city-wide and in other neighbourhoods of Berlin-Neukölln on similar projects of interim use. Nevertheless, the agency is still located in the *Reuterquartier* and maintains substantial contacts in addition to the management of vacancies offered to target group-specific networking, monitoring and moderation of the participation processes as well as the creation of location studies and building expertise about urban spaces etc. Thereby, a former public-private partnership has changed to some extent into a decoupled private one detached from democratic legitimation.

Conclusion

To sum up, a variety of networks arose through projects in public-private partnership funded by the *Soziale Stadt* program. Moreover, third sector organizations are involved in many cases and observe the decision-making process of local politicians and private actors. Therefore, "dynamic interactions and partnerships of multiple stakeholders" are observable as "urban regimes" as well as "horizontal networks of governance", which show the "decreasing role of formal hierarchical administrative-territorial structures" (Rosen & Razin, 2009: 1703). On the one hand this development represents the global and neoliberal trend in privatization and deregulation. It also exemplifies how state intervention like the *Soziale Stadt* program can turn into projects that bring gains for private agencies. On the other hand, assertions on weakening state intervention and strengthening influence of the market, oversimplify the complex interplay of private developers, public planning institutions and third-sector organizations. As shown with reference to the statement of the neighbourhood manager and the procedure of project funding, "neo-liberal urban governance does not imply the demise of regulation, but rather its changing nature" (Rosen & Razin, 2009: 1702). However, as a transfer of neoliberal strategies to the district-level, the *Soziale Stadt* program brings gain mainly for residents who are well appointed with the necessary capital for individual responsibility and self-monitoring. Therefore, these developments support local and societal power constellations rather than to change them. At the same time, public authorities move back from neglected neighbourhoods against the backdrop of extensive cuts (70% of the funding for the *Soziale Stadt* program since 2010, from 95 million to 17 million Euros in 2014), although many of the social problems still exist, leaving horizontal networks acting to some extent with contrary interests and inconsistent strategies, instead of offering specific and well-directed financial aid.

Chapter 8. The Kurds: "A history of deliberate and reactive state-lessness"

Hanifi Barış

"You should get to know these mountains. ...Each of them is a shelter for a people that does not own these mountains, but have chosen to belong to them." Selim Temo (2013: 1)
"Divide that ye be not ruled." Ernest Gellner (Quoted in Scott 2009: 209)

Introduction

I grew up listening to a story that did not strike me much at the time. My father, who was born in 1925, is a dengbêj[1] (folk poet) and he told me a story explaining the reason for the statelessness of the Kurds in their 'failure' to unite under one leader and join a cause. It is a story about the famous Kurdish leader Cemil Çeto[2] who prepared to fight the Kemalist movement. It was the moment when he saw an opportunity to call upon foreign powers to support the Kurds and assist them in founding a Kurdish state. He meets the leaders of seven tribal confederacies and claims that he can bring France's air force to their help in seven days. Only, he insists that a leader must be chosen, either himself or someone else, who will represent the Kurdish coalition internationally and negotiate with the French. Eminê Ahmed,[3] one of the leaders present, stands up and says that he will never relinquish his title or give his father's legacy away to bow to anyone else. Others follow him in that decision. In short, according to the story the chance to establish a Kurdish state was missed because of the

---

[1] "The word dengbêj can be translated with 'master of the voice', deng meaning voice, bêj derived from the verb 'to say'. In the Kurdish region in Turkey it is used for a singer-poet who sings a cappella, or is occasionally accompanied by a bilûr (shepherd's pipe) or mey (woodwind instrument). He or she has a large repertoire of kilams (recital song, see chapter 1), a nice and strong voice, and knows kilams from well-known master dengbêjs. A good dengbêj also composes kilams him/herself and is known by many people in the near environment." (Hamelink 2014: 17).

[2] The head of the Baxtiyaran tribe of Xerzan, a region in today's Batman, in Kurdistan (the Southeast) of Turkey.

[3] He is also known as Eminê Perîxanê, and he was the head of Raman tribal confederacy in Batman.

lack of unity among Kurdish leaders and such an opportunity was never obtained again.[4]

The story did not strike me until recently, when I read that Idris-i Bidlis-i[5] had advised almost the same thing to Sultan Selim (I) five centuries ago, when Selim asked *"which of the begs was most worthy of this paramount leadership."* (Özoğlu 2004: 49). He intended to choose one of the thirty Kurdish nobles as the ruler of Kurdistan. But Idris advised him not to do so, as *"they are all more or less equal, and none of them will bow his head before any other."* (Özoğlu 2004: 49). The similarity between the two historical moments, despite a half millennium of time apart is very striking. It therefore occurred to me that what seemed to be a 'failure' could have been a deliberate and conscious choice, since choices, not coincidences, have the quality to repeat themselves almost identically in history (Maritain 2010: 3)[6]. The appealing theme in the story and the historical account is that they make room for the element of choice. We see a continuous reluctance or rejection to bow before a higher political authority, a preference to remain local and small in scale, and a tendency to stay autonomous. Modernist-nationalist discourses have long suggested that it testifies to the fact that the Kurds had been the victims of their own pre-modern (read *backwards*) socio-political organization and primordial (read *primitive*) traditions (see Yavuz 2001). Yet, now, an alternative interpretation is possible. As Beck and Scott put it:

"The forms that many people identify as primitive and traditional were often creations responding to, and sometimes mirroring, more complex systems." Beck adds: *"Such local systems adapted to and challenged, or distanced themselves from, the systems of those who sought to dominate them."* Social structure, in other words, is, in large measure, both a state

---

[4] Historical records (Kirisci and Winrow 1997: 80) show that Cemil Ceto revolts against the Kemalist leadership in the summer of 1920, after Huseyin Pasha convinces him that a promise to found a Kurdish state in Turkey was made at the Paris Peace Conference, if the Kurds demonstrate the willingness to do so. It is true that Article 64 of the Treaty of Sevres, signed in August 10, 1920, prepared during that conference, makes such a promise.

[5] The Kurdish ruler of Bitlis province who managed to join thirty-odds Kurdish tribal confederacies gathered and army of almost sixty thousand men, and allied with the Ottomans in 1514 in the battle of Caldiran in which the Ottomans won a decisive victory against the Iranians.

[6] "No doubt there are no "raw" facts; an historical fact presupposes and involves as many critical and discriminating judgments, and analytical recastings, as any other "fact" does; moreover, history does not look for an impossible "coincidence" with the past; it requires choice and sorting, it interprets the past and translates it into human language, it re-composes or re-constitutes sequences of events resulting from one another, and it cannot do so without the instrumentality of a great deal of abstraction [emphasis added]."

effect and a choice; and one possible choice is a social structure that is invisible and/or illegible to state-makers. (Scott 2009: 210)

Although this is not a mainstream understanding of freedom and independence in the era of nationalism, it is clearly a valuable line of thought. The rationale is that once one bows to a higher authority it does not matter if this authority is foreign or familiar; it is still domination and subordination.

In this chapter it is argued that the fact that Kurds have no nation-state of their own cannot be explained solely by failure on the part of Kurdish nobility, but the element of choice was also involved. It does so by highlighting historical moments and socio-political phenomena, which demonstrate that the Kurds did not only resist incorporation in state-structures when they were pressured to do so, they also avoided state formation per se for most parts of their history from the sixteenth to the twentieth century; be it in the sense of escaping foreign domination or in the sense "to prevent states from springing up among them" (Scott 2009: X). Even though such an understanding of Kurdish history may seem unconventional, I think many scholars have already cleared the path towards this conclusion. Drawing on Scott's work, The Art of Not Being Governed (2009), I argue that the Kurds have preferred to keep the state at a distance and to remain loyal to sub-state social and political structures. Apart from the literature, this chapter is also based on Hamelink's research on the kilams (recital songs) of dengbêjs (folk poets). These kilams strengthen the view that the Kurds had a distanced relationship to the idea of state and that the borders of nation-states were not seen as legitimate by many Kurds.

I will start with a short discussion of Scott's thesis, and then give some historical examples to apply his thesis to the Kurdish situation. I continue with main arguments that address Kurdish history of evading and avoiding the state as a deliberate choice and a stateless conception of self-rule. The undertaking with Hamelink is not an attempt to prove that even the 'uncivilized' are 'civilized', but to challenge the entire discourse of 'progress' and 'civilization' that puts the state or nation-state at the core of socio-political organization and political activism.

Scott's main thesis in *The Art of Not Being Governed* (2009: IX-X) states that

"[H]ill peoples are best understood as runaway, fugitive, maroon communities who have, over the course of two millennia, been fleeing the oppressions of state-making projects in the valleys—slavery, conscription, taxes, corvée labor, epidemics, and warfare. Most of the areas in which they reside may be aptly called shatter zones or zones of refuge. Virtually

everything about these people's livelihoods, social organization, ideologies, and (more controversially) even their largely oral cultures, can be read as strategic positioning designed to keep the state at arm's length. Their physical dispersion in rugged terrain, their mobility, their cropping practices, their kinship structure, their pliable ethnic identities, and their devotion to prophetic, millenarian leaders effectively serve to avoid incorporation into states and to prevent states from springing up among them."

These "hill peoples" are inhabitants of what he calls 'Zomia', a vast area in South-East Asia with high altitude that used to make physical access difficult for valley states. They needed manpower to produce, maintain and expand domination, which was difficult to accomplish in the highlands. Those who wished to 'keep the state at arm's length' would therefore deliberately settle in the less accessible zones. Scott's thesis is important because "*it shatters the common view that those living outside the nation state are primitive and uncivilized*" (Conyon 2010: 1, 4). However, for Scott, this is not only a matter of a hierarchical dichotomy between highland *people* and lowland *civilizations*; it goes much deeper than that. The book is also a general criticism of associating civilization and progress with forming states and regarding sub-state political structures as uncivilized or backward. Scott argues that the old imperialistic missions of "*civilizing*" or "*Christianizing*" are carried out under the flag of "*development*", "*progress*" and "*modernization*" (2009: 98-102).

There are a number of criticisms regarding Scott's thesis. A well-known set of arguments is that he over-generalizes his insights that he chooses his examples from areas that fit his hypothesis, and that he is too dependent on secondary literature written in English (Sadan 2010; Subrahmanyam 2010). Sadan (2010: 5-7) stresses that 'Zomia' was of central importance in Van Schendel (2002) not as a region, but as an intersection between regions or areas of study. She argues that "*borderlands and process geographies*" are ignored by Scott. She also adds that the peoples that Scott focuses on are those who are either 'peripheral' or 'invisible' in the history books of their neighbours, and thus points out the need to incorporate 'oral history' or 'oral tradition' of those peoples in order to account for epistemological shortcomings.

Scott and the Kurds

Historically, a state with the name *Kurdistan* has never existed. The largest political structures that were formed in the geographical territory called Kurdistan today were several Kurdish principalities under Ottoman and Persian rule, and a province named *Kurdistan*. This province existed for most part of the last millennium in the margins of both empires. Scholars have provided a number of geographical, social and political reasons that prevented the Kurds from forming a state of their own. The most common is that Kurdistan is a mountainous country, a rough geography, which makes it extremely difficult for a single political entity to gain substantial control over the entire region. A well-known idiom suggests that *even Alexander the Great couldn't bring this region under his rule.* This rugged geography, it is further argued, also prevented the formation of a collective social identity, a standard language and the development of a shared goal among Kurds. However, Scott (2009: XI) reverses this argument by stating that *"the mountains as a refuge for state-fleeing people, including guerrillas, is an important geographical theme."* Likewise, Kurdistan has also functioned as a refuge for many. Due to the rugged terrain that allowed no easy access, the Kurds maintained their presence in this region despite many invasions and long centuries of foreign rule.

Another dominant theme is that the Kurds did not develop a national consciousness and a national unity among themselves and thus cold not build a state of their own. However, social practices like the reluctance and even resistance to being incorporated in the spheres of state influence, the inclination to avoid being ruled, regulated, taxed, conscripted and contained by formal state borders, could all be seen as deliberate attempts to keep the state at a distance. For instance, switching sides between imperial powers was a frequent practice for local rulers who occupied the margins of the empires. And crossing state borders has been a common practice for the Kurds who live in borderlands. Many Kurds have grown up hearing stories of fugitives, bandits and ordinary peasants, who used to take shelter in the mountains of Kurdistan to escape state laws and obligations. Hamelink (2014) has shared her analysis of songs and stories of the dengbêjs in which we witness the protagonists pass borders not like they travel from a country to another one, but like they remain within the same country. I argue that these social and political practices of most of the Kurds until the 1930s is a testimony to their determination to escape the iron clutches of the (nation-)state.

Although Scott (2009: 130) limits the options available to the people who escaped subordination to either absorption or resistance, the Kurdish population under the threat of the Safavid and Ottoman empires in the sixteenth century neither resisted through military confrontation nor fled, nor were they absorbed or assimilated. The Kurdish notables adopted a third strategy: they played the two empires against each other and maintained their autonomy in the margins of political and military powers far more superior then themselves.[7] Scott (ibid: 210) also points out to such a strategy later on, when he states:

"when nonstate peoples (aka tribes) face pressures for political and social incorporation into a state system, a variety of responses is possible. They, or a section of them, may be incorporated loosely or tightly as a tributary society with a designated leader (indirect rule)."

It must be highlighted that the indirect rule in the case of Kurdish emirates characterized a high level of autonomy. As Özoğlu (2004) and Ateş (2013) have demonstrated, the authority of the rulers in Kurdistan was not interfered with by the Ottoman Sultan and they maintained hereditary privileges like property of the land and succession. Özoğlu (2004: 57) emphasizes that the administrations of the least accessed territories were named *hükümet*s (government) and behaved accordingly:

"The state preferred not to interfere in their succession and internal affairs, and contented itself with recognizing the authority of the rulers. The sultan issued official diplomas of investiture to show his approval. The hükümets did not have the timar, zeamet, or has. They neither paid taxes to the Ottoman state nor provided regular military forces to the sipahi army"[8].

Ateş (2013: 32) refers to the same phenomenon when he states that:

"apart from the requirement of doing battle and combat with the heresy-embracing "redhead" they were freed from all obligation to pay extraordinary impositions (tekalif) and autonomy was granted to them over their ancestral lands (odjak) and homes (yurt)..."

This helps us to understand two important things. First, the Kurds have played their role in shaping the course of events in Kurdistan, and are thus not mere victims of historical developments. Second, the existence of

---

[7] Notice the almost identical strategy adopted by Syrian Kurds in *Rojava* (Western Kurdistan) since the civil war broke out in the country in 2011: *"the Kurdish movement in Rojava decided to go a third way: it would side neither with the regime nor with the opposition. It would defend itself, but it would not wage war."* Source: "Democratic Autonomy in Rojava" by TATORT Kurdistan, on *New Compass Press*, 10.10.2014. Available on: http://new-compass.net/articles/revolution-rojava; accessed on 24.11.2015.

[8]"The Ottoman lands were divided into three categories: mülk, freehold land; vakif, land granted for pious or charitable purposes which remained or was revised at the sultan's discretion; and arazi-i emiriyye or miri, agricultural land that belonged to the Ottoman state. Revenues for the state were generated exclusively from the latter, which was organized in three types of administrative unit: timar, zeamet, and has. This organization was called the dirlik or timar system. A timar was the smallest unit and produced up to twenty thousand akçes [akçe was the Ottoman currency]. Zeamets produced from twenty thousand to one hundred thousand akçes, and they have produced over one hundred thousand akçes as tax revenues. Most dirlik holders were military men. The timar, village-level revenue, was given to the lowest-level military men (sipahis) for their service to the state." (Özoğlu 2004: 52)

hükümets that had a high level of autonomy as internal political organizations demonstrates that the Kurds did not lack the characteristics attributed to other social and political groups around them. This defies the argument that they are second to categorically superior groups called nations.

Additionally, when the Ottomans implemented modern reforms aimed at centralizing political power and therewith gravely diminish Kurdish autonomy, we see that Kurds followed two trajectories to resist the state. The first one was rebelling against those policies, exemplified by the resistance of Mir Bedirxan, the emirate of the province Botan. The revolt of Mir Bedirxan was an attempt to preserve political autonomy and self-rule in Kurdistan. The other strategy was that they developed new structures and forms of social organization. The Ottomans had eliminated Kurdish aristocracy and destroyed political autonomy in Kurdistan by the mid-nineteenth century. The power vacuum was filled by Dervish/Sufi orders, because the Ottoman state was yet to develop a modern form of citizenship, which could replace feudal political loyalties. But more importantly, the state had nothing to offer the Kurds, because they had already re-organized themselves around religious orders, just when the power of Kurdish emirates started to fade away. While Ateş (2013) and Özoğlu (2004) demonstrated that the autonomy of Kurdish emirates diminished substantially after the seventeenth century, Bruinessen (1990: 2) refers to the ascendance of Sufi orders and religious sects in Kurdistan almost at the same time span. When we put the pieces together, we see that the moment that Kurdish political autonomy was restricted, there appeared an increasing activity of religious orders, which is culminated in the outbreak of the Sheikh Ubeydullah Rebellion in 1880. This revolt is important because it was the first Kurdish resistance that was not organized by Kurdish aristocracy or nobility against Ottoman attempts of centralizing political power in Kurdistan. Sheikh Ubeydullah Nehri was not a Kurdish aristocrat, but a well-respected cleric of a Sufi order known as the Nakşibendi. In this context, it must not be surprising to see that Scott (2009: 209-210) refers to the same dynamics as a strategy of defying or evading the state:

"The Ottomans, in the same vein, found it far easier to deal with structured communities, even if they were Christians and Jews, than with heterodox sects that were acephalous and organizationally diffuse. Most feared were such forms of autonomy and dissent as, for example, the mystical Dervish orders, which deliberately, it seems, avoided any collective settlement or identifiable leadership precisely to fly, as it were, beneath the Ottoman police radar."

Here, we see a clear agency that chooses and/or creates local structures of political organization alternative to larger state-structures, even when classical political forms are not available.

Freedom as evading the state

We know that *Kurdistan* as an administrative unit existed as early as the fourteenth century, and that Kurdish as an identity and Kurdistan as a country clearly appears, with its boundaries and clans, in the fifteenth century (Özoğlu 2004: 26-32). We also know that Ehmedê Xanê stressed the desire of those who would like to see a united Kurdish kingdom as early as the seventeenth century, in the introduction of his epic Mem and Zin (*Mem û Zîn*) (ibid). Although they were incorporated in larger state structures, their own customs, traditions and social practices preserved the Kurds from being totally absorbed by the State. In that sense, Belge's (2011: 105) analyses take us to the heart of the point:

"Kinship networks thus enabled a variety of resistant acts that cumulatively undermined the state-building project. First, they served as networks of information and trust accessible only to the locals, regularly disrupting law enforcement. Second, contacts in the lower-level bureaucracy enabled local society to manipulate crucial records on population, land ownership, and marriage, creating a problem of legibility and posing important challenges for the institutionalization of state law. Third, state officials who were sent from outside the region were occasionally absorbed in the local moral order and began to act according to local rules, favoring "kin" and ignoring the commands from above. On the ground, then, quotidian conspiracies rendered the boundary between state and society fuzzy, undermined the state's infrastructural power, and impeded state rationality and order from deepening its hold over the imagination of citizens."

Fragmented social and political structures and the absence of a centralized political authority in a society, as Bruinessen (1978) emphasizes, may indicate a tendency to remain out of the direct control of the state. Although Kurdish tribes have frequently formed and still form alliances with the state, this mostly serves them to gain more power in the competition with their rivals or to preserve their power and autonomy. It does not necessarily suggest that they are absorbed by or incorporated into state structures[9]. Kurds are loyal, Bruinessen (ibid.) argues, not to an ethnic group, a nation, or a state, but the chief loyalty is that of local

---

[9] The state has also been receptive to this strategy in Kurdistan, because alliance with tribes might buy their support or neutrality against the ones that are seen as immediate threat to state integrity or security. For the state, it might also mean preventing a united front or undermining national aspirations of the Kurds.

characteristics, owed to tribal chieftains (*Agha*) and charismatic religious leaders (*Shaikh*). The (psychological) remoteness of the Kurds to the institutional existence of the idea of the state is a dominant theme in Bruinessen's thesis. One example of this is the word *binxetê*, the word used by Kurds in southeast Turkey to refer to Syria. It means 'below the line', referring to the railway passing through the region. In Kurdish vernacular, Syria was thus not seen as a different country, but as the lands 'below the railway line'. Also the continuous illegal border crossings of Kurds living in these borderland zones show that they do not recognize the border as a legitimate structure. Crossing these artificial state borders is a daily phenomenon for those who live near borderlines. They are preserving relationships with their relatives across borders, they trade with each other and marry their sons and daughters to people at the other side. Belge (2011: 101) stresses that *"The ease with which Kurds crossed the border undermined the government's efforts to institutionalize borders as containers of discrete nations"*.

Furthermore, those practices are not just anachronic strategies that were used almost a century ago. There are contemporary forms of such socio-political activities. For instance, the majority of Kurds still avoid invoking the state and its courts in times of conflict[10]. Those who grow up in Kurdish region will recall that conflicts are mostly solved by a local "*judicial*" mechanism. In rural areas sheikhs and mullahs invoke sharia law when they intervene in conflicts, while local notables apply customary law to issues brought before them. In urban areas, we see that legal or illegal institutions of Kurdish political movement take the role of arbitration and judiciary upon themselves: a role that is generally performed by a sovereign. As the Kurdish journalist Irfan Aktan also stated (my translation):

"The Kurds, at the time being, handle their judicial conflicts on their own. The judicial commissions of the BDP, who were labeled as the "parallel state" and became the target of crackdowns and police operations against the KCK, were indeed a traditional way of Kurdish peace-making "without invoking state institutions". Although belittled, the aşiret[11] system used to provide the Kurds with principles and mechanisms

---

[10] For a detailed discussion on and documentation of judicial practices carried out by various organizations affiliated with Kurdish political movement in Turkey, see the book *Democratic Autonomy in Kurdistan: The Council Movement, Gender Liberation, and Ecology-in Practice;* authored by TATORT Kurdistan, published in 2013 by New Compass Press, Porsgrunn, Norway.

[11] The term aşiret means tribe in Kurdish and Turkish. However, the aşiret system is not only a tribal socio-political system. Özoğlu (2004: 46) clarifies the distinction between different social and political layers of the system, and underlines the fact that it does not

of justice that are necessary for any social organization." (Radikal 22.12.2013)

The aforesaid social and political practices on the other hand also became the ground of a self-orientalist conception, especially in 1990s in Turkey, which implied that the Kurds have not yet developed a sense of nationhood, and that they are not politically mature enough to form a nation. *"You cannot convince me that the Turkish nation (Türk Ulusu) and the Kurdish nationality (Kürt milliyeti) are equal (my translation)"*, said Birgül Ayman Güler[12]. The statement puts 'Kurdish nationality' in a secondary rank as a political category, vis-à-vis the 'superior' one, the 'Turkish nation'. What made the difference was, clearly, mastery over a territory in the ownership of a sovereign state. This self-orientalist understanding had become the ground for some Kurdish nationalists to blame their ancestry of lacking national consciousness as well. Here, we see a clear link between the ages-old colonialist/modernist discourses that imposed dichotomies of 'civilized'-'uncivilized', 'modern'-'backward', 'developed'-'undeveloped'; and the nationalist tendency to rank and hierarchise peoples on the bases of having or not having a sovereign state.

However, there are ways of political activism free from the dichotomy of sovereignty and statelessness. Resistance to political centralization reflected in the practices outlined above is one of those ways that conceives political autonomy in evading the state. As Arendt (1998: 234) suggests:

"If it were true that sovereignty and freedom are the same, then indeed no man could be free, because sovereignty, the ideal of uncompromising self-sufficiency and mastership, is contradictory to the very condition of

---

exclusively refer to only tribal socio-political organization: "Primary sources often use the term aşiret (Arabic, ashira) to refer arbitrarily to all political units—whether clan, tribe, or emirate. These sources do seem to hint that the emirate was a tribal confederacy. The distinction between the tribe and the emirate is particularly important for understanding Kurdish-Ottoman relations. Richard Tapper's definition of tribe and confederacy seems to fit best to the purpose of this work. Therefore, this chapter uses the term "Kurdish tribe" to refer to a sociopolitical entity whose group solidarity is based predominantly upon primordial relations and whose members consider themselves culturally distinct. On the other hand, the Kurdish emirate or confederacy differs from the tribe in terms of its larger size and more heterogeneous culture, its presumed origin and stratified class composition, its more circumstantial solidarity, and its closer relations with the state. The Kurdish emirate is composed of a number of tribes, both nomadic and settled, and of nontribal groups who speak different dialects. The supreme leader of the emirate (mir) has considerable military power and lives usually in a fortified city with his entourage."

[12] An MP of the People's Republican Party (Cumhuriyet Halk Partisi-CHP) and a former professor of politics at Ankara University. Source: Today's Zaman, 24.01.2013.

plurality. No man can be sovereign because not one man, but men, inhabit the earth..."

Therefore, in the case of the Kurds the tendency towards remaining autonomous could testify to a notion of freedom as the will to evade the state. In other words, not having a state of their own and not trying to found one until the early twentieth century, might, after all, just be an alternative vision of freedom.

Conclusion

I highlighted a number of historical arguments that demonstrate that the Kurds did not only resist incorporation in state-structures when they were pressured to do so, they also prevented "states from springing up among them" (Scott, 2009: X), for most parts of their history from the sixteenth to the twentieth century.

I have argued that forming alliances with states, remaining small in scale but choosing autonomy over subordination to one another, taking refuge in the mountains to escape state domination, crossing borders with little regard to their legitimacy when needed and forming internal judiciary mechanisms are all strategies of keeping the state at a distance in Kurdistan.

Although mainstream nationalist discourses in Turkey and academics in Kurdish studies often suggest that statelessness is an indication of the lack of national consciousness on the part of the Kurds. An alternative interpretation of political fragmentation in Kurdistan is offered in this chapter. I have argued that the Kurds prioritized self-rule and local autonomy and that they deliberately avoided being incorporated into larger state structures, due to a different political culture and an alternative understanding of freedom.

Sirkeci, Cohen, Yazgan (eds)

Chapter 9. *As if all life had vanished...* The return of Kurdish villagers to their hometowns

Şemsa Özar

In the early 1990s, more than a million Kurdish villagers had been forced to flee their villages in the course of the armed conflict between the Turkish security forces and the PKK (Partiya Karkerên Kurdistan – the Kurdistan Workers' Party). The inhabitants of thousands of villages and hamlets in the Kurdish region of Turkey had been evicted by the Turkish security forces primarily to deprive the PKK guerrillas of their rural environment and support from the villagers. In the literature it is known as four cuts. It means cutting off the sources of food, funds, intelligence and recruits to the rebel armies. Numerous studies and personal accounts that take up the issue of forced migration of Kurds from a variety of perspectives have been published (TMMOB, 1998; Kurban et al., 2006; Kışanak, nd.; Dinç, 2004; Kalkınma Merkezi, 2010; Demirler & Eşsiz, 2008; Çağlayan, Özar, & Doğan, 2011; Yağız et al., 2012), but to date very little has been written about people returning to their villages (Jongerden, 2008; Göç-Der, 2013). This article aims to elucidate the return of Kurds to their homeland, to those villages they once had been brutally driven out of. On the other hand, it is a known fact that the majority of Kurds have not yet returned to their villages. Kavar people, however, after living in Istanbul for almost a decade, in a metropolis that they had no initial intention to settle, decided to go back to their homeland. I will, thus, often use quotations from face-to-face interviews conducted with the returnees in the villages of Kavar,[1] a region in the southwest of Lake Van, Behra Wanê (Van Sea) as Kurds name it. I attempt, in this article, to disclose the ways in which the Kavar people through all these years of struggle constructed their subjectivities expanding on political and ethical imaginaries.

The plan of the article is as follows: in the next section I first offer an overview of forced migration[2] of Kurds in general. I continue with a brief summary of the years spent in Istanbul. Then, I try to demonstrate the

---

[1] For the interviews, I am very grateful to Nurcan Baysal and her team. Nurcan Baysal has written a magnificent book on Kavar entitled *O Gün* (That Day), Ankara: Iletisim Yayinlari, 2014.

[2] Forced migration, as used in this article, refers to coerced relocations of people as a result of direct military offensives or involuntary movements of people as a result of the conflicts between the state and insurgencies.

struggle given to re-establish a life in the once brutally demolished villages. Needless to say, the challenges and problems faced by the villagers during this whole fleeing and coming back home along with their perseverance in rebuilding a life and a community in their hometowns had, among other factors, revealed the political and ethical nature of their subjectivity vis-á-vis the Turkish state. When I say, political end ethical, I mean that their conduct throughout these years of dislocation and return cannot be understood if we reduce their acts to their narrowly defined economic interests. Nor can we understand their subjectivity if we see them simply as victims of a process they have no control over.

Forced migration of Kurds

Estimates on numbers of forced migrants from the Kurdish region vary according to the source. According to a survey commissioned by the government and carried out by Hacettepe University Institute of Population Studies,[3] the number of internally displaced people from 14 provinces[4] in the eastern and south eastern Turkey was estimated as being around 1 million people. According to the survey, about half of these people moved to urban areas within the same region and the rest migrated to provinces such as İstanbul, Ankara, İzmir, Adana, Mersin, Bursa, to those provinces with relatively higher job opportunities and higher percentage of Kurdish population. On the other hand, Human Rights Association (İnsan Hakları Derneği, İHD) estimated a much higher number for the forced migrants. According to this estimation, 3688 settlements had been evacuated and around 2.3 million civilians had been forced to migrate during the same period.

In the first half of the 1990s, thousands of villages were emptied of their residents and razed to the ground in the Kurdish region of Turkey by the Turkish military forces in the name of securing hegemony over the region and opposing the PKK. Research findings on forced migration of Kurds in Turkey also suggest other, but relatively minor reasons for displacement of Kurds such as, loss of security due to armed clashes, evictions by the PKK, food embargoes and bans put by the security forces on using mountain pastures along with the resultant collapse of the rural economy. Actually,

---

[3] In this study, *Migration and Internally Displaced Population Survey in Turkey*, it is estimated that from 1986 to 2005 between 953,680 and 1,201,200 people migrated for "security reasons" from the villages and towns of the fourteen provinces in eastern and southeastern Anatolia (HÜNEE, 2006: 61). The Migrants' Association for Social Cooperation and Culture (GÖÇ-DER) places the figure of displaced people at approximately three million.

[4] Adıyaman, Ağrı, Batman, Bingöl, Bitlis, Diyarbakır, Elazığ, Hakkari, Mardin, Muş, Siirt, Şırnak, Tunceli and Van.

in the context of forced migration, adverse economic factors that make life impossible in the villages mostly emerge as a result of coercive actions.

In some cases, villagers had been given the 'choice' between joining the village guards (*korucular* in Turkish) or leaving their villages. Village guards are a paramilitary force that was established in 1985 and is still in place, composed of civilians, mostly Kurds.[5] Villagers are given arms on the condition that they remain loyal to the security forces and take part in military operations together with the security forces against the PKK guerrillas. In exchange for their services they receive arms, a monthly compensation and some other employee benefits. Their numbers reached nearly 90,000 in the 1990s, during the period in which the fight between the security forces and the PKK intensified. Now, their number is estimated to be around 65 thousand. This 'divide and rule' strategy aims to disrupt solidarity within a community and tries to generate hostile relations among the members of a community. I will turn to the village guards again, since some of the villagers in Kavar join the village guards.

Kavar

Kavar villages lie between Tatvan and Van, by car it is only 15 to 20 minutes from Tatvan. There are 6 villages[6] in the Kavar region. These villages are not remote mountain villages, all are very close to the main road between Tatvan and Van. Before 1990s the population of the region was around 4,000, now with the returnees it is around 2,000. This is a region that once had also been homeland to Armenians. Most of the villages have both Armenian and Kurdish names and also official Turkish names.

In the end of 1993, incidences of threats, intimidation and assault faced by the villagers of Kavar reached its peak. On the 27th of December 1993 soldiers came to Kavar. They gave the villagers one day time. Either Kavar people would become village guards or all men would be taken away. A man tells what happened on that and the next day:[7]

It was the night of Dec. 28, 1993. Soldiers came. First, they set fire to the mountains. After 1am in the morning Special Operations Troops entered the village with panzers. They shot our uncle. His arms were smashed into bits. Houses were destroyed. 7 houses were burned down.

---

[5] For a in-depth study on village guards see Özar, Uçarlar, and Aytar (2013).

[6] Kolbaşı (Avetax), Bolalan (Şamnis), Dibekli (Sülü), Düzcealan (Çorsin), Tokaçlı (Kurtıkan), Yassıca (Ünsüz).

[7] *28 Aralık 1993 gecesiydi. Askerler geldi, önce dağları ateşe verdiler. Saat 01.00'den sonra Özel Harekât köyün içine panzerlerle birlikte girdi. Bizim amcamızı da vurdular, kolları paramparça oldu... Evleri delik deşik etmişlerdi. Yedi ev yakıldı. Askerler, özel harekât sabah 09.00'da falan çekip, gittiler.*

Soldiers and Special Operations Troops left around 9 o'clock in the morning.

A man who has witnessed the fire from his office in Tatvan says:[8]

They burned down the villages. I have seen all from my office. Villages were burning. We took the road to Kavar, but the military closed the Tatvan-Van road. The villages were burning, we just watched.

Another villager from Kavar tells how they had been driven out of their village:[9]

They said we should immediately leave the village. Otherwise, they said, 'we'll kill you'. In that very short time, we couldn't even bury our dead.

In two villages men joined the village guards in order not to leave their village and animals. In the other four, in which villagers refused to become village guards people were tortured and put in jail and some became victim of unresolved assassination.

In this period, 30 to 35 young people joined the PKK. In two years' time only very few elderly people remained in these four villages that refused to take arms against their own children.

---

[8] *O gün köyleri yaktılar. Ben çalıştığım kurumun camından gördüm. Köyler yanıyordu. Yola çıktık, köylere gitmek istedik. Tatvan-Van yolunu kapadılar. Köyler yakıldı, biz izledik.*

[9] *Bu kadar süre içinde bu köyü boşaltacaksınız. Yoksa hepinizi öldürürüz dediler. O gün, o kısacık sürede cenazelerimizi bile kaldıramadık.*

Kavar people flee their homes leaving their lands, homes, fields, livestock, memories and dead behind as they ventured into the unknown.

İstanbul

Particularly during the first years in İstanbul, in this foreign and in many ways hostile environment, Kavar people encountered huge problems in finding a place to live and a job to secure their daily survival. Men could only get temporary construction jobs while women worked in cheap-labor workshops, usually in the garment sector. These jobs were mostly low-wage and informal jobs with bad working conditions, lacking social security.

Stripped of their livelihoods, environment, and community and even to a certain extent their mother tongue, almost from all their commons that make them who they are, Kurdish villagers worked in İstanbul for mere survival. Often they had to travel all around the country in search of work.

A man tells how he searched work all around Turkey: [10]

I went to other places to find work, just to pay our own way. I left my wife and children in İstanbul. I went to Edirne. I went to Düzce. There was construction work there. I worked in pavement construction of municipalities. I went everywhere. I suffered a lot.

Kurds could only find jobs as temporary contract workers, a category of work that became prevalent in the neoliberal era. The flow of Kurds to urban areas in the context of forced migration coincided with the period of neoliberal restructuring in Turkey. Inevitably, it was the migrant Kurds that were ready to take up these temporary jobs offered by this new system. In İstanbul, along with poor working conditions, Kurds suffered from humiliation, isolation and contemptuous treatment.

Going back to Kavar

In 2000, around a third of the forced migrants from Kavar region decided to go back to their villages with their own means. It is argued that one of the major reasons for their return was the difficulties they faced in earning a living in Istanbul. But, there is enough evidence in these interviews to convince me that an extra economic dimension is in operation here. These people returned not because they made a cost-benefit analysis in economic terms, but because of something that opens to another dimension then the economic one. The stories that I tell will perhaps give a sense of what this other dimension entails.

---

[10] *Çalışmak için başka yerlere gittim, kimseye muhtaç olmamak için. Eşimi ve çocuklarımı İstanbul'da bıraktım. Edirne'ye gittim, Düzce'ye gittim. Tadilat işleri vardı oralarda. Belediyenin yaptırdığı kaldırımlarda çalıştım, hemen her yere gittim. Çok zorluk çektim"*

Administratively, Kavar region belongs to the Province of Bitlis. At almost the same time as Kavar people enter their villages the Governor of Bitlis, Uğur Boran, in March 2001 gives a press release to a newspaper on the issue of returnees:[11]

In Bitlis 83 villages and 124 mezras, 27 thousand 904 citizens had to go to other provinces. As a result of ensuring a peaceful and safe environment, in 2000 our 4 445 citizen from 22 villages and 22 mezras have returned. We have taken necessary measures for the return of people of 23 villages and mezras.

A different perspective for this "peaceful and safe environment" comes from a villager in Kavar:

We entered the village in 2001 together with the headman of the village. Everybody was insulting us: special operations team, village guards, everybody; everybody that did not share our views. Often we were not going to bed at all till in the morning. Village guards, special troops were all keeping guard in front of our houses. We were seeing them but could not do anything. They would shoot us if we went out. Sometimes I was wondering how the morning would break. Shall I die before morning?

Again, a woman with different experiences with this "peaceful environment" says:[12]

Soldiers were not allowing us to stay in the village. For that reason, first we stayed in Tatvan. Every morning, we took the minibus at 6 am. 50 people or so we were getting in the same minibus (laughs). It was unbearable, but believe me, I was falling asleep in that stinky minibus, carrying my two children, Ciwan was then 9, Baran 7 years old. The whole day we were working in the village and in the fields. In the evening we were running to the minibus. Our house was altogether demolished. Soldiers were coming. They were insulting us.

This daily commute with children was so unbearable that the villagers started spending the night in their villages in plastic tents or in houses that were relatively better in shape. While spending the night in their own homes, they had to find ways to hide themselves from the soldiers.

---

[11] *Bitlis'te 83 köy ve 124 mezra boşaltılmış, 27 bin 904 vatandaşımız, başka illere gitmek zorunda kalmıştır. Bölgede huzur ve güven ortamının sağlanması sonucu.... 2000 yılında 22 köy ve 22 mezraya 4 bin 445 vatandaşımız geri döndü. 23 köy ve bu köylere bağlı mezraların geri dönüşü için gerekli önlemler alındı.* (aa) Hürriyet, 12.03.2001.

[12] *Köyde kalmamıza izin vermiyordu askerler. O nedenle önce Tatvan'da ev tuttuk. Her sabah minibüse 6'da biniyorduk. 50 kişi belki bir minibüse biniyorduk (gülüyor). İnsan kokuya dayanamaz ama inan ben o kokuda uyuyordum. 2 çocuğumu da kucağıma bırakıyordum. Ciwan 9, Baran 7 yaşındaydı. Tüm gün köylerde iş yapıyorduk, tarlada. Akşam yine minibüse koşuyorduk. Bizim ev tamamen yıkılmıştı. Askerler geliyorlardı, bize bir dolu laf söylüyorlardı.*

A woman says:[13]

They were saying: 'Forbidden, why are you here?' We were hiding the mattresses and telling them that we were not staying at night. We were hiding the mattresses in the fields, so that they don't find them in our houses and become abusive. They allowed us to stay in our houses after a year.

The villages where they returned to were not places that offered better housing, infrastructure or opportunities for education of the children. Most of the trees were dead. The houses were in ruins. A woman entering her village the first time after so many years expresses her feelings as:

It was as if all life had vanished...[14]

Nevertheless, it was a return to the homeland, to a place where they belonged to. With perseverance, the villagers were carving out a life for themselves.

Meanwhile, the European Court of Human Rights (ECtHR) had issued more than thirty judgments in which Turkey was made to pay compensation for violation of villagers' rights in the course of displacement. Moreover, the acceptance of Turkey for candidacy to the European Union (EU) was made conditional upon its fulfilment of a number of political criteria including addressing the problems faced by the displaced Kurdish population. As a result of these developments, a law called the Compensation Law was enacted and put into effect in 2004 to compensate the losses of villagers due to the armed conflict since 1987. However, this law and related projects and programs implemented by the state have proven to be entirely insufficient.[15] Additionally, in numerous regions law enforcement officers, the gendarmerie and special troops have prevented people from returning to their villages, just as it happened in Kavar. Furthermore, the government's refusal to take responsibility for the evacuation of the villages has opened the way for further aggravation of existing injustices.

Most of the Kavar villagers did not receive any compensation for their loss of family members, land, houses and animals. A villager tells us one of the reasons:[16]

---

[13] *'Yasaktır, niye kalıyorsunuz?' diyorlardı. Yatakları saklıyorduk askerler geldiğinde, 'gece kalmıyoruz' diyorduk. Yatakları bahçelerin içinde saklıyorduk, evin içinde yatak görmesinler bize hakaret etmesinler diye. Ben, kocam çocuklar hepimiz böyle yaşıyorduk. 1 yıl sonra izin verdiler köyde kalmamıza.*

[14] *Ne bileyim sanki yaşam yok olmuştu...*

[15] For an assessment of the Compensation Law, see Kurban, D. & Yeğen, M. (2012).

[16] *15 yıl sonra köye dönüş projesi çıktı. Bize dediler ki şu kağıdı imzalayın. Kağıtta köyü PKK'nin yaktığı yazıyordu. Kabul etmedik. Onlar yaksaydı, onlar yaktı derdik ama devlet yaktı. Önce hayvanların samanlarını ateşe verdiler. 15 yıl biz ne yaptık, kimse sormadı.*

After 15 years, there was this project. We were told to sign the documents. On that document it was written that the PKK burned down the village. We refused. If they had, we would say PKK burned down the village, but the state burned it. They first set the animal hay to fire. Nobody asked us how we survived all these 15 years. Nobody... After 15 years without any help or support, some people returned to the village. Still we are struggling to build up an existence here.

Struggle for livelihoods – 'beri' road

I suppose what happened to 'beri' road vividly demonstrates the extent of struggle villagers have gone through for their livelihoods and the role, if any, the state plays in this struggle.

In May, herds of sheep and goats are taken by shepherds to high pastures and they stay there until the end of September. Mountain pastures are 2.5 to 4 km away depending on the village women set off. Women go to these pastures on foot two times a day, once in the morning and the second time in the afternoon for milking the sheep. Milking the sheep means 'beri' in Kurdish. After milking the sheep, they walk the same way back to their homes with plastic containers full of milk. The way to 'beri' is called 'beri road'. In fact, this is a women's work, men do not go to 'beri'. Men are the shepherds. 'Beri' road is steep and stony.

Because of this steep and stony 'beri' road, this type of animal husbandry depends on the presence of physically strong women that can go to 'beri'. Some families because of the difficult climb to 'beri' have

Kimse... 15 yıl sonra köye bazı insanlar kendi çabalarıyla dönmeye başladı. Hala da bir hayat kurmak için mücadele ediyoruz.

sold their animals and given up sheep husbandry. If the 'beri' road could be built, then the transfer of milk would be done by vehicles.

After long negotiations with the officials, the villagers and the representatives of a foundation working in the area were successful in convincing the officials (kaymakam) to lend the machinery to the villagers required for building the 'beri' road. The promise was made in June 2010. The 'beri' road, to date, is still in the shape it was 100 years ago.

In September 12, 2010 a referendum was held for several changes in the Constitution. On the 13th of September, the governor cancelled the construction of the 'beri' road without a stated reason. The reason, however, is not difficult to guess. The majority of the Kavar villagers following the call made by the BDP (Peace and Democracy Party, the political party that represents the Kurdish Movement then) boycotted the referendum against the wishes of the ruling party.

The 'Wise Men' committee meet Kavar women

Lastly, I will conclude with a rather recent event that I think discloses the ways in which the Kurdish villagers are reshaping the political space and power relations.

Kavar people were informed that the Eastern Anatolia group of Wise Men along with some officials will be visiting Kavar region to hear about their problems regarding the peace process. Wise Men Commissions were appointed by the government. They include prominent figures and celebrities representing social, academic, cultural, historical, economic, and political domains. Their mission was to create an environment conducive to a more favourable state of mind in the whole country for facilitating the peace process.

After long discussions, the villagers decide to host the Commission in the village that was exposed to the most brutal treatment in 1993 by the Turkish security forces.

The house of condolence was prepared for the meeting. Table cloths were laid down and flowers were put on the tables. Actually, the table cloths were not only for decoration, they were also representing the identity of the villagers, the colours of the table cloths were representing the Kurds (red, yellow and green). Here, we can recall those times that once one of the governors in the region have attempted to ban even the traffic lights because of their colours: red, yellow and green. I read the distance between these two moments of the symbolic politics of colour configurations as a result of the political persistence of the Kurdish people. In my opinion, it is still very difficult to conceive of these Wise Men sitting in front of these colours for example in İstanbul.

That day of the visit, women come to the meeting with the pictures of their guerrilla children that have died during the clashes between the Turkish security forces and the PKK.

While women were telling the Wise Men what happened in their village on the 28th of December 1993, they were video recorded by the officials of the prime ministry. I think it shows how the villagers in their own territory have, if any, crossed the borders of fear.

One of the women starts telling her story. A woman with her husband's picture in hand tells the Wise Men what happened that day when the soldiers raided their village: [17]

---

[17] *28 Aralık 1993 gecesi askerler akşam üzeri köyümüze geldiler. Eşimi evden çıkardılar. Eşimi şehit ettiler. Hiçbir şeyi yoktu. Eşim müteahhitti. Bizi taradılar. Tank, top ateşiyle. Askerlerin arasında 3 kişi de maske takmıştı. Beni de dövdüler. Eşimin önce bacaklarını kırdılar çocukların önünde. Sonra evden dışarıya çıkardılar. O'nu vahşice*

Conflict, Insecurity and Mobility

katlettiler. Sonra da panzerle üzerinden 4-5 kez geçtiler. Soruyorum size: Bunu niye yaptılar? Bunca yıl geçti hala cevabı bulamadım. Eşimin etlerini yerden kazıdım. Bütün parçaları yere yapışmıştı, tek tek topladım.
    Heyet Başkanı: *Peki, devletten beklentiniz nedir?*
    Kadın: *Önce Öcalan'ın özgürlüğü, sonra dilimiz ve kimliğimiz.*
    Heyetten biri: *Senin yaşadıklarınla bunun ne ilgisi var.*
    Kadın: *20 yıldır kendime aynı soruyu soruyorum. Kocama niye bunu yaptılar? Aslında niyenin bir cevabı yok. Biliyorum ki, niyenin bir cevabı yok. Kendimi inandırmaya çalışıyorum, kocam bir mücadele için öldü, bizler için öldü, Kürt halkı için öldü diye.*

Soldiers came to our village in the evening of Dec 28th 1993. They took my husband out of the house and then he was martyred. My husband was in the subcontracting business. 3 of the soldiers had masks on their face. They hit me. They first broke my husband's legs in front of our children. Then they took him out of the house and killed him brutally and then ridden over him with a panzer 4-5 times. I am asking you all why they did this. So many years have gone, I still don't know the answer. Why? Why? My husband had no gun, he was a builder. I scraped his flesh from the ground. One by one I collected his pieces from the ground.

One of the wise men asks:
What do you want from the state?
She responds:
First, freedom for Öcalan (the leader of the PKK, who is in jail since 1999), then our mother tongue and our identity.
A man from the Commission asks:
What all these have to do with what you have encountered?
She says:
I spent all these years thinking about why my husband was killed. Why they did this to my husband? Actually there is no answer to this? I try to make myself believe that my husband died for a cause, for us, for the Kurdish people.

In lieu of conclusion

We have heard time and time again that the Kurdish 'problem', which has been around for over a hundred years, is the result of 'underdevelopment' in the east of the country. According to this claim, if the government had instituted a proper development program in the east and if people's level of income increased, we would not have such a problem. The story about Kavar tears down this superficial evaluation. The residents of Kavar left behind their lives in the cities, choosing to live in a place that had been razed to the ground and where they are constantly subjected to the harassment and insults of the gendarmerie and the special troops.

Kavar people confronted with tough choices at every turn of fleeing and returning to their homeland. Each choice they made was an indication of their ethical and political stance: Rather than taking arms against their own children, against those that were defending their existence as Kurds, they chose to leave their villages to an unknown. In spite of all the gendarmerie violence and lack of livelihoods, they chose with all their perseverance to rebuild a life and community in their homeland. Although they had almost no means for this whole rebuilding process, they did not give up from what they knew was right and chose to refuse the compensation money offered by the state. As a consequence, they paid heavy prices for these and many other choices they made. However, at the same time, in the struggle of the people of Kavar we bear witness the ways in which their choices opened up spaces of freedom through the agency offered to them by a collective identity.

Acknowledgement
The first version of this article was presented at *Translocal Commons: a Colloquium with Susan Buck-Morss* at Boğaziçi University on 31st of October 2013. A Turkish version of this article appeared as "*Sanki Yaşam Yok Olmuştu... Kürtlerin Köylerine Dönüşü*" in Yahya M. Madra (ed.), *Türkiye'de Yeni İktidar Yeni Direniş. Sermaye-Ulus-Devlet Karşısında Yerelötesi Müşterekler,* Istanbul: Metis Yayınları, 2015. I am grateful to Yahya M. Madra, Müge Sökmen and the participants of the Colloquium for their valuable comments and constructive suggestions.

Chapter 10. Negotiating identity and coping with urban space among young Kurdish migrants in Istanbul

Karol P. Kaczorowski

Many existing studies on Kurdish migration concentrate on displacement and expulsion experienced by Kurds in various parts of Kurdistan and especially between 1970 and 1999 in Turkey. However it can be observed that since the beginning of the twenty-first century migration have also played a substantial role in the mobility of Kurds, owing to stabilization in Southern Kurdistan (i.e. Autonomous Kurdistan Region in Iraq) and improvement of minority rights in Turkey due to the accession process with the EU, the economic and educational needs became more influential in the decisions of Kurdish migrants in twenty-first century. To my best knowledge, it appears that there is a shortage of studies examining economic migration and new spatial movements of the Kurds in the twenty-first century Turkey[1].

This chapter presents partial results of an ongoing research examining social construction of ethnic identity of young Kurdish migrants in Istanbul. First, the theoretical context is explained with emphasis on the importance of Istanbul for Kurdish culture and conceptualization of identity and migration. Environment of human insecurity (EOHI) is introduced as the model for understanding the studied case of migration. Preliminary results of in-depth interviews with migrants are presented in the second section. Respondents' understanding of key notions (migration, homeland and Kurdish culture), their attitudes towards Istanbul, the perceived qualities and flaws of conditions that the city provides, and the potential relevance of the metropolis to Kurdish culture are presented.

Significance of Istanbul to Kurdish culture and society

The largest part (often referred to as *Northern*) of the geographical and cultural region treated by Kurds as their homeland, Kurdistan, falls within the borders of modern Turkey. The estimations of Kurdish population in Turkey vary between 14 and 20 million (CIA, 2008; Sirkeci, 2000)[2]. The

---

[1] One of few examples of such studies is an article by Femke Sonnenschein and Toon van Meijl (2014) examining multiple identifications of Kurdish workers in Istanbul's tourist industry.

[2] Both global and Turkish populations of Kurds are hard to estimate. Resettlement and assimilation processes forced by inhabited states are obstacles in this matter. Some

population of Istanbul, the largest city in Turkey, is over 14 millions. Headquarters of Turkish corporations and national media are located in this great metropolis. Since the creation of the Republic of Turkey in 1923, and thanks to dynamic economic development and urbanization rate especially after the 1970's, Istanbul has significantly expanded – it remains as the main destination for many families migrating to the city from less developed parts of Turkey. Although the city produces approximately more than a quarter of the whole country's Gross Domestic Product, it is characterized by visible economic inequalities (see Karpat, 2004; Ciplak, 2012).

Istanbul bears a great significance for the Kurdish culture as many Kurdish organizations were active in the city over the 19th and 20th century. It is believed that first Kurds lived in this region during the Byzantine Empire (see Alakom, 2011: 19-21; Pirbal, 2008). First Kurdish organizations were created in Istanbul, and moreover, throughout the years it has been a base for headquarters of many Kurdish cultural societies and newspapers (Alakom, 2011: 9-91). Idris Bitlisi - an Ottoman diplomat and prominent negotiator with Kurdish tribes under the rule of Sultan Selim I (1512-1520) also lived in Istanbul. Idris Bitlisi's most known work was a book on the history of Ottoman Empire - *Heşt Beheşt* (Eight Glories) (see Özoğlu, 2004: 47-51). The city was for some time a home to such notable Kurdish characters as poet Hacî Qadirî Koyî, Abdullah Cevdet - one of the founders of Committee of Union and Progress and propagator of secularism, religious leader Said Nursî, Celadet Bedirxan - writer and author of Hawar - latin alphabet for kurmanci dialect. *Kürdistan* one of the first Kurdish newspapers was founded and published in Istanbul by Mikdat Midhat Bedirxan in the years from 1892 to 1902.

Since the beginning of Second Constitutional Period in 1908 until the declaration of Turkish Republic in 1923, several Kurdish societies aimed at integrating elites and promoting Kurdish language, culture, history and political views operated in the city. Alakom (2011: 95) categorizes them into intellectual communities, nationalist organizations, periodicals and women organizations. Among them, the two were very important for the development of Kurdish nationalist thought: Society for the Mutual Aid and Progress of Kurdistan (*Kürt Teavün ve Terakki Cemiyet*) and Society for the Advancement of Kurdistan (*Kürdistan Teali Cemiyeti*).

The largest Kurdish community in the world lives in Istanbul (The Economist, 2005). The metropolis has been for years called as "the biggest

---

estimations from the first decade of the 21st century implicate that there are 30-38 millions of Kurds worldwide and 12-20 millions live in Turkey (see. Yıldız 2005: 6). Therefore it can be assumed that probably Turkish Kurds are half of world's Kurdish population.

Kurdish city" (see Alakom, 2011: 9-19). Research carried out by Rüstem Erkan in 2009 demonstrated that over 5 million Turkish Kurds live outside the eastern regions of the country (which are named by the Kurds as the Northern Kurdistan). The highest percentage of this group lives in Istanbul (TimeTurk, 2010).

The city of Istanbul is also special due to domination of Turkish culture. Here, cultural dominance is understood not only as majority of citizens of Istanbul of Turkish descent, but also as cultural phenomenon which show their hidden diameter at both symbolic and societal level, i.e. interactive level (Mucha, 1999: 27-31). Norms and values of the dominating ethnic (Turks) and religious group (Hanafi Muslims)[3] are taken for granted and perceived as cultural universals. Furthermore the nationalistic ideology [often called Kemalism (see Yavuz, 2003: 31)] of state that for many years sought to erase Kurdish identity (e.g. by calling them Mountain Turks) can be treated as "predatory identity" in Appadurai's (2006: 51-59) sense.

Despite the demographic and cultural importance of Istanbul for Kurds, there are not many studies on Kurds in this city. Most notable are Alakom's (2011) monography that analyzes functioning of Kurds in the city until 1925 and the works of Turkish political scientist Çelik (2002, 2005, 2012). Çelik's doctoral dissertation analyzing migration of Kurds to Istanbul and their participation in public organizations remains unpublished. In her published works, Çelik (2005) have analyzed mainly refugees and resettled Kurds. Secor (2004) studied spatial perception of Istanbul and practices of resistance through usage of space by conducting focus group interviews with Kurdish Women.

Theorizing identity and ethnicity

Identity as a theoretical notion and a subject of social studies has gained popularity in last decades of the twentieth century. Various approaches to this problem and its complexity led to ambiguity of the term. Scholars from different backgrounds disagreed on to whom *identity* can be attributed (e.g. people, animals, objects, individual, groups), what are its main characteristics (e.g. stability or change) and to what extent its construction and negotiation can be conscious and voluntary (see. Jenkins, 2004: 8-14). Some social psychologists and micro-sociologists tend to put more emphasis on individual self and even state that such thing as *collective identity* is non-existent. Other scholars - often macro-oriented sociologists and historians study only dominant traits of large groups (usually nations, societies). There are however also contemporary social

---
[3] Majority of Turkish Kurds are Shafi Muslims (see Heper, 2007).

scientists who suggest that studies of individual and collective identity should be connected with themselves (e.g. Jenkins, 2004: 15-18). They point out that individual manifestations of the dominant culture are at the heart of the study of identity, and thus collective values are fundamentally important for the identity of the individual (see Westin, 1983; Berger and Luckmann, 1991: 194-204).

Ethnic identity is often regarded as one of the key components of individual identity, as the ethnic group is one of the main reference groups. Belonging to a particular ethnic group in the eyes of society and the state can influence one's economic, legal and political situation, hence there is a need to negotiate ethnic identity. (Fenton, 2010: 190-213). The ethnic identification (both in theory and practice) may consist of a number of factors such as, inter alia: ancestry, language, religion, territory of residence and political affiliation. These compounds are not always clear, and the boundaries of belonging to an ethnic or national group are often not sharp. In addition, these factors are inextricably linked with one's whole identity. In the foreword to *Ethnic Groups and Boundaries,* Barth (1969) stated that despite earlier theories of ethnicity in social anthropology, its constitutive features are largely not objective and not biological. Barth did not, however, overestimate the cultural interpretation of ethnicity, noting that in conducting research an anthropologist has access only to socially effective traits of ethnicity and in practice cultural values are often used instrumentally by ethnic groups (e.g. for gaining political or economic support). In contemporary cultural anthropology and sociology of ethnicity there is an emphasis on treating cultural practices as mainly rational and conscious (see Comaroff i Comaroff, 2009).

In this chapter, ethnic identity is treated as connected with cultural identity (e.g. Hall, 2006; Comaroff i Comaroff, 2009), subject to changes in time and socially constructed. Therefore I will concentrate on how it is constructed, negotiated and cultivated rather than on the nature of the essence of Kurdish identity.

In anthropological and sociological studies of ethnicity urban space and migration were taken into consideration since works of Park's Chicago School (see Park, McKenzie & Burgess, 1925; Fenton, 2010: 56-58). Antagonistic relations between the metropolis (treated as place of exile) and villages in Kurdistan (treated as homeland) are also often depicted in Kurdish literature (see. Bocheńska, 2011; van Bruinessen, 2013). Barth (1969: 12-13) underlined the importance of consideration of ecological factors in studying ethnicity as people who identify themselves as members of the same ethnic group can practice their ethnic identity completely differently in different environments. The urban environment can be crucial to the construction and negotiation of all elements of identity (Mach, 1989: 153-193).

Conceptual framework for Kurdish migration in Turkey

One of the most important theoretical and analytic divisions in migration studies concerns forced and voluntary migration. Such categorization remains troublesome and was criticized by several scholars, as even under relatively peaceful conditions when choice about leaving one's hometown appears to be not restricted, there may be some factors that to an extent necessitate migration (e.g. bad economic situation, poor living standards and underdeveloped health care facilities) – often called push factors. Despite this complexity, Abu-Lunghold (1988: 61-62) notes that there is still an enormous difference between the situation when a migrant is pulled by needs and an exile when he is pushed from his homeland. Drawing from these differences, the present project is a study of spatial mobility which is affected by personal decisions. In the situation of Kurds in Turkey such migration contrasts with forced resettlement led by state in the country's South-East especially from 1980's until the beginning of the twenty-first century (see Jongerden, 2007).

Migration that is not connected with expulsion and armed conflict is usually theorized with a focus on (more or less) rational calculation of potential loss and gain analysing spatial mobility similarly to economic dilemma. Scholars often enumerate push and pull factors for migration while putting emphasis on different dimensions of decision making. Researchers who analysed migration in developing countries have underlined the role of process of urbanization and economic underdevelopment of rural areas (Todaro, 1969). From the point of world systems theory, the importance of core-periphery mobility has also been stressed (Wallerstein, 1974). Parnwell (1993) proposed a multi-level migration theory which takes into consideration personal decisions at the micro-level, socioeconomic conditions that constitute meso-level and large-scale development processes and transformations that occur at the macro level. While searching for the main factors of migration scholars conceptualized it as: an investment (Sjastaad, 1962), a kind of social system (Masey et al., 1993), risk diversification (Stark, 1991), the management of uncertainties (Ghatak et al., 2006), a result of existing social networks (Bauer and Gang, 1998) and a response to insecurity and conflict (Sirkeci, 2006). The last theory has been developed by Sirkeci initially for his analysis of Kurdish migration from Turkey to Germany, and it was used by various scientists to explain Iraqi, Turkmen, Lebanese and Alevi migrations (see Sirkeci, 2009: 8). It draws on the observation that no decision of migrant is solely based on individual perspective and calculation, it is rather a result of the environment that puts the potential migrant in a situation that he is inclined or have to decide about the place of his working and living. As often ethnic conflict and migration are studied separately, Sirkeci notes that analyzing spatial movement under the framework of the environment of human insecurity can encompass both phenomena (see Sirkeci, 2003: 9-15; Sirkeci, 2009).

Theoretical framework of environment of human insecurity (EOHI) is treated by its author as a part of transnational studies. As he points out transnational shift in study of migration offered more complex approach to such problems as multiplicity of sending and hosting areas or rigidness of bureaucratic and academic definitions of the notion of migration. Moreover it overcame fixation on nation-states and the dangers of analysing migration in linear way as classic theories and international documents often did (see Sirkeci, 2009: 4; Vertovec, 1999). It has been however noted that while giving opportunity to recognition of variety of mobility forms transnational theories may lack in clarity of explanation. Integrating a model of environment of human insecurity, its material and non-material aspects and taking from classical approaches (such as pull and push factors) from this perspective may improve both the clarity and complexity of migration studies (see Sirkeci, 2009: 3-9). The model sees a social actor as being influenced by an environment of insecurity that manifest itself both on material (access to e.g.: housing facilities, income, health and educational services and material wealth) and non-material levels (possibility to maintain ones identity, language and sense of belonging) which are mutually correlated and often intertwined (Sirkeci, 2003: 11-12; Sirkeci, 2009: 6-9). The actor has to choose between *status quo* and *exit* from EOHI. The second choice can lead him to entering another type of EOHI as its factors are relative and gradual. The most visible examples of impact of EOHI on migration are armed conflicts, however, the model is still relevant in a situation of no direct physical conflict. As classic sociological conflict theories (such as authored by Ralf Dahrendorf or Lewis Coser) underline, conflict is a permanent state of the society, although its intensity and level of manifestation strongly varies. Therefore in a time of peace the migrant is still under the influence of EOHI, although his choice has relatively more impact on migration than in case of people who are subject to war or resettlement policy. The conflict and insecurity have just different scope and intensity (see Sirkeci, 2009: 7-12). This appears to be the case for Kurdish migrants of the waves considered by scholars as voluntary – before the 1980's and after the 1990's (see Çoban, 2013; Kaczorowski, 2015).

Internal migration flows in Turkey

Often cited push factors for internal migration in Turkey are: lack of services, inadequacy or low standard of infrastructure and insecurity. According to Gedik (1997), who analyzed internal migration in Turkey (in the years of 1970, 1980, 1985), pull factors influence potential migrant to the same extent during the decision making. These would be: existing social networks in the migration area (usually ties with family members or people from the same village) job-opportunities and communication and transportation facilities. Psychological distance may be more important than physical one as proximity of a destination place seems to be irrelevant if only family members, neighbours or friends reside there.

Apart from the pull factors (e.g. better socioeconomic conditions in destination area) which are most frequently mentioned by migration scholars, the less evident factors of cultural and social advantages in cities providing wider range of pastime activities and social environment for migrants to participate might be important. International Organization for Migration (2003) have noticed while studying international migrants from Kurdistan Autonomous Region in Iraq (Southern Kurdistan) to United Kingdom, that the general environment of freedom (including leisure activities) played a substantial role in respondents' decision and evaluation of migration. These so called "social advantages" represent access to art provided by availability of museums, theatres, libraries and cinemas, chances to engage in various activist organizations but probably most notably the opportunity to freely spend time without being frowned upon by the community. This "social" difference may be a result of heterogeneity of inhabitants of destination area, which leads to different norms and interaction schemes that may be perceived by migrants as more open and that bring chances to make relations with other people more easily. Perception of these cultural and social factors can vary much more frequently (making them rather micro factors rather than meso-level ones). These perceptions are also much more difficult to assess for social scientists compared to the evaluation of economic, educational and health care standards in the places of migration. Individual evaluation of norms and importance of cultural life may be influenced by various variables such as the attitude towards tradition and relations with primary groups, personal socialization, ethos, and degree of cultural homogeneity of homeland. Although "social advantages" are hard to quantify and scientifically measure, they remain to be important pull factors that are mirrored also in narratives of young Kurdish migrants in Istanbul (see below). These advantages and their paucity in the places of origin represent a non-material form of environment of human insecurity – e.g. in this example, the impossibility to maintain one's identity through activities in the leisure time.

It is important to note that contrary to theories of internal migration in developing countries it is not rural to urban but urban to urban that is the most popular type of migration within Turkey. Analysis by Gedik (1997) proved that migration from city to a city (even in the least urbanized provinces) since 1970's have become the most frequent type of migration. Although during 1995-2000, the rural to urban migration rate was higher, owing to state's resettlement policy in the Southeast (see Filiztekin and Gökhan, 2008), urban to urban migration may also be very popular in contemporary migration of the Kurds. The road to a new home for many forced migrants in 1990's followed a multi-step pattern: first from South-East to some cities closer to the region but situated usually in more western part of country, and from those cities to other urban areas further afield, often Istanbul. Kurds who migrate today may also do it in a multi-step fashion. For example, one may be studying (or complete a part of their education e.g. undergraduate) in one city and then she can move to another (as was the case with some of my respondents).

Internal migration flows were apparent also in the times of Ottoman Empire, as Karpat (2004) argues mobility of new bureaucrats have transformed existing local relations and created new elites. Until the 1960s, when Import Substitution Industrialization policies were introduced Turkey was a rural country with a relatively limited urbanization. Then a need for labor was arisen and it created a wave of internal migration from economically less developed parts of country to urban industrial centers. These urban centres often lacked facilities for newcomers, who resorted building homes illegally on state-owned lands – the so called *gecekondu's* (which means - *built overnight*) (see Çoban 2013: 5; Karpat 2004). As Romano (2006: 112) points out the migration of Kurdish youth to university cities and their participation in urban life and activism allowed a creation of a new political class that formed Kurdish Left in following decades, also resulting in the creation of PKK.

Different kinds of insecurity – Current and past waves of Kurdish migration

As noted by Alinia (2008: 30) general Kurdish migration (regardless of the origin state) can be divided before 1975 and after. While the first phase was largely economic and more voluntary, the second phase was connected with armed and political struggle (see van Bruinessen, 1999). Waves of internal migration in Turkey can be divided between pre-1960's era, rapid industrialization and urbanization in the 1960's and 1970's, dominance of forced migration due to armed conflict between the state with PKK and resettlement policy in the 1980's and especially in the 1990's and potential new wave of voluntary migration connected with economic growth in the beginning of the twenty-first century. Kurds who were relatively free in their migration decisions could have relied on social networks (both formal and informal) involving people coming from same villages, cities or regions of Turkey (we are referring to the concept of *hemşehri*). Those who migrated for economic reasons before the mass resettlement in the 1990s, would find it easier to integrate and internalize Turkish culture while internally displaced people have problems with speaking the official Turkish language properly. They were also not recognized by the state and were not able to receive support until the beginning of the twenty-first century.

Thus there is a difference between the environment of human insecurity where the dominant problem is socio-economic deprivation and the one in which armed struggle and forced resettlement are dominant. Internally displaced people faced economic, political, social, relational and security issues as categorized by Çelik (2012). Despite the fact that the Turkish state eventually abolished the policy of resettlement, migration-rate among the Kurds was still high in the 2000s. We can argue that a new wave of Kurdish migration would be a voluntary one driven mostly by economic and educational needs.

However, the problem of forced migration in the 1990's remains relevant also for the new wave of migration. It can affect it in a way that new migrations may follow the patterns of the previous forced resettlement. In fact some of my respondents recalled that when they were very little their villages were burnt or their relatives had experienced problems with the Turkish troops. These can also be new migrants who are children of IDPs and following, or moving with the help of the networks created by the IDPs.

Narratives of my respondents (who are migrants of the new wave) show the relevance of the conflict across all levels: macro agent level - Turkish state is discriminating the Kurdish community or at least the discrimination is perceived as such (as expressed by the respondents below); individual (micro) actors level – Kurds experiences as members of minority in western Turkey (see Sirkeci 2009: 8-11). This conflict was violent especially in 1990's and resulted in mass resettlement (see Jongerden, 2007). However the conflict's nature was rather non-material at the time of migration for most of my respondents (they represent the new wave of internal migration in Turkey in the beginning of the 21st century).

It happens that the most dominant factor is at the micro level – i.e. lack of employment and economic career opportunities. Hence my respondents often mentioned the difference in education level and job opportunities between Istanbul and their hometowns. This discrepancy has been underlined in previous studies of migration in Turkey, including those focused on the Kurdish issue (see Gedik, 1997; İçduygu et al., 1999; Sirkeci, 2000). Although a more open climate for social activism, social life, and expressing individual identity are pointed out by respondents, lack of educational and economic opportunities in their hometowns appear to be the dominant factor in their migration. Presence of more political freedom in Istanbul was acknowledged by respondents, but for many of them this can be rather a new thing they realised only after migration. On the other hand multiculturalism in citiesand educational and economic opportunities were mentioned frequently (see in following paragraphs).

Respondents understanding of migration *(göç)*, homeland *(memleket)* and culture (kültür)

Preliminary research results presented below are based on 22 semi-structured in-depth interviews with young Kurdish migrants resident in different districts of Istanbul and one group interview with 6 conservative Kurdish women (among whom two were recent migrants). Participants were recruited by snow-ball technique. Interviews were conducted in Turkish in August and September 2014. Interview schedule focused on three broad topics: History of migration, social construction of Kurdish identity and attitudes towards Istanbul.

6 of the 22 interviewees were women. Almost all of respondents were Sunni Muslim (except 2 Alevi women) and Kurmanci dialect speakers (except one speaker of Zazaki). The youngest respondent was a 19 years old student, the oldest was 35 years old. Majority of the respondents were students or graduates of one of the universities in Istanbul, two of them were studying in other cities but stated Istanbul as their place of residence. Among graduates, there were newly qualified lawyers, high school teachers, physiotherapists, one entrepreneur and one unemployed person. Most of participants of in-depth interviews were leftist Kurds, although not all of them were voters of pro-Kurdish *Peoples Democracy Party* (*HDP* in Turkish) whereas one respondent described himself as former AKP voter.

Interviews and conversations with Kurds and Kurdish migrants in Istanbul led to discovery of specific understanding of key notions - migration *(göç)*, homeland (*memleket*) and culture (*kültür*). Probably as a result of endured deep experiences in the family or heard from others and surrounding climate of forced migration in the 1990's, many Kurds in Istanbul only recognise forced migration.

Some respondents were underlining the fact that they came to the city for educational rather than settlement - *I did not came to migrate [settle], I came to university* (respondent from Konya). I wanted to interview one of my Kurdish friends, who works as a teacher of English language and she said she is not a migrant, she just stayed in Istanbul after her studies. As conversation continued she realised that in fact she is a voluntary migrant as she lives in Istanbul for around ten years now. Such immediate connotation between migration and displacement led me to see the necessity to emphasis on voluntary migration in my study. Turkish word describing a refugee - *mülteci,* was used to describe forced migrants from abroad, during my fieldwork most notably these were people fleeing Syria. My friend suggested that the most appropriate word for "voluntary migration" would be *gönüllü göç* in Turkish. Then I have used it when I invited potential participants. Among Kurds in Istanbul, migration *(göç)* can be associated with forced migration *(zorunlu göç)*. The definition of a migrant may also depend on a situation as one person can feel that he or she is a voluntary migrant while other would not consider himself or herself that way, noting that their stay in Istanbul may be temporary or task oriented.

During these interviews, I asked respondents to describe the characteristics of their homeland (and other places from which they might have migrated) and everyday life in those places prior to their movement. I also planned to compare these descriptions with their characterization of Istanbul. Therefore understanding of the village, city or district from which they descended (i.e. *memleket*) was also a key point in this study. This word of Arabic origin is also used by the citizens of Turkey abroad to refer to their home country (i.e. Turkey) but more often to a geographic area (town, city, village, etc.) in Turkey from which they come from. While inviting people for interviews, I have found out that this term may be used not only to describe the location of a birthplace but more often the homeland (place of origin) of a family. Many young Kurds who were born in Istanbul name their *memleket* differently as their family descends from other regions. Thus, some members of Kurdish youth visit their homelands but never lived there and some have never been there (one of the reasons for this can be the fact that some settlements were destroyed during the clashes between Turkish military forces and PKK). Some might have just followed their parents to a new place of residence. A graduate student with whom I made a pilot interview during summer 2013 admitted that he was born in a village near Diyarbakır which was burnt when he was an infant. Another respondent had moved to Istanbul with her parents and her younger sisters were born there. *Memleket* can be therefore associated with the area of origin of the family which one might only know through second hand information. It is however interesting that despite the remoteness or even loss of the homeland its name is still preserved as an important part of self-identification in interactions with other Turkish citizens.

Culture is understood broadly in this study. It is varyingly interpreted in every-day use and by different scholars. Kroeber and Kluckhohn (1954) analysed 168 different uses of the term in the early 1950s. An earlier definition by Kluckhohn and Kelly (1945) is adopted here: *All those historically created designs for living, explicit and implicit, rational, irrational, and nonrational, which exist at any given time as potential guides for the behavior of men.* I have asked respondents if in their opinion Istanbul is somehow connected with Kurdish culture, what customs would they describe as characteristics of Kurdish culture and do they perceive any features of their lives which indicates that they are maintaining Kurdish culture. Responses point an association of culture with tradition and art. Thus my questions concerning broadly understood Kurdish culture where perceived as mainly about so-called "high culture". Many respondents have emphasized that their homeland was a place of cultivation of Kurdish customs while maintaining them is almost impossible in the conditions of city of migration: *You cannot live the life by Kurdish culture in Istanbul, you can in Mardin...* said a respondent from Mardin. This may have to do with connotations of Turkish phrase *örf ve adetler* which denotes customs and habits, but at the same time word *örf* is connected with traditional code representing more formal side of the notion.

Young migrant's attitudes towards the city of Istanbul

Majority of the respondents have migrated to Istanbul in order to study in one of so many universities in the city. Its multiculturalism, educational prestige, economic opportunities and availability of rare majors were cited as reasons for choosing Istanbul as a destination. Some respondents have completed part of their higher education in other cities and moved to Istanbul for graduate studies, or for a second major or to pursue a career. Almost all of them, when they first arrived, felt overwhelmed by Istanbul's enormous size and crowdedness. Respondents underlined the difference between their homeland and Istanbul in terms of direct contacts they used to have with almost every one living in their places of origin. However, there were thousands of anonymous people passing by in Istanbul – *very crowded, very hectic, everyone was in a hurry* said the third respondent from Mardin about his first impressions of the city. *I came to university, in our place people talk with each other while walking, here they talk very rarely, no one looks the other in the face...* said a respondent from Bitlis. Reactions to vastness of cities' landscape was mentioned a few times as they felt the fear of being lost.

Conflict, Insecurity and Mobility

Narratives on the links between Istanbul and Kurdish culture differed depending on one's general attitude to the city. While discussing Kurdish population in Istanbul, respondents would often point out that many Kurdish migrants are getting assimilated into Turkish culture in the city – *For Kurdish culture Istanbul is disadvantageous... people living in metropolis became similar to each other (...)* said a respondent from Bitlis. This can be treated as non-material form of insecurity – i.e. a perceived threat of assimilation. Some respondents pointed out that Istanbul is not a Kurdish homeland in a way the cities of Kurdistan are - *Istanbul is important for Kurdish culture...but more for Turks... as for lives of Kurds... Diyarbakır, Erbil, Mohabad, Qmişlo, Kobane, Efrin...* said a respondent from Batman. Some underlined that Kurdish traditions cannot be cultivated there. Many respondents stated that the city has a place in Kurdish history as it was a home for Bedirxan and is a destination for Kurdish migrants. Many respondents accented that the city was a place of cross-cultural exchange – *Istanbul is important for every culture* said a respondent from Şırnak. This difference in views on the city was mirrored also in varying emphasis on its advantages and disadvantages. Most of respondents pointed to the availability of jobs and variety of possible activities that one can find in the city as its main qualities. *You can find everything that you want* said a respondent from Konya while another respondent from Mardin said *if you want to work in Istanbul you can find the job.*

It was like going to Disneyland, it was a city like Disneyland, and everything looked great said a respondent from Batman on his first impression of Istanbul. *In our place, in the evening, everybody altogether stop for the call for prayers - ezan - and life ends. Here it's not like this, in Taksim, in Kadıköy, at night at any hour you can sit with your friends* said another respondent from Bitlis. At the same time, majority of interviewees have found living and working in the city difficult. One of the respondents noted that Istanbul is a great city for the rich while there is a widespread economic exploitation and exclusion of many Kurdish migrants. *In other Kurdish districts, if you live with Kurds there (...) they are poor... they are oppressed...* said the second respondent from Mardin. Overpopulation, pollution, traffic and more indirect inter-personal relations were also cited as disadvantages of living in the city. They were comparing Istanbul with their places of origin, reflecting perhaps other elements of an environment of human insecurity which is also linked to economic circumstances.

When asked about changes in their lives and opinions after they moved to Istanbul, respondents would often deny any major differences. Many of them, however, noted that living in Istanbul provided them with possibilities of meeting new people, engaging in new activities. Some of them admitted that they socially become more liberal than they were in their homeland. For example, some started drinking alcohol while some are now living with an unrelated person of the opposite sex without marriage. It appears, however, that their political views and opposition to Turkish nationalist ideology were matured prior to migration.

Maintaining Kurdish identity in Istanbul

Being born to Kurdish parents makes one Kurdish and this line of thinking was common among my respondents. This does not however mean that every person who was raised in a Kurdish family would publicly and openly admit that he or she is a Kurd. Some sees their ethnicity just as a simple fact of life while valuing religious affiliation and community higher. Some others underline Kurdish identity strongly and often politically emphasise to show that they are opposed to those who discriminate Kurds in Turkey. It is however important to note that majority of respondents when asked about the meaning of being Kurdish and how Kurds differ from others would begin with an emphasis on that one's ethnicity does not matter much and people of different origins have similarities. This is to imply that, while being Kurdish, they are not nationalists and Kurds are not fundamentally different from other cultures, ethnic groups or nations. *Being Kurdish... so ...normally... if it's necessary to express then... It's nothing. Being Turkish does not matter, being English does not matter, being German, being French does not matter...*says a respondent from Batman. Many of my interviewee's have stated that if they would have to describe, in some way, Kurdishness they would refer to resistance, oppression and discrimination, thus referring to the difficult history of Kurds and their homeland as put by a respondent from Van: *Being Kurd in this country means death, means pain, means tears.* Many of them also referred to them having darker skin color than Turks, being generally warm in social relations (phrase used was - *sıcak kanlı* – literally it means having warm blood in Turkish), and being hospitable as characteristics of the Kurds.

Maintaining Kurdish identity was usually linked to the use of Kurdish language (most respondents spoke Kurmanci), collective memories of for example *Newroz* celebrations and knowing Kurdish history. Although respondents did not always explicitly mentioned the last point, preserving collective Kurdish memory was often considered important. Many of them also mentioned important historic Kurdish figures and tragic events such as Halabja massacre (in Iraq) or killing of Kurdish smugglers in Roboski (in Turkey).

Political activities were also part of their belonging. Some respondents were active members in youth organisation of pro-Kurdish People's Democratic Party (*Halkların Demokratik Partisi*) or other leftist parties close such as the Socialist Party of Opressed (*Ezilenlerin Sosyalist Partisi*). Most respondents could name some Kurdish institutions based in Istanbul such as Mesopotamia Cultural Center (*Mezopotamya Kültür Merkezi*) and Kurdish Institute of Istanbul (*Enstîtuya Kurdî Ya Stenbolê*). Some took part or were involved in organization of activities of those institutions but many of them would not recall the addresses of these organizations.

Although majority of respondents would think mainly about Kurdish traditions and high culture when asked about cultural practices and customs, they would say, for example, they still drink ceylon tea (the so-called smuggled tea – *kaçak çay* as it is used to be smuggled from Arab countries) instead of Turkish tea from Black Sea region or eating a special recipe cheese with herbs - typical for Şırnak province. Many listen to Kurdish music most notably Şivan Perwer, Ciwan Haco and Ahmet Kaya.

Various ways of preserving ethnic identity was evident in the narratives of my respondents. However, some were not easy to practice due to the official denial policy. This would lead to cross level conflicts between individuals and the state[4] over the practice of Kurdish culture. Perceived discrimination was evident as Kurds often hide their ethnic identity in public. However it is important to note that Istanbul was generally viewed as a multicultural city with rather liberal environment compared to other cities such as Izmir or Adana. Even disclosing their birth places would solidify discrimination under certain circumstances. Many respondents mentioned that they could not find flats for rent when the vendors figure out they were born in a South-East province as one from Hakkari stated: *I came to Istanbul, I was a student, I was supposed to find a flat, I searched, but I couldn't find a place. In most places, I approached, they asked me where am I from, what is my homeland. When I said Hakkari, they would say, we are not letting it*. This was a clear case for an environment of human insecurity faced by Kurds after migrating to Istanbul. It was about facing discrimination in finding a house to rent implying a material and non-material insecurity (an indication of individual level - micro - and community level conflict - meso) at the same time. At the same time, this place of origin based belonging and ties can help migrants find accommodation and economic opportunities.

---

[4] See Sirkeci (2003).

Conclusion

At the beginning of the twenty-first century, it seems a new wave of Kurdish internal migration emerged in Turkey. As Istanbul is a city hosting the largest Kurdish population in the country, there is need to study new Kurdish migration to this city.

The findings based on the in-depth interviews with young migrants from different districts of the city show migrants do not necessarily perceive Istanbul in relation to the Kurdish culture. Tradition is associated with collective life in Kurdistan. Istanbul is rather a place with wider freedoms and enables Kurdish organizations' activities. Migrants see this metropolis as an endless source of possibilities – a *Disneyland* but also as an urban space of difficult work life. It also facilitates assimilation while being a place of exile. Young Kurdish migrants exited one kind of environment of human insecurity characterised by lack of economic and educational opportunities and they ended up in another environment of (relative) human insecurity marked by other difficulties and threats such as high prices, indirect contacts, and potential ethnic assimilation.

Preserving Kurdish cultural habits in Istanbul is evident in publicly visible, collective actions but also in everyday lives of young migrants. While multiculturalism and job opportunities make Istanbul a better place than other Turkish cities in the eyes of migrants, this climate of opportunities is not free from obstacles for maintaining Kurdish identity. Respondents highlighted this conflict over official recognition of their culture while acknowledging the opportunities. Place of origin (e.g. district, city or village) of the family is a strong marker of identity and it appears critical in discrimination faced by migrants in Istanbul. This is another example for conflict at the meso level (based on stereotypes about Kurds common among Turks) forming part of the new environment of human insecurity emerging after migration.

Acknowledgement

The article was written in the scope of project financed by Polish National Science Center by the decision number DEC-2013/09/N/HS3/02014.

Chapter 11. Perspectives on communal violence against Kurds in Turkey

İmren Borsuk

The second half of the 2000s saw an "expedited process" for the Kurdish question in Turkey as many reforms regarding cultural and linguistic rights were put into place by the AKP (Justice and Development Party, *Adalet ve Kalkınma Partisi*) government at an unprecedented speed compared to earlier governments. Moreover, the negotiations to disarm the PKK (Kurdistan Workers' Party, *Partiya Karkerên Kurdistan*), which were also unimaginable before, started in late 2012 and came to a halt after the elections on 7 June 2015. The reforms shattered the pre-existing relationship between Kurds and state authorities that viewed Kurdish identity as an existential threat to the unity of Turkish state. Ironically, the betterment of Kurdish rights coincided with the increase in communal violence incidents against Kurds. My study on communal violence against Kurds is compiled from the archives of *Özgür Gündem* and *Dicle Haber Ajansı* (Dicle News Agency) and it finds more than 600 communal violent acts against Kurds between 1999 and 2012. Communal violent acts can be described as violence in which one of the motives of mobilization is "communal" that targets the communal identity of certain persons or groups. The change from vertical state-rebel group violence to horizontal society-society violence in Turkey points out fault lines of potential social frictions in society. Moreover, these communal attacks are a litmus test to scrutinize the resonance of democratization reforms with state and political authorities since their investigation and prosecution illustrate whether these authorities are able to defend recently recognized cultural rights and treat these matters in a fair and equitable manner. In this chapter I discussed the reasons of communal attacks against Kurds and shares some of the findings of my ongoing investigation the data of which came from fieldwork and archives of *Cumhuriyet*, *Özgür Gündem* and *Dicle Haber Ajansı*.

In doing so, this chapter firstly presents some general characteristics of communal violence against Kurds in Turkey. Secondly, it provides some examples from the most common types of communal violent acts against Kurds. Thirdly, theoretical framework on the reasons of communal violence is briefly discussed. Then, communal violence incidents against Kurds are examined through these arguments and hypotheses.

Some general features of communal violence in Turkey

Since 1984, the rise of armed conflict with the PKK, Turkey has witnessed a civil war that is characterized as an intrastate violence challenging a sovereign state. Unlike other civil wars that also involved communal violence such as in Northern Ireland, Rwanda, Sudan, Yugoslavia and Sri Lanka; Turkey's civil war did not face communal violence apart from sporadic communal disturbances (Kılıç, 1992). The communal attacks against Kurds came into public limelight in the second half of the 2000s as many journalists and scholars began to discuss "lynching" incidents against Kurds that were more frequent in the Western cities of Turkey. Contrary to many declarations of local and national politicians that deny the ethnic character of these incidents, there are "communal" violent acts against Kurds in Turkey. Their precipitating reasons involve expressions of Kurdish identity such as speaking, listening, singing in Kurdish or participating in demonstrations that reveal the possible attachment to a pro-Kurdish cause such as protests by the pro-Kurdish party, Newroz celebrations, civil disobedience acts and commemoration of wartime losses. I do not want to detail the reasons of commonplace usage of the word "lynching" to describe these incidents as it is beyond the scope of this chapter but it is necessary to highlight that lynching, as it is used, involves execution of victims by many tactics such as hanging, shooting, burning, lacerating, stabbing, dismembering or mutilation. In Turkey, many communal attacks against Kurds are not *"lynching"* in its proper sense (fortunately) but can be described as *"violent rituals"* (Tilly, 2003). It is defined as collective violence with high salience of short-run damage and high-coordination between violent actors. Tilly defines violent rituals as *"at least one relatively well-defined and coordinated group follows a known interaction script entailing the infliction of damage on itself or others"* (ibid.: 14). Being different from mob attacks against leftists that do not adopt certain rituals, rituals play an important role in mobilizing people during communal attacks against Kurds. In many events, Turkish nationals sing their anthem, Turkish flags are waved, the slogans of soldier funerals *"Şehitler ölmez, vatan bölünmez"* (the martyrs will never die, the country will never be divided), *"Kahrolsun PKK"* (Damn PKK), *"PKK def'ol"* (PKK Get out) are shouted.

Communal violence against Kurds in Turkey is directed mainly against the pro-Kurdish party, its members, activists and supporters. There are also a significant number of cases against Kurds who were not involved in any kind of political activity at the time of communal attacks. Anything that connotes Kurdish identity may turn according to circumstances into the triggers of mass anger such as wearing an Ahmet Kaya[1] t-shirt, speaking Kurdish, singing or listening to Kurdish songs. The symbols that recall the PKK also ignite mass fervour such as wearing things that recall the PKK colours or joining in a militant's funeral. The victims are diverse; Kurdish families from Eastern and Southeastern Turkey such as Van, Şanlıurfa, Muş or Kurdish shopkeepers in Western cities; Kurdish construction and seasonal workers; Kurdish students. Perpetrators are also various and not necessarily the hot-core supporters of Turkish nationalism such as *Ülkücü* or *Alperen* Institutions. Shopkeepers, craftsmen and men on the street participate in these incidents. When the rumours about the links of an alleged offender to the PKK spread, the number of mobs grew bigger.

In my research, inspired by the studies of Tilly (1966), Tilly and Zambrano (1989), Wilkinson (2004) and Varshney (2002), I define a communal violent event as '*an occasion on which at least more than two persons gathered in a publicly-accessible place and some seize or damage at least one person or objects by the motive of targeting their communal identity*'. I present some of the incidents below to illustrate these types of communal violent acts.

Illustrative examples

Violent attacks against Kurdish workers

In a park of the Akyazı district of Sakarya, a conflict over "shoulder strike" between youths of the district and seasonal workers that came to collect hazelnuts from Southeastern Turkey turned into a PKK fight. Following the fight that was said to include a dispute over the PKK, four people were taken into custody. The local people that learned the news gathered in front of the provincial police station and shouted slogans against the PKK. The protesters tried to enter into the police station. When the tension did not appease, the governor of Sakarya came up and talked to the crowd "You showed reaction by gathering here. Furthering this reaction means reacting against the state. I ask you to disperse complacently. The children whom you reacted to are in the hands of the state. The grand state will apply whatever necessary. You do not commit the same fault, too". The protesters were dispersed by the hand of police and gendarmerie forces (see Akyazı'da gergin saatler [Tense hours in Akyazı], *Cumhuriyet*, 9 September 2006).

---

[1] Ahmet Kaya is a singer with Kurdish origins. He was exposed to public humiliation by Turkish media after he announced his willingness to sing music in Kurdish in a music awards ceremony. He had to go into exile in Paris where he also died in 2000.

Violent attacks against Kurdish students

Three students at Giresun University Tirebolu Mehmet Bayraktar Vocational School were attacked by *ülkücü*[2] and people from Tirebolu. While students were going to their home, a group of *ülkücü* approached and said "*we will not shelter PKKs here*" and assaulted the students, two males and one female. The male students took blows to their heads and some people from Tirebolu joined the group of ten who attempted to lynch the female student. After taking blows to her head and body, she sought refuge in a student dormitory for males as *ülkücüs* attacked with knives. The person in charge of security at the dormitory shouted "the PKKs among you get out" and took the female student out. After the attack, students were transferred to Tirebolu State Hospital. Police did not launch an investigation for perpetrators but took the statements of the three students who were attacked. These Kurdish students cannot go out of their homes for fear of being lynched (see Tirebolu'da Kürt öğrenciler linç edilmek istendi [Kurdish students in Tirebolu are attempted to be lynched], *Dicle Haber Ajansı*, 28 June 2010).

Violent attacks against Pro-Kurdish party

The BDP (Peace and Democracy Party, *Barış ve Demokrasi Partisi*) Diyarbakır office where hunger strikes were initiated was attacked by 50 people with stones and sticks. The windows of the building were broken down and the party signboards were damaged. After the incident, the group was taken to the police station (see Diyarbakir'da gergin gün [Tense day in Diyarbakır], *Cumhuriyet*, 18 November 2012).

Violent attacks against demonstrators for a Pro-Kurdish cause

After the public declaration in Taksim Square where protests regarding the incidents in Diyarbakır were staged, police intervened in the demonstration. Fırat Kaplan was involved when the police intervened. He was attacked by Roma people equipped with chopper knives and sticks. Biyet Kaplan, brother of Fırat Kaplan, said that his brother had nothing to do with the demonstration. Biyet Kaplan spoke for Firat Kaplan, who is unable to talk because of injuries, "*While my brother was going to my elder sibling, 15-20 people stopped him in the road. Since my brother is dark-skinned and likens to Kurds, they attacked him with chopper knives, daggers and sticks. They blew his head with chopper knives. All the veins in his left hand are dead. Doctor said: 'his hand can remain disabled'. There are serious blows in the upper side of his left hand. The bone is squashed. I do not understand what they want from my brother*". He told

---

[2] Ülkücüler (Idealists) are known as Turkish ultra-nationalist youth organization of Nationalist Action Party.

that police blamed his brother for the incidents (see Romenlerin saldırısına uğrayan Kaplan'ın sağlık durumu ciddi [the health conditions of Kaplan who is exposed to attacks of Roma people are serious], *Dicle Haber Ajansı*, 4 April 2006).

An example of non-occurrence

One group attempted to attack the building of the BDP after the killing of two police officers by the explosion in front of Osmaniye Credit and Dormitory Institution. While the groups began to gather in front of the Osmaniye branch of the BDP, police took preventive measures. The head of the BDP Osmaniye Branch, Maşallah Çetin said that the group was dispersed by the police. Police took the group to the nearby station before the assault. Maşallah Çetin said that "*I think that they could not attack because we were too many and police took care of them. There were groups down there anyway. Police checked the IDs of these people and brought them to Carşı police station nearby. We also saw a police later standing in front of the entrance of our building. I called the police and they came to the scene. They said 'we are not related to this incident. We are trying to ensure your safety'. Police intervened and dispersed the groups around the BDP building. Police took serious measures [to prevent an attack]*" (see BDP Osmaniye İl binasına gündüz ortası saldırı [Attacks against the BDP Osmaniye City Building in the middle of the day], *Dicle Haber Ajansı*, 26 August 2012).

Reasons for communal violence: A theoretical overview

The power-threat hypothesis is widely discussed in the USA in order to explain lynching events against Blacks (Reed, 1972; Corzine et al., 1983; Tolnay et al., 1989). Blalock's (1967) power-threat hypothesis argues that the rise in racial tensions stemmed from the fears of the majority about their dominant status that was affected by the participation of a subordinate population to economic and political competition. Soule (1992) argues that lynching rates against Blacks increased because interracial political and economic competition intensified with migration to the Southern manufacturing areas, Black participation in the cotton economy after the enfranchisement of the Black population and the rise of black participation in the populist movement. Olzak (1990) demonstrates that economic competition and populist threats simultaneously increased rates of lynching and urban violence at the national level in the USA from 1890 to 1900. For Carrigan and Webb, the mob violence against Mexicans also aimed at eliminating economic and political competition by sustaining the displacement of the Mexican population from the land characterized by denial of access to natural resources, political disfranchisement and economic dependency upon an Anglo-controlled capitalist order (Carrigan & Webb, 2003:418).

Many studies on ethnic conflict also developed theories to explain the role of political and economic grievances on the onset of ethnic violence. Couched as relative deprivation "*a perceived discrepancy between men's value expectations (the goods and conditions of life to which people believe they are rightfully entitled) and their value capabilities (the goods and conditions they think they are capable of attaining or maintaining)*" (Gurr, 1970:13), Gurr argues that deprivation increases human tendency to collective violence. Stewart (2008) enlarges the scope of relative deprivation with the horizontal inequality concept. He argues that horizontal inequality between groups that involves political, economic, social and cultural dimensions enables inter-ethnic animosities and enhances the risk of intergroup violence. This hypothesis is also confirmed by large-N studies (Østby, 2008; Cederman, Weidmann & Gleditsch, 2011). Political competition between ethnic groups may also lead to ethnic violence especially when political cleavages coalesce with sharply polarized and cohesive ethnic groups. Notably ethnic outbidding strategies, in which political leaders heighten the ethnic tone in order to capture the political leadership of their ethnic groups, are considered to be detrimental to inter-ethnic peace as they can backfire the ethnicization of social conflicts (Rabushka & Shepsle 1972; Rothschild, 1981; Horowitz, 1985; Kaufman, 1996). Many studies reveal a dynamic relationship between politics and ethnic violence. Gagnon (2004) contends that elites in Yugoslavia provoked ethnic tensions in order to defy reformist challenges to their political power. By the same token, many researchers demonstrate that ethnic violence displays a variation within the same country since type, size and nature of cleavages change according to cities. For example, caste cleavages thrive on ethnic cleavages in many southern states of India and forestall the radicalization of ethnic tensions (Wilkinson, 2004). Brass (1997) argues that in riot-prone cities, institutionalized riot systems, which denote the networks between militant groups, police forces and politicians, stir up ethnic disagreements in order to unite ethnic groups around ethnic political entrepreneurs. Wilkinson (2004) shows in his analysis of India that Hindu-Muslim violence occurs less in states run by governments that rely on minority support because politicians use more effectively security forces under their control to halt inter-ethnic tensions in these areas. Hence, he puts emphasis on the role of electoral incentives as a catalyst of abating inter-ethnic tensions.

Another argument relates communal violence to the activation of boundaries, more generally, to boundary crises. Inverarity (1976) argues that racial tensions in the USA increased due to disruption of white solidarity in the South. Two facts threatened white community. On one hand, rising populist movements unifying both poor whites and blacks threatened white supremacy. On the other hand, black participation in economy after enfranchisement intensified economic competition in the South by purchasing lands, producing cotton and competing with white labourers. According to Inverarity, the extent to which a given community responds to a boundary crisis with repressive justice depends directly on the magnitude of mechanical solidarity in that community (Inverarity, 1976: 278). Many constructivist accounts of ethnic violence display the activation and hardening of boundaries under war conditions that undercut inter-ethnic trust networks (Dale, 1997; Dean, 2000; Peterson, 2000). Negative catalysts such as regime crises or state decline destabilize ethnic boundaries. Contrary to many surveys showing inter-ethnic collaboration in Yugoslavia, the economic crisis and state dissolution brought about the crystallization of boundaries (Woodward, 1995). Dumitru and Johnson (2011) demonstrate that deliberate state policies regarding citizenship and nationality that construct inclusive or exclusive boundaries of nationhood have an impact on the scope of inter-ethnic violence under war conditions.

Communal violence against Kurds: Why now and not before?

In Turkey, communal violence against Kurds increased notably after 2005 and intensified more specifically after the attempt of burning the Turkish flag in Newroz celebrations in Mersin. During the economic contraction of 2001 in which Turkey's economy downsized by 9.5 percent (Akyüz & Boratav, 2003), communal violence against Kurds was not a significant phenomenon. Conversely, the rise in communal violence coincides with economic development. Turkey managed to combine high rates of economic growth, 7.5 percent per annum in the 2002 - 2006 period (Öniş & Bayram, 2008). There are socio-economic inequalities between Turks and Kurds (Table 11.1), however, one can easily assume that in the 1990s where thousands (or millions) of Kurds migrated to urban areas, the socio-economic rift between Turks and Kurds was even more amplified because of the impoverishment of Kurds ensuing from displacement (see Jongerden, 2007). Kurds compose the majority of displaced persons due to security reasons. Hacettepe University Institute of Population Studies conducted a comprehensive survey on displaced persons for security reasons (HÜNEE, 2006) that reveals the scale of this impoverishment: the majority of displaced households contain 5 or more people, 78.2% of displaced persons are uneducated, while close to half of displaced individuals suffer unemployment and the other half of them are working without social security. My interviews also revealed that in some areas, seasonal Kurdish workers are paid very little which in turn decreases the wages of other labourers in economic competition. Thus, local resentment may emerge. Nonetheless, this was also the case in the 1990s and between 2000 and 2005 during which communal violence against Kurds was less abundant. Hence, I do not consider the economic competition as the main trigger of communal violence.

Table 11.1. Socio-Economic Inequalities between Turks and Kurds, %

2010/2011	**Turks**	**Kurds**
People whose father are not educated	20	53
People who live below 700 TL	29	48
People who are not educated	7	26
People who live with a population of 9 person in the house	2	17
People who got state support	4	9

Source: The report of findings about the research on perceptions and expectations concerning Kurdish question by Konda (2011).

Political fragmentation in Turkey has declined in the 2000s (Table 11.2). Political representation of Kurds was enhanced not only due to the significant Kurdish support for the AKP government but also due to the fact that a pro-Kurdish party won seats in the parliament by running independent candidates to bypass the 10% electoral threshold. Moreover, the period of instable and fragile coalition governments in the 1990s seemingly ended. Turkish political system has turned into a dominant party system (Çarkoğlu, 2011) and sustained stabilization with four political parties (Şekerçioğlu & Arıkan, 2008: 215): AKP, representative of a conservative peripheral segment, CHP (Republican People's Party, *Cumhuriyet Halk Partisi*), representative of a secular segment, MHP (Nationalist Action Party, *Milliyetçi Halk Partisi*), representative of Turkish nationalism and BDP, representative of Kurdish nationalism.

It might be easy to assume that ethnic boundaries are activated by the official recognition of different sub-ethnic identities as a result of reforms regarding Kurdish identity. Nonetheless, the activation of boundaries remains a vague hypothesis. Many events that brought about structural shifts in Turkey can be counted as triggers of activation of boundaries such as the foundation of Turkey as a nation-state or the onset of the war with the PKK. Thus, it is necessary to question how the boundary crisis of the 2000s in Turkey is different from the earlier ones.

Table 11.2. Party competition and Government Formation between 1999-2012

General Elections	Government Formation	Ruling Party	Effective Number of Parties	Ruling party's vote share (%)	Support for ruling party in cities with largest Kurdish population (%)
1999	Coalition	DSP-MHP-ANAP[3]	6.78	55.58	26.01
2002	Single-Party	AKP	5.43	34.43	23.43
2007	Single-Party	AKP	3.48	46.58	46.44
2011	Single-Party	AKP	2.97	49.95	41.95

Sources: The elections results are compiled using the electoral results of Belgenet.[4]The index on effective number of parties in Turkey is taken from Tezcür (2012) who calculated the effective number of parties according to vote shares. The cities with largest Kurdish populations are Ağrı, Bingöl, Bitlis, Diyarbakır, Hakkari, Mardin, Muş, Siirt, Tunceli, Van, Şanlıurfa, Şırnak, Adıyaman, Batman, Elazığ according to Mutlu (1996). The cities with largest Kurdish populations founded after 1990, Batman, Şırnak, Ardahan and Iğdır are added into calculations.

The ideal of Turkish nationhood was implanted in the belief that all ethnically diverse Muslim populations of Turkey, including Kurds, were future Turks who would be assimilated into Turkish identity as long as modernization progressed (Aktürk, 2009). Kurdish insurgencies which were erupted in the aftermath of the foundation of the Republic fuelled the fears of bureaucratic-military elites about the dissolution of state by secessionist movements. Kurdishness was constructed as an existential threat and conceived as an obstacle the ideal Turkish citizen who was secular, Western and loyal to Turkish nation (Yeğen, 1999). None of the constitutions of the Turkish republic, 1924, 1961 and 1982 authorize expressions of ethnic identity. The armed conflict with the PKK reawoke the securitization discourse that considered the use of extraordinary violence against Kurdish identity legitimate to protect the integrity of Turkish nation-state. Turkey applied the worst case scenario of a counter-terrorist representation strategy that thwarted the political articulation of the Kurdish problem (Chowdhury & Krebs, 2010). The state authorities drew a close line between 'cultural' and 'political'. Any defence of basic rights for Kurds was considered political and was represented in public sphere as 'treacherous' or '*Kürtçü*' [pro-Kurdish] in search of Kurdish ethno-nationalist goals. Cultural expressions of Kurdish identity were qualified by the Constitutional Court as a threat to unitary and progressive

---

[3] DSP (Democratic Left Party) and ANAP (Motherland Party).
[4] Received from http://www.belgenet.net available on: 23 May 2011.

nature of state and constituted one of the motives for the closure of pro-Kurdish parties (Koğacıoğlu, 2004). The supporters and activists of pro-Kurdish parties which rose onto the political scene after the 1990s endured excessive repression of security forces and they were portrayed as PKK members (Watts, 1999). Furthermore, democratic claims based on Kurdish rights were represented as deviant and divisive in Turkish media (Sezgin & Wall, 2005; Somer, 2005). In sum, the language of armed conflict was in effect conflict-generating for the multicultural nature of society as any expressions of Kurdish identity evoked anxiety-laden discourse and was stigmatized with terrorism and separatism.

2000s were years of transition not only for the Kurdish problem but also for the Turkish political sphere. The AKP, a scission of closed conservative and pro-Islamic Welfare Party rose to power in 2002 as a coalition of peripheral forces and put forth substantial reform programs that not only tamed the bureaucratic-military tutelage but also strengthened cultural rights for Kurds. Among these reforms are teaching of Kurdish in private institutions, broadcasting in Kurdish, lifting of emergency rule in the Kurdish southeastern provinces, ratifications of certain parts of the international law related to minority rights, 24-hour Kurdish broadcasting in state-sponsored TV channel TRT 6, inauguration of a language department for Kurdish at Mardin Artuklu University. Nonetheless, the democratization of Kurdish problem endured grave shocks and setbacks in this process. On one hand, the resumed fight of the PKK in 2004 fed Turkish nationalism and stoked mass anger against Kurds which prepared a convenient social environment for the rise of communal attacks. On the other hand, the AKP reforms which concentrated more on individual rights neglecting the collective ones remained below expectations. In addition, the AKP underwent domestication in power (Tezcür, 2010) and frustrated an important part of Kurds by its *statu quo* profile at critical moments such as the bombardments of Hakkari in 2005 and death of civilians in Uludere (Roboski) by military bombardments in 2011. The Kurdish opening initiated by the government in 2009 proposed no coherent map and finally was abandoned in the face of oppositions. Moreover, the AKP could not generate a widespread public consensus on reforms for the Kurdish problem not only because these reforms drew the ire of parties in opposition, the CHP and the MHP, but also the AKP alienated the electorate of opposition parties through the heavy-handed use of state repression against social movements and by a culturally-loaded political rhetoric polarizing the society along a *Kulturkampf* (see Kalyacıoğlu, 2012). The AKP did not give up also its reflex majoritaire which criminalized the demands of pro-Kurdish parties by the hand of prosecutors and security forces during the KCK (Union of Communities in Kurdistan) operations and it sought to isolate politically pro-Kurdish parties presenting them as the political façade of the PKK.

New tensions emerge during times of transition. Communal violence, which is a symptom of divided societies, is among these new tensions of Turkey that coalesce with the de-securitization of Kurdish problem. Their resurgence avows that identity boundaries are now recognizable in the public sphere and can turn into a justification for the use of violence. Contrary to many expectations about the reflections of macro-political developments into the micro-sphere in a parallel direction, *"[T]here is a disjunction, and sometimes a strong one, between personal inter-ethnic relations and political inter-ethnic relations"* as Horowitz (2004:246-247) underlines. The perceptual rigidity produced by the armed conflict over Kurdish identity still overshadows interpersonal relations in the urban sphere and cannot be expected to overturn in one decade. While many people in Eastern and Southeastern Turkey lived through the political, social and economic dynamics of the Kurdish problem day by day; the consciousness of people in Western Turkey was shaped more by the state discourse and the fight against the PKK. The remark of one participant of TESEV research is illustrative in this regard:

"Here only the martyrs are known. Kurds are ignored. In fact, Kurds here are mostly assimilated or they are mostly out of sight. Here Kurd means terrorist, and solving the Kurdish Question means finishing terror. Therefore, the problem needs to be explained well here" (Ensarioğlu & Kurban, 2011:43).

Today, the ethnic microcosm of urban cities is more vibrant with the recognition of ethnic identities. However, identities are not conceived in the same way as they were before the war. Civil wars generate endogenous dynamics transforming the boundaries of ethnic groups (Kalyvas, 2008) and end up, in most cases, with hardening them. The social, political and economic repercussions of war changed what it means to be Kurdish and Turkish in urban life. The nationalist spirit fed by the war accorded to all Turkish citizens a vigilant duty to "react against terror", which targeted not only the PKK but also the expressions of Kurdish identity. Moreover, the horizontal inequality between Turks and Kurds and inter-ethnic interaction in urban context multiplied the stigmas used to describe Kurds as Saraçoğlu's research (2011) demonstrated. He found five main stigmas used by *Izmirli* toward Kurdish migrants in the city a) ignorant and uneducated b) benefit scroungers c) disrupters of urban life d) invaders e) separatists. Ethnicity is no more a private matter as it was reduced to be before the war but connotes social and political resonances and communitarian associations in public sphere. Considering that "*identity is often in the eye of the beholder*" (Jenkins, 1996: 2), there are "*moments of becoming Kurdish*" in public life that may spark interpersonal tensions in Western cities such as speaking Kurdish, singing and listening to Kurdish songs, organizing weddings in conformity with Kurdish customs, participating in pro-Kurdish parties' demonstrations or expressing their support, empathy or opposition to the PKK and pro-Kurdish party. In urban life of Western cities, different from other Muslim ethnic groups, people associate Kurdish identity more easily with "territorial ethnicity" rooted in the social and political space of Kurdish-inhabited areas of Eastern Turkey. For example, many interviewees stated that people have a tendency to associate more easily and swiftly people from Hakkari or Şırnak with the PKK and the support of pro-Kurdish party compared to those from Malatya or Gaziantep. Thus, the saliency of Kurdish identity is adjusted during interpersonal interactions upward or downward according to these moments of "becoming Kurdish".

Democratization reforms not only changed the nature of the Kurdish problem but also the nature of civil society. Civil society organizations (CSOs) proliferated in the public sphere and found a larger opportunity structure to mobilize. These civil society actors are not always supportive of rights and liberties for Kurds. The establishment and nationalist CSOs are sceptical about reforms and view them as concessions to terrorism (see Kaliber & Tocci, 2010). With the acceleration of the European Union accession process and democratization reforms, there has been a mushrooming of nationalist and statist CSOs in the public sphere. For example, Red Apple Coalition (*Kızıl Elma Koalisyonu*) composed of statist-nationalist network of (un)civil associations emerged in 2003 (Jacoby, 2011). Among others, new nationalist CSOs were founded such as VKGB (*Vatansever Kuvvetler Güç Birliği*, The Union of Patriotic Forces) and KMD (*Kuvayi Milliye Derneği*, the National Forces Committee). Called as *Ulusalcılar,* these types of organizations are organized around three common themes: "uncompromising anti-Westernism; externalization of Islam from Turkish nationalism; and ethnic exclusionism" (Uslu, 2008: 73). This neo-national resurgence is supported by certain media organizations and by popular culture that depict Kurds as internal traitors in collaboration with foreign powers in pursuit of vengeance (Uslu, 2008; Dönmez, 2008).

The preliminary findings of my data on communal violence incidents against Kurds in Turkey confirm Wilkinson's argument (2004) and show that communal violence against Kurds take place more in cities governed by political parties which cannot appeal to Kurdish voters, in the MHP and the CHP controlled municipalities compared to the AKP controlled-municipalities. The establishment and nationalist CSOs benefit from a greater opportunity structure to mobilize in the CHP and the MHP-controlled municipalities compared to the AKP-controlled ones. In many communal violence incidents against Kurds, nationalist CSOs play the role of brokers linking unconnected groups and mobilizing them in a single movement (McAdam et al., 2001). Moreover, people with a certain status in public coined as "riot specialists" by Brass, *"persons who are active at all times in monitoring the daily life of the town or city in the areas in which they reside or which they frequent"* (Brass, 1997: 285) such as gang groups, landlords, shopkeepers and civil society actors etc. have a greater mobilization capacity to gather people in case of PKK-related rumours due to more statist and nationalist social environments of these cities. Besides, there is enough resentment that can be mobilized by riot specialists under favourable conditions due to the intensity of victims out of war: "approximately one over ten Turks and one over five Kurds affirms the existence of wounded or dead as a result of the conflict situation in the last 30 years" according to KONDA research (Konda, 2011: 21). The same research also points out worrisome signs of a psychological divide (Table 11.3).

Table 11.3. Tolerance toward different ethnic identities

The question: Would you accept the persons asserted (Turks for Kurds and Kurds for Turks) as a spouse, as a colleague or as a neighbour?

Position of those who say "yes"	**Turks**	**Kurds**
As husband or wife	57,6	26,4
As colleague	53,5	24,8
As neighbour	47,4	22,1

Source: The report of findings about the research on perceptions and expectations concerning Kurdish question by Konda (2011:45-46).

Many incidents of non-occurrence regarding attacks against the pro-Kurdish party, as one of them was aforementioned, show that police have the capacity to intervene efficiently to halt the mobs. In many cases of communal violence incidents, police forces are often accused of late intervention or remaining spectators. Police forces intervene when violent incidents begin to exacerbate. Local cleavages are also involved in these violent acts since pro-Kurdish parties find their rivals and/or other Kurdish victims find their acquaintances attacking their workplaces or houses.

Thus, for those who are disturbed by political and economic competition in local context, ethnic tensions serve them to solve local conflicts without any prosecution process since many cases are closed without any liability and result with the displacement and investigation of victims. Communal violence reframes the conceptualization of popular justice in local context. Law is not just a mere code that regulates relationships and judges them but it also has the *"cultural power"* that shapes and reshapes relationships, defines and produces meaning and identities (Merry, 2000). People who would be afraid to break legal rules at normal times dare to participate in group beatings or looting because they feel omnipotent as a mob and probably think that security forces will be empathetic to them or at least will not intervene. Police takes the provocateurs into custody in case of serious injury or death. The investigation and prosecution process of communal violence incidents are also difficult to pursue since people often are scared to report the criminals. In many cases, those who report are becoming victims and end up being investigated by the police. For example, in the case of seventeen year old E.C. who was beaten by a group for singing a Kurdish song, Istanbul Usküdar Children Bureau [of the Police] sent him to prosecution for *"being sympathizer of PKK and provoking the population"*. Many communal attacks against Kurdish workers ended up with victims being investigated by the police and their displacement to other cities. Courts are also affected by the racialization of the Kurdish problem. For example, a Kurdish family attacked in Denizli was forced to move away from the city while the court considered *"regional differences"* as a plausible reason for ethnic violence (Çivril Assize Crime Court cited by Bayır, 2013:138).

Conclusion

In one comprehensive study, Horowitz (2001) points out three conditions of deadly ethnic riots. First, a hostile relationship between groups that can entice them to killing is pre-existent. Second, they rely on social support; backed by local leaders who justify these incidents. Third, security forces leave the door of communal violence incidents open by implicitly letting them, not interfering directly or being sympathetic to the rioters.

In Turkey, although there are worrisome signs of intolerance against Kurds, there is not an entrenched animosity between Turks and Kurds. Communal violence against Kurds rarely ends up with death. Thus, it is plausible to assume that the general aim of these kinds of violent events is to intimidate rather than to destroy. I observed in my research a variation among cities in Turkey related to public support for such acts since communal violence against Kurds increases in areas with strong statist and nationalist political stance.

While the myth of homogeneity of Turkish national identity is shattered irreversibly in the last era, ethnic heterogeneity has now become more visible. This may not only lead to a multicultural society but also to the possibility of exploitation and manipulation of ethnic boundaries in the public sphere. Security forces, community activists and politicians should take a stronger public stand against these hate crime incidents and not downplay them as "public reaction". Often these violent attacks are triggered by rumours that link some organisations or individuals to the PKK. This kind of rumours offer a clear warning for the police to take measures against potentially violent attacks against Kurds.

Chapter 12. Military service-migration nexus in Turkey

Ulaş Sunata

The engagement between military and migration calls to mind either migration of soldiers or migrations at the time of war or military coup. Military migrants and their families (Ware, 2012; Cooke & Speirs, 2005), as well as comparisons of veterans and non-veterans (London & Wilmoth, 2006: 135) have received attention since World War II in the literature, particularly from life course approaches (Wilmoth & London, 2013). Special interest has gone to experiences of American soldiers and their psychological and health problems. But this chapter is not related, in this sense, to military migration.

The term "military migrant" (Ware, 2012) is generally identified as people who migrate in order to "fight for their country" beyond the national border. However, this definition ignores the existence of non-combatants' migration at the time of war. Moreover, the definition of military migration excludes military-related migrations out of wartime, such as migrations caused by military coupes or military service obligations. In sum, there are two problematic areas in this definition: (i) the subjects and (ii) the temporal and causal dimension. Therefore, the terms including military migrant and military migration are not used in this study, but instead military-related migrant and military-related migration are used.

In this chapter, the focus is on the military-migration nexus in Turkey, particularly military service-motivated migration. In the literature, the impact of military service on population mobility is initially examined within the 19th and early 20th centuries' French experience (Weber, 1976; Baker, 1998). However, this instance and other similar experiences are related to migrations for military service, but we will discuss migrations when dealing with military service. In other words, this chapter deals with the question of how the military service shapes civil men and their families' life course trajectories in the context of migration, particularly the impact of conscription on emigration, which we shall define below.

There is a considerable lack of research on military sociology in Turkey. Therefore, we propose here that there is a need for research on the relationship between military and migration. In terms of military-migration nexus in the Turkish case, two major areas can be investigated: (i) exiles, asylum seekers and refugees as a result of military coups and (ii) conscription-related migration. This chapter aims to explore the relationship between the military service system and migration. The Turkish experience differs from the French experience, because the latter is portrayed with migrations for military service but the former covers migrations to escape from military service and mostly to acquire the chance for a much shortened military service. Sunata (2002) argued that Turkish military service obligation is seen by highly educated strata as a reason of emigration. Sunata (2011) also presented that the opportunity of military service by payment in foreign currency is one of the main motivations among these people to go abroad and work there. In other words, military service obligation comes into existence as one of the main push factors and the shortened option as a boomerang effect. The request for evading military service obligation and the one for acquiring the shortened military service option are mostly two sides of the same coin. Consequently, this study will address the whole impact of the military service system on emigration from the historical and comparative perspective of the Turkish case.

It can be argued that the military service system and the related institution of armed forces are part of the main organs in the nation-state structure. Nevertheless, international migration is generally debated as a challenge to this structure. It is possible to state that military-related migration and the above mentioned military migration have opposite characters in this context. But, this study considers it from a different angle: management of military-related migration in the Turkish case. We will concentrate on the questions whether Turkish emigration history and the emerging diaspora affect military service politics for the migrants or these politics affect new migration, and whether this management empowers the nation-state structure contrary to what is believed.

This chapter will first discuss military-migration nexus in the Turkish case and the relevance of the military service system in Turkey to labour emigration. Then, it will present main features of this kind of migration. The subsequent section will address the variety of ideal male migrant types due to the military service, and a basic model of gendered migration that can be used as a frame of reference to explain the dynamics of feminization, rationalization, and nationalization. Finally, migration as a challenge to the military service (as a social nation-state institution) or military service as a challenge to migration will be debated.

Military-(nation-state)-migration nexus

I

The institution of military service held a special place in the context of the regular army for more than two hundred years. It is obvious that institutionalized conscription has a universal meaning for nation-states. Levi (1996: 162) emphasizes that the military service requires and helps to build a modern nation-state. Conscription is institutionally read as "the obligations of male citizens and the reach of the state" (Levi, 1996: 132). It is a social contract between the state and its citizens in favour of the state in exchange for government protection of property and life. Compulsory-universal male conscription began in France in 1798. In fact, it is not a coincidence that military service was institutionalised one decade after the French Revolution. Henceforth, it was the institutionalized military service that promoted a new social type: "citizen-soldier".

Levi (1996: 134) separated the French model of military service from the Anglo-Saxon democracies' model, which was institutionalized during World War I. In addition, historian Eugen Weber (1976) mentions the social transformation of the population in rural France in the period between 1870 and 1914 in his influential book *Peasants into Frenchmen*. Besides work carried out on roads, railways, and schooling; Weber argues that military service was a new way of civilising (daily life such as diet, hygiene, dressing or bedding) and particularly nationalising the countryside. The role of military service is to make people understand the language of the dominant culture and its values as well as, amongst others patriotism (Weber, 1976: 494). It is possible to state that single language and standardization of behaviour imply nationalisation, rather than modernisation.

To sum up, conscription is viewed as a form of national education for the adult male population at large. Weber (1976: 302) concludes that "the army turned out to be an agency for emigration, acculturation, and, in the final analysis, civilisation, an agency as potent in its way as the schools about which we tend to talk a great deal more". Weber points out here that military service is seen by the authorities not only as a means of supplying the army with troops but also a political strategy for the citizen-army. It is also evaluated as virility/manhood/masculinity school (Baker, 1998: 195). More importantly, it is an introduction to urbanization (Moulin, 1991: 118). It is even seen as encouraging permanent emigration (Weber, 1976: 302).

It is believed that the Turkish model of military service is very similar to the French one. The Ottoman Empire initially established its regular army in 1826 in spite of a lacking script (code). The military regulations were enacted in 1869, while the military service law came into force in 1886. The temporary statute for military obligations was legislated in 1914. In Turkey, mandatory national conscription began in 1927 by enacting the military law. Like Weber in France, Stirling (1951: 165) initially mentions the effects of compulsory conscription on the rural population of Turkey in his book *The Structure of Turkish Peasant Communities*. They are also related to the form of education and initiation of rural-to-urban migration. In the Turkish case, military service is often identified by the state as a mechanism for individual (male) members of the military-nation and for young males as a rite of passage to manhood (Narlı, 2000: 118; Altınay, 2004).

II

The military-migration nexus in Turkey is not to be restricted to the rural-to-urban continuum at the national level. Turkish army has caused emigration several times and affected some international affairs in the past. The essential part of military-related emigration contains coup-related migrations. In spite of the 1973 recruitment stop, Germany and some other European countries did not require visas for Turkish citizens until the 1980 military coup d'état (Martin, 2004: 142). After the military intervention in Turkey, most European countries imposed visas on people from Turkey, along with others, in order to halt the growing number of asylum seekers. The 1980 military coup also stimulated the outbreak of the military conflict between Turkish security forces and the Partiya Karkerên Kurdistan (PKK) in the 1980s and 1990s. Both the military coup and the following armed conflict predominantly in Kurdish provinces were responsible for the refugee flows from Turkey. The main countries granting asylum to refugees throughout this period were Germany, France, the United Kingdom, and the Scandinavian countries. The military coup sent over 50,000 Turkish asylum seekers to Germany (ibid). Based on the Turkish International Migration Survey 1996, Sirkeci determines that migration from Turkey to Germany underlines the role of economic motives in comparison with other destinations but also points the multiple motivations including ethnic conflict leading to emigration (Sirkeci, 2002:8; Sirkeci, 2003: 150). He stresses that "because compulsory military service in Turkey is drafting all men when they reach age of twenty regardless of ethnicity, many Turkish men, as well as the Kurds, try to escape from it by migrating abroad." (Sirkeci, 2002:8-9; Sirkeci, 2003:149).

Despite the question of the equality principle, military service by payment (*bedelli askerlik*) that has been in existence in different periods since the Ottoman Empire as an alternative to compulsory military service meant that an implementation based on the payment in full or in installments was used to sharply shorten the period of military service. This implementation is generally performed in order to (i) cover the financial needs of the army and state, (ii) reduce the accumulated amount of draft evaders, and (iii) avoid individuals' job losses. More importantly, this has been another option for potential male migrants in the Turkish case since 1980.

It is possible to argue that 1980 is the most critical year not only for coup-related migration but also conscription-related migration. On the eve of the military coup, on 20th of March 1980, the 'military service by foreign currency' scheme was launched. It means individuals will be considered they have done their military service if they pay a set fee in a foreign currency (*dövizli askerlik*). Turkish citizens who have lived and worked abroad for at least three years can also be exempt from military service (long- or short-term) by paying a certain fee in foreign currencies albeit - they were still required to go on a 21-day basic military training in Turkey. This basic training requirement was abolished recently. The sum to be paid in foreign exchange is according to the current regulation which was about 6,000 Euros (previously it was 10 thousand German Marks, 5,112 Euros and 10,000 Euros) (ASAL, 2014).

III

Sunata (2011: 171) argued that the dominance of the military is not a speculation but rather a social phenomenon since the establishment of the Republic of Turkey. It became visible through routine discrete military coups and interventions in the last six decades. Moreover, it has been consolidated in the face of continuous stress. Turkish military has always claimed a dominant role in society, while legitimizing its own existence with the purpose of "protecting the country and its official ideology from enemies inside and outside". Furthermore, the military has become a political power, while not only preserving the status quo against leftists, but also reducing the Kurdish question into the war against the PKK and secularism into the struggle with the Islamists. The Justice and Development Party (AKP), the current government of Islamists altered the official ideology paradigm in this context taking Kurds' support. This caused a decrease in military authority in the last decade, and culminated in the Kurdish-Turkish peace process started in 2013.[1] As well as, it has made inroads into prevail religious representation in public spaces. In parallel with the Syria crisis, radical Islam organisations became stronger

---

[1] The process was however abruptly stopped in 2015.

in Turkey. In spite of the changing paradigm, the army has had root-bound power in Turkey.

In Turkey, the obligation to do military service is particularly strict in comparison with practices in many other countries. In Turkish law there is neither the possibility for conscientious objection nor civil service, although these rights were gained in the 1970s in almost all European countries. The duration of the military service has been dropping steadily, except during the World War II and in the period between 1993 and 2003 (during when, as mentioned above, Turkey was experiencing a civil war). There are some plans to increase the number of professional soldiers in the future, but it has no plan to abolish conscription (Sunata, 2011: 169). The duration of the compulsory military service in Turkey still depends on the level of education. For male citizens with no higher education, the service lasts one year, and for male citizens holding a Bachelor's degree or higher it varies as follows: They can either do 12 months as reserve officers or do six months as short-term privates.

The Government justifies military service as an important aspect of the principle of equality before the law, arguing that allowing any person or group to be excluded from performing compulsory military service would compromise the equality principle of the law. Nevertheless, obligation of conscription to men (gender difference) and the availability of military service by payment (class difference) remain in conflict with the principle of equality principle of Turkey's constitution (Sunata, 2011: 169-170).

In Turkey, a large surveillance system operates in the name of the military service (Sunata, 2011: 171). For instance, men are questioned about their military service when checking in a hotel, when applying for a driving license, or when crossing a border of Turkey. Furthermore, a person liable for military service needs to present documentation annually in order to be able to postpone it. Also, additional documentation required from all academic institutions in Turkey must be forwarded to the government to prove whether male students are attending lectures and writing exams. Unlike female students abroad, male ones must present their official transcripts and verifications of enrollment from their academic institution to the Turkish embassy in the country of residence.

The military service status is also an indicator of socio-economic status (Sunata, 2011: 172). Being a conscience objector, a draft evader (an evader of enlistment or an examination evader), being exempt from the draft, or being deferred indicate social deprivation in different levels. It is explicit that completing military service brings status and prestige for men. When a man applies for a job or an academic position or even decides to marry, he will often be questioned whether he has served in the army or not. But more importantly, having done a long-term or a short-term military service, or a military service by payment shows the person's economic background.

The military service obligation is still not open to be questioned in Turkey as a strong nationalist understanding prevails. The authoritarian power of the military has caused a widespread social anxiety, as well as cowed silent resistance strategies regarding military service. To explain the relations between the military and the citizen of Turkey, Sunata drew a father-son analogy (Sunata, 2011:171). The sons address their father, the military, with deference to his authority, thereby reproducing this authority again and again. Some sons do not show deference and resist the reproduction of their father's authority. For example, a lot of male university graduates try to keep student status in Turkey in order to delay military service. Still, it is not an ultimate solution for escaping from service, but serves to lengthen the period of anxiousness. The second possibility for postponing military service obligation is to work abroad. Working abroad for three years extends the delay and makes military service for three weeks by payment possible. Furthermore, to avoid military service completely or to be eligible for the military service by payment scheme, one has to become citizen of another country. Yet, a new citizenship may come with another military service duty (Sunata, 2011: 175). Avoiding military service can also direct individuals towards education as many enrol for Master's programmes. Both working abroad and studying longer are strategies of a silent societal resistance.

IV

The phenomenon of Turkish compulsory military service affects the lives of many men and their families. Military service evasion (*askerden kaçma*), that is draft dodging, is a common issue among men of Turkey. About 42 per cent of the population in military age prefer to defer service legally or illegally (Sunata, 2011: 172-173). Many young men in Turkey often move to different parts of the country or go abroad to avoid conscription. Therefore, the military service system in Turkey remains a highly important factor that has an impact on migration (Sunata, 2011: 167-175).

It is clear that evading Turkish compulsory military service is seen as a motive for going abroad (Sirkeci, 2002; Sunata, 2002: 69-70). Based on a parliamentary question in May 2002, it is estimated that since 1980, each year, around 10,000 men benefit from the shortened military service by payment in foreign currency scheme (Sunata, 2011: 170). Another finding is that military service obligation is also an indirect reason to leave Turkey for some young women in order to join their partners (Sunata, 2011:243).

Sunata (2011) conducted 66 semi-structured in-depth interviews with highly skilled labour migrants from Turkey in Germany in 2005-2006. She then analyzed their approaches to the military service system. She revealed that they consider military service as a problem, a reason to migrate, unwanted, unnecessary, dreaded, waste of time, a condemnation, an obligation, which is irrational, suboptimal, unproductive and militarist. There are five different types of male migrants in terms of initiation, perpetuation and completion of migration in relation to the military service: (i) persons whose migration is irrelevant to military service, (ii) persons who migrate to be eligible for military service by payment scheme, (iii) persons who initiates migration to avoid military service without any plan but then go for the military service by payment scheme, (iv) persons who migrate to avoid military service completely, and (v) person who apply for asylum on the grounds of avoiding military service (Sunata, 2011).

The first type does not pay attention to military service in migration decision. It is either irrelevant to his migration (if he has already completed it) or it is an accidental by-product of his migration, and he does not show any interest in this topic (becoming migrant for unintended consequence). The second type organizes his migration specifically with the intention of earning the right to reduced military service by payment. He saves money to pay the fee while working abroad. Having enough funds saved and the required minimum amount of time spent abroad, he enrols for the three-week draft by payment during his vacation. He can then decide to return or to continue working abroad (becoming migrant for unintended consequence). The third type initiates his migration as ad hoc plan to escape from this compulsory military service duty but he has no certain plan about the future (becoming migrant as a last resort). Through the challenges of his migration experience, he converts into the second or the fourth type. The fourth type, like the second and third, goes abroad without the intention of return in the near future since he is against military service and military service by payment (becoming migrant without an absolute solution). He may then denounce his Turkish citizenship, or become a dual citizen, or he may change his mind to go for the military service by payment (i.e. the second type). The second type is apparently prevalent. Sunata (2011: 247) argued that the conscription-related male migration is socially and institutionally constructed.

According to Sunata (2011: 243), obligatory military service becomes the main tangible and intelligible reason to leave Turkey for young professional men, as well as an indirect reason for female migrants mostly including young married professionals. The problem of Turkish military service suffices to explain at least some temporary (three year) labour emigration. A significant amount of young highly educated men from Turkey work abroad for at least three years and pay a significant sum in order to reduce their compulsory military service to three weeks. This kind of military service does not result in any discontinuity in their careers, since they can perform their draft in vacation time. This motivation "legalizes" their movement not only in their eyes but also, curiously, in the public opinion of Turkey. Labour migration is seen as a respectable option and is often recommended to young men in Turkey. This not only refers to a personal political strategy but also reflects a silent social resistance.

V

Recent studies pay attention to this military service avoidance issue in relation to migrant's ethnic, educational and socio-economic backgrounds. Sirkeci (2002: 8) argues that this motivation regarding "environment of human insecurity" is more likely among Turkish Kurds instead of Turks. İçduygu, Romano, and Sirkeci (1999) proposed the concept of insecurity in relation to material and non-material circumstances in order to explore an ethnic question in Turkey. Sirkeci (2002: 1) then defines environment of human insecurity as "a combined set of background factors interacting with international migration." Moreover, Sirkeci (2006) operationalizes migration derived from the environment of insecurity as an "opportunity framework" for an environment of relative security. For him, an environment of insecurity, including socio-economic and political deprivation facilitates migration. Like Sirkeci, other scholars (Göktürk, 1999; Sunata 2011: 242) emphasize the liberating character of migration. Sunata (2014) suggests that Turkish migrants who experience the environment of insecurity in Turkey in relation to ethnicity, gender or sexual orientation are less likely to re-migrate, arguing that migration alleviates their deprivations.

Sunata (2011: 174) argues that military service can be seen as a push factor of highly skilled labour migration. In other words, conscription contributes to the brain drain. About 5 per cent of highly-educated young men in Turkey prefer to emigrate in order to evade military service (Sunata, 2002: 69). Their motivation is not necessarily related to their anti-militaristic stance but rather to their career-related anxieties (Sunata, 2002: 70). This anxiety is about a delayed transition from university to work because of conscription. On the one hand, most employers do not offer formal jobs to young men until they have completed their military service. On the other hand, conscription can be considered as waste of time and money in young men's career planning period. Length of compulsory military service appears as a significant barrier to career planning and development. However, the military service by payment schemes allow continuity in career without a long break. Almost all men do the military service by payment during their vacation time – which is less than one month. Compulsory military service is not only a reason for brain drain, but also a factor for not returning after study abroad (Tansel & Güngör, 2003: 64). Sunata (2011: 243) even contends that going and working abroad in order to solve this problem are considered as institutionalized expulsion with imperative remittances.

Men with lower socio-economic status are much more likely to benefit from military service (MacLean and Elder Jr, 2007; Lutz, 2008). Men with high socio-economic status are unlikely to enrol for the army to pursue a professional career. Military service evasion based on ethnicity and sexual orientation can be considered as a warrant for refugee status. However, military service evasion due to career anxiety is often considered as "voluntary migration", and not forced migration. Nevertheless, most highly skilled people and people with high socio-economic status prefer not to apply for asylum on the grounds of avoiding military service. Instead, they prefer to be called expatriates, highly skilled labour migrants, or elite migrants.

Conclusion

The military service system in Turkey leads to labour migration. The Turkish state appears to be anxious about losing highly skilled people, yet at the same time, the military service obligation directs them to emigration. The selection of military service destinations, salaries for privates and reserve officers are all disincentives for highly skilled men. As a consequence, draft evasion is an institutionalized phenomenon in Turkey for highly educated people. Going and working abroad in order to avoid military service is also an institutionalized phenomenon: institutionalized expulsion. Sunata described this phenomenon as "brain flight" (2011: 175).

The military service by payment in foreign currency designed for labour emigrants is a mechanism for collection of imperative remittances and it prevents the boomerang effect. In the 1960s and 1970s, Turkey first referred to the importance of remittances. As Abadan-Unat (1976: 24-5) describes, there are two effects of remittances for the sending country: a rise in potential purchasing power and a rise in hard foreign currency at the disposal of the state organs. She also stresses the existence of the "boomerang effect" i.e. the re-export of remittances to the host country. On the other hand, it is known that highly skilled workers are less likely to send remittances. The military service by payment in foreign currency scheme then also appears a kind of compulsory remittances scheme.

Military service can be avoided by emigration, through a special program which permits Turkish citizens living and working abroad to opt for military service by paying a fee in foreign currency (Aydas et al., 2005: 57). This scheme was initially set up to ensure foreign currency flows to the country but then it became a mechanism to avoid military service and a facilitating factor for emigration.

Except multiple citizenship and dual citizenship in certain countries allow individuals to renounce Turkish citizenship which automatically releases them from compulsory military service. However as a rule men are not allowed to renounce Turkish nationality unless they completed or legally deferred military service (OECD, 1998: 173). Although in recent decades, Turkey have adjusted rules and regulations around military service by payment programme to accommodate varying demands and circumstances of Turkish migrant workers abroad, this issue of compulsory military service remain to be a variable in understanding international migration from Turkey.

References

Aalbers, M. B. (2010). The Revanchist Renewal of Yesterday's City of Tomorrow.*Antipode*, 42, 1-29. Received from http://onlinelibrary.wiley.com/doi/10.1111/j.1467-8330.2010.00817.x/pdf available on: 05.03.2011.

Abu-Lunghold, J.L. (1988). Palestinians: Exiles at Home and Abroad, *Current Sociology* 36 (2): 61-69.

Adler, P. S., & Kwon, S. W. (2002). Social capital: Prospects for a new concept. *Academy of management review*, 27(1), 17-40.

Afet ve Acil Durum Yönetimi Başkanlığı [Prime Ministry Disaster &Emergency Management Presidency]. (2013, September 09). *Syrian Guests Circular on Health and Other Services*. Circular No.08. Retrieved from: <https://www.afad.gov.tr/TR/IcerikDetay.aspx?ID=44>

Ahmed, A. S. (1995). *Postmodernizm ve İslam* (Postmodernism and İslam: Predicament and Promise), İstanbul: Cep Kitapları, (in Turkish).

Aktürk, Ş. (2009). Persistence of the Islamic Millet as an Ottoman Legacy: Mono-Religious and Anti-Ethnic Definition of Turkish Nationhood. *Middle Eastern Studies*, 45(6): 893-909.

Akyazı'da gergin saatler [Tense hours in Akyazı]. (2006). *Cumhuriyet*, 9 September, 15.

Akyüz, Y. & Boratav, K. (2003). The Making of the Turkish Financial Crisis. *World Development*, 31 (9): 1549–1566.

Al Jazeera. (2013, December 26). Kürtlerin ana talepleri. Retrieved July 26, 2014, from *Al Jazeera*: http://www.aljazeera.com.tr/dosya/kurtlerin-ana-talepleri

Alakom, R. (1998). *Eski İstanbul Kürtleri*, Istanbul: Avesta Basın Yayın.

Ali, S. (2007). 'Go West Young Man': The Culture of Migration among Muslims in Hyderabad, India. *Journal of Ethnic & Migration Studies*, 33(1), 37-58. doi: 10.1080/13691830601043489

Alinia, M. (2008). Spaces of Kurdish Diasporas. Kurdish identities, experiences of otherness and politics of belonging. *Göteburg Studies in Sociology* No. 22

Alisch, M. (2002). Soziale Stadtentwicklung in Deutschland. Fachstelle für Stadtentwicklung Zürich (Hrsg.). Aufwertung als Programm? Ansätze und Folgen integrierter Stadtteilentwicklung. Eine internationale Fachtagung in Zürich. Gottlieb Duttweiler Institut (GDI). Zürich: Fachstelle für Stadtentwicklung, 15-23.

Altınay, A. G. (2004). *The myth of the military-nation: Militarism, gender, and education in Turkey*. Palgrave Macmillan.

Amnesty International (2009). *Stranded, Refugees in Turkey denied Protection*. London: Amnesty International Publications.

Amnesty International (2010). Greece: Migrants, Refugees and Asylum-seekers; Conscientious Objectors and Excessive Use of Force by Law Enforcement Officials: Amnesty International Submission to the UN Universal Periodic Review.Received from http://www.amnesty.org/en/library/info/EUR25/008/2010/en available on: 13.10.2013.

Amnesty International (2013). *Frontier Europe: Human Rights Abuses On Greece's Border with Turkey*. London: Amnesty International Ltd.

Andersson, M. (2003). Immigrant youth and the dynamics of marginalization. *Young, 11*(1): 74-89.

Appadurai, A. (2006). *Fear of Small Numbers: An Essay on the Geography of Anger*, Durham and London: Duke University Press.

Arendt, H. (1998). *The Human Condition*. Chicago: University of Chicago Press

Arslan, D. (2015, October 24). Syrian refugee crisis forces closer cooperation between EU-Turkey. Received from: http://www.todayszaman.com/diplomacy_syrian-refugee-crisis-forces-closer-cooperation-between-eu-turkey_402296.html available on: 28.20.2015.

ASAL. (2014). T.C. Milli Savunma Bakanlığı, Akseralma Dairesi Başkalığı (ASAL) Official web site. Received fromhttp://www.asal.msb.gov.tr/available on: 05.04.2014.

Ateş, S. (2013). *Ottoman-Iranian Borderlands: Making a Boundary, 1843-1914*. Cambridge: Cambridge University Press

Ayata, B. (2011). *The Politics of Displacement: A Transnational Analysis of the Forced Migration of Kurds in Turkey and Europe*. Baltimore: John Hopkins University.

Aydas, O. T., Metin-Ozcan, K., & Neyapti, B. (2005). Determinants of workers' remittances: the case of Turkey. *Emerging Markets Finance and Trade*, 41(3): 53-69.

Babická, K. (2013). Towards a human rights dimension of FRONTEX?. Received from http://aa.ecn.cz/img_upload/6334c0c7298d6b396d213ccd19be5999/babick_frontex_ii_1.pdf available on: 13.04.2014.

Baker, A. R. (1998). Military Service and Migration in Nineteenth-Century France: Some Evidence from Loir-Et-Cher. *Transactions of the Institute of British Geographers*, 23(2), 193-206.

Baker, W. E. (1990). Market networks and corporate behavior. *American journal of sociology*, 589-625.

Baldaccini, A. (2010). Extraterritorial border controls in the EU: The role of FRONTEX in operations at sea. Ryan, B. and Mitsilegas, V. (eds.) *Extraterritorial immigration control: Legal challenges*. Leiden: Martinus Nijhoff. pp. 229-256.

Baldaccini, A. and Guild, E. (Eds.). (2007). *Terrorism and the Foreigner*. Leiden: Koninklijke Brill NV.

Balzacq, T. (2008). The policy tools of securitization: Information exchange, EU foreign and interior policies. *Journal of Common Market Studies*, 46 (1), 75–100.

Barkey, H. J., & Fuller, G. E. (1998). *Turkey's Kurdish Question*. Maryland: Rowman & Littlefield.

Barth, F. (1969). Ethnic Groups and Boundaries in: idem, Ethnic Groups and Boundaries: The Social Organization of Culture Difference, London: Allen and Unwin: 9-37.

Başer, B. (2011). *Kurdish Political Activism in Europe with a Particular Focus on Great Britain*. Berlin: Berghof Peace Support and Centre for Just Peace and Democracy.

Baud, M. & Schendel, W. van (1997). Toward a Comparative History of Borderlands *Journal of World History*, 8, (2), 211-242.

Bauer, T. and I. N. Gang. (1998). Temporary Migrants from Egypt: How Long Do They Stay Abroad? *IZA Discussion Paper* No: 3.

Bauman, Z. (2007). *Liquid Times: Living in an Age of Uncertainty*. Cambridge: Polity Press.

Bayer, P., Hjalmarsson, R., & Pozen, D. (2007). *Building criminal capital behind bars: Peer effects in juvenile corrections* (No. w12932). National Bureau of Economic Research.

Bayer, P., Pintoff, R., & Pozen, D. E. (2003). *Building criminal capital behind bars: Social learning in juvenile corrections*. Economic Growth Center, Yale University.

Bayır, D. (2013). Representation of the Kurds by the Turkish Judiciary. *Human Rights Quarterly*, 35 (1), 116-142.

BBC (2014, January 22). Inquiry calls after migrants die under tow in Greece. *BBC*.

BDP Osmaniye İl binasına gündüz ortası saldırı [Attacks against the BDP Osmaniye City Building in the middle of the day], *Dicle Haber Ajansı*, 26 August 2012. Received from http://www.diclehaber.com/1/4/466/view News/320409 available on 30 August 2012).

Becker, H., & Löhr, R.-P. (2000). "Soziale Stadt". Ein Programm gegen die sozialräumliche Spaltung in den Städten. *Aus Politik und Zeitgeschichte, No. B 10-1*, 22-29.

Belge, C. (2011). "State Building and the Limits of Legibility: Kinship Networks and Kurdish Resistance in Turkey". *Int. J. Middle East Studies, Vol.* 43: 95–114.

Berger, P. L. and T. Luckmann. (1991 [1966]). *The Social Construction of Reality - A Treatise in the Sociology of Knowledge*, London: Penguin Books.

Bermudez, A. (2013). A Gendered Perspective on the Arrival and Settlement of Colombian Refugees in the United Kingdom. *Journal of Ethnic and Migration Studies*, 1-17. doi: 10.1080/1369183x.2013.778139.

BİA Haber Merkezi. (2012, May 14). Türkiye AİHM'de Birinciliği Kaptırmıyor. Retrieved July 10, 2014, from BİANET: http://www.bianet.org/bianet/ diger/138322-turkiye-aihm-de-birinciligi-kaptirmiyor.

Bigo, D. (2000). When Two Become One: Internal and External Securitizations in Europe. Kelstrup, M. W. (ed.) *International Relations Theory and the Politics of European Integration. Power, Security and the Community*. London: Routledge. pp. 203-241.

Bigo, D. (2002). Security and Immigration: toward a critique of the governmentality of unease. *Alternatives*, 27(1), 63-92.

Bigo, D. (2005). Frontier Controls in the European Union: Who is in Control?'. Bigo, D. and Guild, E. (eds.) *Controlling Frontiers. Free Movement Into and Within Europe*. Burlington: Ashgate: 49-99.

Bilgen, B. (2014). Katı Bir Bağ mı, Dinamik Bir Ağ mı? Güvenlik ve Kalkınma İlişkisini Güneydoğu Anadolu Projesi (GAP) Bağlamında Yeniden Yorumlamak. Received from http://researchturkey.org/tr/a-static-nexus-or-a-dynamic-network-rethinking-the-security-development-relationship-within-the-context-of-southeastern-anatolia-project/ available on: 15.06. 2014.

Blakeley, G. (2010). Governing Ourselves: Citizen Participation and Governance in Barcelona and Manchester. *International Journal of Urban and Regional Research, 34(1)*, 130-145.

Blalock, H. M, Jr. (1967). *Toward a Theory of Minority-Group Relations*. New York: Wiley.

Bocheńska Joanna. (2011). Między ciemnością i światłem. O kurdyjskiej tożsamości i literaturze. Kraków: Księgarnia Akademicka.

Böhme, C., Franke, T., & Strauss, W.-C. (2008). *Statusbericht 2008 zum Programm Soziale Stadt*. Berlin: Bundesministerium für Verkehr, Bau und Stadtentwicklung.

Bosniak, L. (2000). Universal Citizenship and the Problem of Alienage. *Northwestern Law Review*, 94, 963-984.

Bourdieu, P. (1999). "Rethinking the State: Genesis and Structure of the Bureaucratic Field". In *State/Culture: State Formation After The Cultural Turn*, Edited By George Steinmetz, Cornell University Press, 1999; p. 53-75.

Bourdieu, P. (2011). The forms of capital. (1986). *Cultural theory: An anthology*, 81-93.

Braddock, J. H., & McPartland, J. M. (1987). How minorities continue to be excluded from equal employment opportunities: Research on labor market and institutional barriers. *Journal of Social Issues, 43*(1), 5-39.

Brammer, M. (2008): Zwischennutzung in Berlin Neukölln. Kreativwirtschaft als Motor in einem sozial benachteiligten Binnenquartier. *Zeitschrift für Angewandte Geographie, 32*, 71-77.

Brass, P. R. (1997). *Theft of an Idol*. Princeton, NJ: Princeton University Press.

Britton, M. L. (2013). Latino Spatial and Structural Assimilation: Close Intergroup Friendships among Houston-Area Latinos. *Journal of Ethnic and Migration Studies*, 40(8), 1192-1216. doi: 10.1080/1369183x.2013.858017.

Bruinessen, M. V. (1978). *Agha, Shaikh, and State: On the Social and Political Organization of Kurdistan*. Phd Thesis, Submitted To The University of Utrecht. Available from: www.hum.uu.nl/medewerkers/ m.vanbruinessen/ publications/bruinessen_agha_shaikh_and_state_1978.htm.

Bruinessen, M.V. (2000). *Mullas, Sufis and Heretics: The Role of Religion in Kurdish Society*. Collected articles. Istanbul: The Isis Press.

Buur, L., Jensen, S. and Stepputat, F. (2007). The Security-Development Nexus. Buur, L., Jensen, S. and Stepputat, F. (eds.). *The Security-Development Nexus: Expressions of Sovereignty and Securitization in Southern Africa*. Uppsala: Nordiska Afrikainstitutet and Cape Town: Hsrc Press.

Byrne, D. (1999). *Social exclusion*. McGraw-Hill International.

Çağlayan, H., Özar, Ş. & Doğan, A.T. (2011). *Ne Değişti? Kürt Kadınların Zorunlu Göç Deneyimi*, Ankara: Ayizi Kitap.

Çakır, R. (2010, November 17). Kürt Sorununda Silah Kapı Açmıyor, Tam Tersine Kapatıyor. Retrieved June 30, 2014, from *Gazete Vatan*: http://www.gazetevatan.com/rusen-cakir-341223-yazar-yazisi--kurt-sorununda-silah-artik-kapi-acmiyor--tam-tersine-kapatiyor-/

Çarkoğlu, A. (2011). Turkey's 2011 general elections: towards a dominant party system? *Insight Turkey*, 13 (3): 43-62.

Carrera, S. (2007). The EU Border Management Strategy: FRONTEX and the Challenges of 'irregular' Immigration in the Canary Islands. *CEPS Working Document 261*, Brussels: Centre for European Policy Studies.

Carrera, S. and Guild, E. (2010). Joint Operation RABIT 2010' – FRONTEX Assistance to Greece's Border with Turkey: Revealing the Deficiencies of Europe's Dublin Asylum System. Justice and Human Affairs, Liberty and Security in Europe Papers. Received from http://www.ceps.be/book/%E2%80%98joint-operation-rabit-2010%E2%80%99-%E2%80%93-frontex-assistance-greece%E2%80%99s-border-turkey-revealing-deficiencies available on: 13.10.2011.

Carrigan, W. D. & Webb, C. (2003). The Lynching of Persons of Mexican Origin or Descent in the United States, 1848 to 1928. *Journal of Social History*, 37 (2): 411-438.

Casier, M. (2011). The Politics of Solidarity: The Kurdish Question in the European Parliament. In M. Casier, & J. Jongerden, *Nationalisms and Politics in Turkey. Political Islam, Kemalism* (pp. 197-217). New York: Routledge.

Castles, S., & Miller, M. J. (1998). *The Age of Migration*. New York: The Guilford Press.

Çavuşoğlu, M. (2014, March 13). Statement by Mevlüt Çavuşoğlu on the European Parliament Resolution on Turkey 2013 Progress Report. Retrieved from Republic of Turkey, Ministry for EU Affairs: http://www.ab.gov.tr/index.php?p=49475&l=2

Cederman, L.E., Weidmann. N. & Gleditsch, K. (2011). Horizontal Inequalities and Ethno-Nationalist Civil War: A Global Comparison. *American Political Science Review*, 105 (3), 478-495.

Çelik, A. B. (2002). *Migrating Onto Identity: Kurdish Mobilization Through Associations in Istanbul*, Doctoral Dissertation, Binghamton: State University of New York.

Çelik, A. B. (2005)."I miss my village!": Forced Kurdish migrants in Istanbul and rheir representation in associations, *New Perspective on Turkey*, vol. 32: 137-163.

Çelik, A. B. (2012). State, Non-Governmental and International Organizations in the Possible Peace Process in Turkey's Conflict-Induced Displacement, *Journal of Refugee Studies* Vol. 26, No. 1.

Çetin, S. (2011). 2010 Turkey Monitoring Report on Right to Refugee and Asylum. Received from http://www.ihad.org.tr/file/reports/2011/2010%20TURKEY%20MONITORING%20REPORT%20ON%20RIGHT%20TO%20REFUGE%20&%20ASYLUM.pdf available on: 14.09.2013.

Chowdhury, A. &. Krebs, R.R. (2010). Talking about terror: Counterterrorist campaigns and the logic of representation. *European Journal of International Relations,* 16(1), 125–150.

CIA Central Intelligence Agency. (2008). *The World Factbook – Turkey: People and Society,* online: https://www.cia.gov/library/publications/the-worldfactbook/geos/tu.html#People [02.02.2015].

Ciplak, B. (2012). *The Relationship between migration and crime in Istanbul, Turkey - and social support in practice*, ISZU Sosyal Bilimler Dergisi online http://www.academia. edu/3052392/Migration-Crime_Relations_in_Istanbul_Turkey   [23.05.2013].

Çivril Assize Crime Court (Asliye Ceza Mahkemesi), E.2007/252, K.2008/423 (11 July 2008).

Claffey, M., Bugua, M. M., & Sisk, R. (1999, February 17). Kurds protests capture with violence, threats. Retrieved June 22, 2014, from *New York Daily News*: http://www.nydailynews.com/archives/news/kurds-protest-capture-violence-threats-article-1.825808.

Çoban, C. (2013). *Different Periods of Internal Migration in Turkey from the Perspective of Development,* American International Journal of Contemporary Research, Vol. 3 No. 10; October 2013.

Cohen, J. H., & Sirkeci, I. (2011). *Cultures of migration: the global nature of contemporary mobility*. Austin: University of Texas Press.

Coleman, J. S. (1988). Social capital in the creation of human capital.*American journal of sociology*, S95-S120.

Comaroff, J. and J. Comaroff. (2009). *Ethnicity Inc*. Chicago and London: University of Chicago Press.

Conway, D., & Cohen, J. H. (2002). Local dynamics in multi-local, transnational spaces of rural Mexico: Oaxacan Experiences. *International Journal of Population Geography*, 9(1), 141-161.

Cooke, T. J., & Speirs, K. (2005). Migration and Employment among the Civilian Spouses of Military Personnel. *Social Science Quarterly*, 86(2), 343-355.

Corzine, J., Creech, J. & Corzine, L. (1983). Black Concentration and Lynchings in the South: Testing Blalock's Power-Threat Hypothesis. *Social Forces,* 61 (3), 774-796.

Council of the European Union (2004). Council Regulation (EC) No 2007/2004 of 26 October 2004 establishing a European Agency for the Management of Operational Cooperation at the External Borders of the Member States of the European Union, OJ L 349/1, 25.11.2004.

Coyne, C. (2010). *Review of James C. Scott, The Art Of Not Being Governed: An Anarchist History Of Upland Southeast Asia*. Online article, available from: http://www.ccoyne.com/review_of_james_scott.pdf. Accessed on March 20, 2014.

Dale, C. (1997). The dynamics and challenges of ethnic cleansing: The Georgia-Abkhazia case. *Refugee Survey Quarterly*, 16(3), 77-109.

De Genova, N. & Ramos-Zayas, A. Y. (2003). Latino Crossings: Mexicans, Puerto Ricans, and the Politics of Race and Citizenship. New York: Routledge Press.

Dean, R. (2000). Rethinking the civil war in Sudan. *Civil Wars*, 3(1), 71-91.

Debenedetti, S. (2006). Externalization of European Asylum and Migration Polices.*Paper Presented at 2nd Session of the Florence School on Euro-Mediterranean Migration and Development*, 15–30 June 2006. European University Institute, Florence.

Dede, O., & Kaya, E. (2013, October 31). AB'nin 2013 İlerleme Raporu Üzerine Bir Değerlendirme. Retrieved June 28, 2014, from Bilgesam:

http://www.bilgesam.org/incele/737/-ab%E2%80%99nin-2013-turkiye-ilerleme-raporu-uzerine-bir-degerlendirme/

Deliso, C. (2011). Safeguarding Europe's Southern Borders: Interview with Klaus Roesler, Director of Operations Division, Frontex. Balkananalysis.com. Received from http://www.balkanalysis.com/greece/2011/09/23/safeguarding-europe%E2%80%99s-southern-borders-interview-with-klaus-roesler-director-of-operations-division-frontex/ available on: 01.09.2011.

Demirler, D. & Eşsiz, V. (2008). Zorunlu Göç Deneyimini Kadınlardan Dinlemek: Bir İmkân ve İmkânsızlık Olarak Dil. In N. Mutluer (Ed.), *Cinsiyet Halleri*, İstanbul: Varlık.

Deutsches Institut für Urbanistik (Difu) (2013). Gutachten. Verstetigungs möglich keiten Berliner Quartiersmanagementverfahren. Berlin, Mai 2013.

Dicle, A. (2014, July 19). (Ş. G. Sağnıç, Interviewer)

Diener, A. C. & Hagen, J. (Eds). (2010). Introduction: Borders, Identity, and Geopolitics, (Edited by: Alexander C. Diener and Joshua Hagen), *Borderlines and Borderlands: Political Oddities at the Edge of the Nation-State*, New York, Rowman & Littlefield Publishers, 1-14.

Dinç, N.K. (2004). *Göç Hikâyeleri*, İstanbul: GÖÇ-DER.

Dinesen, C., Ronsbo, H., Juárez, C., González, M., Estrada Méndez, M. Á., & Modvig, J. (2013). Violence and social capital in post-conflict Guatemala. *Revista Panamericana de Salud Pública*, 34(3), 162-168.

Diyarbakır'da gergin gün [Tense day in Diyarbakır]. (2012). *Cumhuriyet*, 18 November, 7.

Dönmez, Ö.R. (2008). Vigilantism in Turkey: Totalitarian Movements and Uncivil Society in a Post-9/11 Democracy. *Totalitarian Movements and Political Religions*, 9 (4), 551-573.

Donnan, H. & Wilson, T. M. (2002). *Sınırlar: Kimlik, Ulus ve Devletin Uçları*, (Borders: Frontiers of Identity, Nation and State), Ankara: Ütopya Yayınevi.

Duffield, M. (2007). Development, Security and Unending War: Governing the World of Population. Cambridge: Polity Press.

Dumitru, D. & Johnson, C. (2011). Constructing Interethnic Conflict and Cooperation Why Some People Harmed Jews and Others Helped Them during the Holocaust in Romania. *World Politics*, 63 (1), 1–42.

Eccarius-Kelly, V. (2002). Political Movements and Leverage Points: Kurdish Political Activism in the European Diaspora. *Journal of Muslim and Minority Affairs*, 22(1): 91-118.

Eccarius-Kelly, V. (2008). Interpreting the PKK's Signals in Europe. *Perspectives on Terrorism*, 2(11), 10-15.

Eccarius-Kelly, V. (2014). The Kurdish Conundrum in Europe: Political Opportunities and Transnational Activism. In W. Pojman, *Migration and Activism in Europe since 1945* (pp. 57-80). New York: Palgrave Macmillan.

Elwood, S. (2002). Neighborhood Revitalization through 'Collaboration': Assessing the Implications of Neoliberal Urban Policy at the Grassroots. *GeoJournal*, 58(2-3), 121-130.

Ensarioğlu, Y. & Kurban, D. (2011). *How Legitimate are the Kurds' Demands? The Kurdish Question through the Lens of Turkey's West*. Istanbul: TESEV (Turkish Economic and Social Studies Foundation, TESEV).

European Commission (2010). Statement by Cecilia Malmström, European Commissioner in charge of Home Affairs on the request of the Greek government to get assistance via Rapid Border Intervention Teams at the land border between Greece and Turkey. European Commission - MEMO/10/516 24/10/2010.

European Commission (2011). Frontex and the RABIT operation at the Greek-Turkish border. European Commission - MEMO/11/130 02/03/2011.

European Commission (EC) (2010). Statement by Cecilia Malmström, European Commissioner in charge of Home Affairs on the request of the Greek government to get assistance via Rapid Border Intervention Teams at the land border between Greece and Turkey. Received from http://europa.eu/rapid/press-release_MEMO-10-516_en.htm?locale=en available on: 10.09.2012.

European Parliament and the Council of the European Union (2007). Regulation (EC) No 863/2007 of the European Parliament and of the Council of 11 July 2007 establishing a mechanism for the creation of Rapid Border Intervention Teams and amending Council Regulation (EC) No 2007/2004 as regards that mechanism and regulating the tasks and powers of guest officers, OJ L 199/30, 31.7.2007.

Fenton, S. (2010). *Ethnicity* (2nd edition, revised and updated), Cambridge: Polity Press.

Ferho, D. (2014, July 16). (Ş. G. Sağnıç, Interviewer)

Filiztekin, A. and A. Gökhan. (2008). *The determinants of internal migration in Turkey* online: http://core.kmi.open.ac.uk/display/11740745 [31.12.2014].

Foucault, F. (1991). *Discipline and Punish. The Birth of the Prison.* Harmondsworth: Penguin.

Foucault, F. (2003). Society must be defended: Lectures at the College de France, 1975-76. London: Allan Lane, the Penguin Press.

Foucault, M. (2004). *Society must be defended.* Lectures as the Collège de France, 1975-76. New York: Picador.

Franke, T., & Löhr, R.-P., & Sander, R. (2000). Soziale Stadt – Stadterneuerungspolitik als Stadtpolitikerneuerung. *Archiv für Kommunalwissenschaften, 39*, 243-268.

Frontex (2006). Decision of the Management Board laying down practical arrangement regarding public access to the documents of the European Agency for the Management of Operational Cooperation at the External Borders of the Member States of the European Union (Frontex), 3402, 22.09.2006. Received from http://www.europarl.europa.eu/document/activities/cont/201005/20100531ATT75236/20100531ATT75236EN.pdf available on: 14.06. 2008.

Frontex (2010). Beyond Frontiers, Frontex: The First Five Years. Michałowice: Offset-Print.

Frontex (2010a). Extract from the Annual Risk Analysis 2010. Received from http://frontex.europa.eu/assets/Publications/Risk_Analysis/Annual_Risk_Analysis_2010.pdf available on: 10.07.2011.

Frontex (2010b). FRAN Quarterly, 2, April-June. Received from http://frontex.europa.eu/assets/Attachments_News/fran_q02_2010_public.pdf available on: 10.07.2011.

Frontex (2013). Frontex Programme of Work 2013. Received from http://frontex.europa.eu/assets/About_Frontex/Governance_documents/Work_programme/2013/PoW_2013.pdf available on: 05.01.2014.

Gagnon, V. P. (2004). *The Myth of Ethnic War: Serbia and Croatia in the 1990s.* Ithaca: Cornell University Press.

Gallo, E. (2013). Migrants and their money are not all the same: Migration, remittances and family morality in rural South India. *Migration Letters*, 10(1), 33-46.

Gargiulo, M., & Benassi, M. (1999). *The dark side of social capital* (pp. 298-322). Springer, US.

Gedik, A. (1996). Internal Migration in Turkey, 1965-1985: Test of Some Conflicting Findings in the Literature. *ANU Working Papers in Demography*, 66.

Ghatak, S., P. Levine and S. W.Price. (1996). *Migration Theories and Evidence: An Assesment*, Journal of Economic Survey 10: 159-98.

Giddens, A. (1997). *Sociology*, Polity, Cambridge, UK.

Giddens, A. (2008). *Sosyoloji*, çeviren: Cemal Güzel, Kırmızı Yayınları, İstanbul.

Gil-Bazo, M. T. (2006). The practice of Mediterranean states in the context of the European Union's Justice and Home Affairs External Dimension. *International Journal of Refugee Law*, 18 (3-4), 571-600.

Gill, P. and Phythian, M. (2006). *Intelligence in an Insecure World*. Cambridge: Polity.

GÖÇ-DER. (2013). *Türkiye'de Koruculuk Sistemi: Zorunlu Göç ve Geri Dönüşler*, İstanbul, Retrieved from: http://panel.stgm.org.tr/vera/app/var/files/t/u/turkiye%E2%80%99de-koruculuk-sistemi-zorunlu-goc-ve-geri-donusler.pdf

Göktürk, D. (1999). *Turkish Delight-German Fright: Migrant Identities in Transnational Cinema*. University of Oxford. Transnational Communities Programme.

Goldring, L. & Landolt, P. (2013). The Conditionality of Legal Status and Rights: Conceptualizing Precarious Non-citizenship in Canada. In L. Goldring & P. Landolt (Eds.), *Producing and Negotiating Non-citizenship: Precarious Legal Status in Canada* (pp. 3-30). Toronto: University of Toronto Press.

Grossberg, L. (1996). Identity and cultural studies: is that all there is? *Questions of cultural identity*, 87-107.

Gruber Foundation. (2011). 2011 Justice Prize: Kurdish Human Rights Project. Retrieved July 10, 2014, from Gruber Foundation: http://gruber.yale.edu/justice/kurdish-human-rights-project-khrp

Guild, E. and D. Bigo (2010). The transformation of European border controls. Ryan, B. and Mitsilegas, V. (eds.). *Extraterritorial Immigration Control: Legal Challenges*. Leiden: Martinus Nijhoff. pp. 252-273.

Gunter, M. M. (1991). Transnational Sources of Support for the Kurdish Insurgency in Turkey. *Conlict Quarterly*, 7-30.

Günter, S. (2007). *Soziale Stadtpolitik*. Bielefeld: transcript Verlag.

Gupta, A. & Ferguson, J. (1992). Beyond "Culture": Space, Identity, and the Politics of Difference, *Cultural Anthropology* 7 (1), 6-23.

Gurr, T. R. (1970). *Why Men Rebel*. Princeton, NJ: Princeton University Press.

Hackworth, J. (2007). The Neoliberal City.Governance, Ideology, and Development in American Urbanism.Ithaca/ London: Cornell University Press.

Hainmueller, J., & Hiscox, M. J. (2010). Attitudes toward Highly Skilled and Low-skilled Immigration: Evidence from a Survey Experiment. *American Political Science Review*, 104(1), 61-84. doi: 10.1017/s0003055409990372

Hall, S. (2006). *Cultural Identity and Diaspora.* In: J. E. Braziel and A. Mannur (eds.) *Theorizing Diaspora*, Malden, MA: Blackwell: 233-246.

Hamelink, W. (2014). *The Sung Home: Narrative, Morality and the Kurdish nation.* PhD thesis, University of Leiden, Netherlands.

Hansen, T. B. and Stepputat, F. (2005). Introduction. Hansen, T. B. and Stepputat, F. (eds) *Sovereign Bodies: Citizens, Migrants, and States in the Postcolonial World.* Princeton: Princeton University Press. pp. 1-36.

Hassan, R. (2010). Socio-economic marginalization of Muslims in contemporary Australia: implications for social inclusion. *Journal of Muslim Minority Affairs*, 30(4), 575-584.

Häußermann, H. (2004). Zwischenevaluation des Bund-Länder-Programms „Stadtteile mit besonderem Entwicklungsbedarf – Die Soziale Stadt". *Walther, U.-J. und Mensch, K. (Hrsg.). Armut und Ausgrenzung in der „Sozialen Stadt".* Darmstadt: Schader-Stiftung: 268-287.

Helliwell, J. F., & Putnam, R. D. (2004). The social context of well-being. *Philosophical transactions-royal society of London series B biological sciences*, 1435-1446.

Heper, M. (2007). *The State and Kurds in Turkey. The Question of Assimilation,* New York NY: Palgrave Macmillan.

Heyman, J. (2007). Environmental Issues at the U.S.-Mexican Border and the Unequal Territorialization of Value. In A. Hornborg, J. R. McNeill, & J. Martinez-Alier (Eds.) *Rethinking environmental history: world-system history and global environmental change* (pp. 327-344). Lanham: AltaMira Press.

Hobolth, Mogens (2006). Governing the borders of Europe: the establishment of the Frontex agency. Paper presented at the Challenge Training School 'Security, Technology, Borders. EU responses to new challenges. Center for European Policy Studies, Brussels, 6 – 7 October 2006.

Horowitz, D. L. (1985). *Ethnic Groups in Conflict.* Berkeley: University of California Press.

Horowitz, D. L. (2001). *The deadly ethnic riot.* Berkeley: University of California Press.

Horowitz, D. L. Some realism about constitutional engineering. In: Wimmer, A., Goldstone, R.J., Horowitz, D.L., Joras, U., Schetter, C. (Eds.). (2004). *Facing Ethnic Conflicts: Toward a New Realism*, Boulder: Rowman and Littlefield: 245-257.

House of Commons (2011). Implications for the Justice and Home Affairs area of the accession of Turkey to the EU. Received from http://www.statewatch.org/news/2011/aug/eu-hasc-turkey-jha-report.pdf available on: 02.09.2011.

Human Rights Watch (2008). Stuck in a Revolving Door. Received from http://www.hrw.org/reports/2008/11/26/stuck-revolving-door-0 available on: 08.10.2010.

Human Rights Watch (2011). *The EU's Dirty Hands: Frontex Involvement in Ill-Treatment of Migrant Detainees in Greece*. New York: Human Rights Watch.
HÜNEE (Hacettepe Üniversitesi Nüfus Etütleri Enstitüsü). (2006). *Türkiye Göç ve Yerinden Olmuş Nüfus Araştırması*, Ankara: HÜNEE. Retrieved from http://www.hips.hacettepe.edu.tr/tgyona/TGYONA_rapor.pdf
Huysmans, J. (2006). *The Politics of Insecurity: Fear, Migration and Asylum in the EU*. London and New York: Routledge.
İçduygu, A., Romano, D., & Sirkeci, I. (1999). The ethnic question in an environment of insecurity: the Kurds in Turkey. *Ethnic and Racial Studies*, 22(6): 991-1010.
İneli-Ciğer, M. (2014). Implications of the New Turkish Law on Foreigners and International Protection and Regulation no. 29153 on Temporary Protection for Syrians. *Oxford Monitor of Forced Migration*, 4(2), 28-36.
Institut für Stadtforschung und Strukturpolitik GmbH (IfS) (2004): *Die Soziale Stadt. Ergebnisse der Zwischenevaluation*. Bewertung des Bund-Länder-Programms "Stadtteile mit besonderem Entwicklungsbedarf – die soziale Stadt" nach vier Jahren Programmlaufzeit. Im Auftrag des Bundesministeriums für Verkehr, Bau und Wohnungswesen, Berlin.
International Crisis Group. (2013, October 07). *Crying "Wolf": Why Turkish Fears need not Block Kurdish Reform*. Europe Report no. 227. Retrieved from: < http://www.crisisgroup.org/~/media/Files/europe/turkey-cyprus/turkey/227-crying-wolf-why-turkish-fears-need-not-block-kurdish-reform.pdf>
Inverarity, J. M. (1976). Populism and Lynching in Louisiana, 1889-1896: A Test of Erikson's Theory of the Relationship between Boundary Crises and Repressive Justice. *American Sociological Review*, 41, 262-268.
IOM International Organization for Migration. (2013). *Perspectives on Migration from Iraq - A Survey of Migrants and Potential Migrants in Iraq and the UK 2013*, online: http://iomiraq.net/file/152/download?token=NB2ev20y [18.02.2015].
Jacoby, T. (2011). Fascism, Civility and the Crisis of the Turkish State. *Third World Quarterly*, 32 (5), 905-924.
Jenkins, R. (1996). *Social Identity*, London and New York: Routledge.
Jongerden, J. (2007). *The Settlement Issue in Turkey and the Kurds: An Analysis of Spatical Policies, Modernity and War*. Leiden & Boston: Brill Academic Publishers.
Jongerden, J. (2008). *Türkiye'de İskân Sorunu ve Kürtler. Modernite, Savaş ve Mekân Politikaları Üzerine Bir Çözümleme*, İstanbul: Vate Yayınevi.
Junger-Tas, J. (2001). Ethnic minorities, social integration and crime. *European Journal on criminal policy and research*, 9(1), 5-29.
Kaczorowski, K. P. (2015). *Towards The Study of New Kurdish Migration in Turkey*, Fritillaria Kurdica, no. 7-8: 38-55, online: http://www.kurdishstudies.pl/ files/Fritillaria_Kurdica_2014_07_08.pdf [01.02.2015].
Kalaycıoğlu, E. (2012). Kulturkampf in Turkey: the constitutional referendum of 12 September 2010. *South European Society and Politics*, 17 (1), 1-22.
Kaliber, A. & Tocci, N. (2010). Civil Society and the Transformation of Turkey's Kurdish Question, *Security Dialogue*, 41(2), 191–215.

Kalkınma Merkezi. (2010). *Zorunlu Göç ve Etkileri. Diyarbakır:* Kalkınma Merkezi.

Kalyvas, S. N. (2008). Ethnic defection in civil war. *Comparative Political Studies*, 41(8), 1043-1068.

Karagül, M., & Masca, M. (2005). Sosyal sermaye üzerine bir inceleme. *AİBÜ-İİBF Ekonomik ve Sosyal Araştırmalar Dergisi.*

Karanja, S. K. (2000). The Schengen co-operation: Consequences for the right of EU citizens. *Mennesker og rettigheter Årgang*, 18 (3), 215 - 222.

Karpat, K. (2004). The Genesis of the Gecekondu: Rural Migration and Urbanization (1976), *European Journal of Turkish Studies.*

Kasparek, B. and Wagne, F. (2012). Local Border Regimes or a Homogeneous External Border? The Case of the European Union's Border Agency Frontex. Geiger, M. and Pécoud, A. (eds.) *The New Politics of International Mobility: Migration Management and its Discontents.* Osnabrück: Steinbacher Druck GmbH. pp. 173-190.

Kaufman, S. J. (1996). Spiraling to ethnic war: elites, masses, and Moscow in Moldova's civil war. *International Security*, 21(2), 108-138.

Kawachi, I., Kennedy, B. P., & Glass, R. (1999). Social capital and self-rated health: a contextual analysis. *American journal of public health*, 89(8), 1187-1193.

Keller, S. (2014). New Rules on Frontex Operations at Sea. *Statewatch.*

Khayati, K. (2008). *From Victim Diaspora to Transborder Citizenship?* Linköping: Linköping Studies in Arts and Science 435.

Kılıç, Ş. (1992). *Biz ve Onlar: Türkiye'de Etnik Ayrımcılık* [We and They: Ethnic Discrimination in Turkey]. Istanbul: Metis Yayınları.

Kindler, M., & Szulecka, M. (2012). The Economic Integration of Ukrainian and Vietnamese Migrant Women in the Polish Labour Market. *Journal of Ethnic and Migration Studies*, 1-23. doi: 10.1080/1369183x.2013.745244

Kirişçi, K. (2000). Disaggregating Turkish Citizenship and Immigration Practices. *Middle Eastern Studies*, 36(3), 1-22.

Kirisci, K. and Winrow, G. M. (1997). *The Kurdish Question and Turkey: An Example of Trans-state Ethnic Conflict.* London: Frank Cass & Co. Ltd.

Kışanak, Z. (undated publication). *Yitik Köyler,* İstanbul: Belge Yayınları.

Kluckhohn, C. and W.H. Kelly. (1945). The concept of culture. In: Ralph Linton (Ed.). *The Science of Man in the World Culture.* New York, NY. (pp. 78-105).

Koğacıoğlu, D. (2004). Progress, Unity, and Democracy: Dissolving Political Parties in Turkey. *Law & Society Review,* 38 (3), 433-462.

KONDA. (2011). *Kürt Meselesi'nde Algı ve Beklentiler Araştırması* [Research on Perceptions ad Expectations about Kurdish Problem]. Bulgular Raporu [Report of Findings]. May.

Koser, K. & Black, R. (1999). Limits to Harmonization: The "Temporary Protection" of Refugees in the European Union. *International Migration*, 37(3), 521-538.

Kroeber, A. L. and C. Kluckhohn. (1954). Culture. A Critical Review of Concepts and Definitions. *Papers of the Peabody Museum of American Archaeology and Ethnology, Harvard University* Volume 47, No. 1, Cambridge MA.

Künkel, J. (2008). Das Quartier als revanchistische Stadtpolitik: Verdrängung des Sexgewerbes im Namen eines neoliberalen Konstrukts. Schnur, O. (Hrsg.). *Quartiersforschung. Zwischen Theorie und Praxis.* Wiesbaden: VS Verlag für Sozialwissenschaften: 169-192.

Kurban, D. & Yeğen, M. (2012). *Adaletin Kıyısında: 'Zorunlu' Göç Sonrasında Devlet ve Kürtler. 5233 Tazminat Yasası'nın Bir Değerlendirmesi: Van Örneği.* İstanbul: TESEV. Retrieved from: http://www.aciktoplumvakfi.org.tr/pdf/TESEV_2012_Adaletin_Kiyisinda.pdf

Kurban, D., Yükseker, D., Çelik, A.B., Ünalan, T. & Aker, T.A. (2006). *"Zorunlu Göç" ile Yüzleşmek, Türkiye'de Yerinden Edilme Sonrası Vatandaşlığın İnşası.* İstanbul: TESEV.

Laakso, M. & Taagepera, R. (1979). Effective' Number of Parties: A Measure with Application to Western Europe. *Comparative Political Studies*, 12, 3-27.

Lanz S. (2009). Powered by Quartiersmanagement: Füreinander Leben im "Problemkiez". Drilling, M. und Schnur, O. (Hrsg.). Governance der Quartiersentwicklung. Wiesbaden: VS Verlag für Sozialwissenschaften: 219-225.

Lees, L. (2008). Gentrification and Social Mixing: Towards an Inclusive Urban Renaissance? *Urban Studies, 45(12)*, 2449-2470.

Lelyveld, J. (1986, March 2). The Swedish Officials Pursue 2 Theories in Palme Slaying. Retrieved July 7, 2014, from The New York Times: http://www.nytimes.com/1986/03/02/world/swedish-officials-pursue-2-theories-in-palme-slaying.html?pagewanted=1

Leonard, S. (2010). EU Border Security and Migration into the European Union: FRONTEX and Securitisation through Practices. *European Security*, 19 (2), 231-254.

Levi, M. (1996). The institution of conscription. *Social Science History*, 20(1), 133-167.

Levitt, P., & Lamba-Nieves, D. (2013). Rethinking social remittances and the migration-development nexus from the perspective of time. *Migration Letters*, 10(1), 11-22.

Lianos, T. P., & Cavounidis, J. (2010). Immigrant Remittances, Stability of Employment and Relative Deprivation. *International Migration*, 48(5), 118-141. doi: 10.1111/j.1468-2435.2008.00482.x

Lin, N. (2000). Inequality in social capital. *Contemporary Sociology*, 785-795.

Lin, N. (2008). A network theory of social capital. *The handbook of social capital*, 50, 69.

Lindstrom, D. P., & Giorguli Saucedo, S. (2007). The interrelationship of fertility, family maintenance and Mexico-U.S. Migration. *Demographic Research*, 17(28), 821-858.

London, A. S., & Wilmoth, J. M. (2006). Military Service and (Dis) Continuity in the Life Course Evidence on Disadvantage and Mortality from the Health and Retirement Study and the Study of Assets and Health Dynamics among the Oldest-Old. *Research on Aging*, 28(1), 135-159.

Lutterbeck, D. (2006). Policing Migration in the Mediterranean. *Mediterranean Politics*, 11 (1), 59-82.

Lutz, A. (2008). Who joins the military? A look at race, class, and immigration status. *Journal of Political and Military Sociology*, 36 (2), 167-188.

Mach, Z. (1989). *Symbols, Conflict and Identity*, Kraków: WUJ.

MacLean, A., & Elder Jr, G. H. (2007). Military service in the life course. *Sociology*, 33(1), 175.

Malkki, L. (1995). Purity and Exile: Violence, Memory, and National Cosmology among Hutu Refugees in Tanzania. Chicago: University of Chicago Press.

Manrique Gil, M., Barna, J., Hakala, P., Rey, B. and Claros, C. (2014). Mediterranean flows into Europe: Migration and the EU's foreign policy. Received from http://www.europarl.europa.eu/RegData/etudes/briefing_note/join/2014/522330/EXPO-JOIN_SP(2014)522330_EN.pdf available on: 16.04.2014.

Maritain, J. (2010). *On the Philosophy of History*. Published by University of Notre Dame Jacques Maritain Center; available on http://www3.nd.edu/Departments/Maritain/etext/philhist.htm, accessed on 06.01.2015.

Marshall, G. (2003). Sosyoloji Sözlüğü, Bilim ve Sanat, çevirenler: Osman Akınhay, Derya Kömürcü, Ankara.

Martin, P. (2004). Germany: Managing Migration in the 21st Century. In: Cornelius, W. A. Tsuda, T. Martin, P. L. and Hollifield, J. F. (eds.) *Controlling Immigration: A Global Perspective*. Stanford, California: Stanford University Press.

Massey, D. S. (1990). Social Structure, Household Strategies, and the Cumulative Causation of Migration. *Population Index*, 56(1), 3-26.

Massey, D. S. and F. G. España. (1987). The Social Process of International Migration, *Science*, 237: 733-738.

McAdam, D.; Tarrow, S. & Tilly, C. (2001). *Dynamics of Contention*. Cambridge: Cambridge University Press.

McArdle, N. (2004). Racial Equity and Opportunity in Metro Boston Job Markets.

McCarthy, B., & Hagan, J. (2001). When crime pays: Capital, competence, and criminal success. *Social forces*, 79(3), 1035-1060.

Menjívar, C., & Abrego, L. J. (2012). Legal Violence: Immigration Law and the Lives of Central American Immigrants. *American Journal of Sociology*, 117(5), 1380-1421.

Merry, S. E. (2000). *Colonizing Hawai'i: The cultural power of law*. Princeton, NJ: Princeton University Press.

Messner, S. F., Baumer, E. P., & Rosenfeld, R. (2004). Dimensions of social capital and rates of criminal homicide. *American Sociological Review*, 69(6), 882-903

MFA (Republic of Turkey Ministry of Foreign Affairs) (2012). Press Release Regarding the Signing of the Memorandum of Understanding on Cooperation with FRONTEX. Received from http://www.mfa.gov.tr/no_-148_-28-may-2012_-press-release-regarding-the-signing-of-the-memorandum-of-understanding-on-cooperation-with-frontex.en.mfa available on: 13.07.2013.

Migdal, J. S. (2004). Mental Maps and Virtual Checkpoints: Struggles to Construct and Maintain State and Social Boundaries, (Edited by Joel S. Migdal), *Boundaries and Belonging: States and Societies in the Struggle to*

Shape Identitiesand Local Practices, Cambridge, Cambridge University Press, 3-23.

Mitchell, Timothy. 1999. "Society, Economy, and the State Effect". In *State/Culture: State Formation After The Cultural Turn,* Edited By George Steinmetz, Cornell University Press; pp. 76-97.

Mocan, H. N., Billups, S. C., & Overland, J. (2005). A dynamic model of differential human capital and criminal activity. *Economica, 72*(288), 655-681.

Mohan, G. & Mohan, J. (2002). Placing social capital. *Progress in Human Geography* 26(2): 191–210.

Moulin, A. (1991). *Peasantry and Society in France since 1789*. Cambridge University Press.

Mountz, A., Wright, R., Miyares, I., Bailey, A.J. (2002). Lives in Limbo: Temporary Protected Status and Immigrant Identities. *Global Networks*, 2(4), 335-356.

Mucha, J. (1999). Dominant Culture as a Foreign Culture. Dominant Groups in the Eyes of Cultural Minorities. Introduction, In: idem (Ed.), *Dominant Culture as a Foreign Culture. Dominant Groups in the Eyes of Minorities*, New York: Columbia University Press and East European Monographs: 7-23.

Mutlu, S. (1996). Ethnic Kurds in Turkey: A Demographic Study. *International Journal of Middle East Studies*, 28 (4), 517-541.

Narlı, N. (2000). Civil-military relations in Turkey. *Turkish Studies*, 1(1), 107-127.

Neal, A. W. (2009). Securitization and Risk at the EU Border: The Origins of FRONTEX. *Journal of Common Market Studies*, 47 (2), 333-356.

Nieszery, A. (2008). Class, race, gender... neighbourhood? Zur Bedeutung von Quartierseffekten in der europäischen Stadtforschung. Schnur, O. (Hrsg.): *Quartiersforschung. Zwischen Theorie und Praxis.* Wiesbaden: VS Verlag für Sozialwissenschaften: 107-126.

Nolin, C. L. (2002). Transnational ruptures and sutures: questions of identity and social relations among Guatemalans in Canada. *Geojournal*, 56(1), 59-67.

Oberwittler, D. (2006). Social Exclusion and Youth Crime in Europe-The Spatial Dimension. *Publication Series – European Institute for Crime Prevention and Control, 48*, 27.

OECD. (1998). Trends in International Migration 1998 Continuous Reporting System on Migration. OECD Publishing.

Olzak, S. (1990). The Political Context of Competition: Lynching and Urban Racial Violence, 1882-1914. *Social Forces*, 69 (2), 395-421.

Öniş, Z. & Bayram, I. E. (2008). Temporary star or emerging tiger? Recent Turkish economic performance in a global context. *New Perspectives on Turkey,* 39, 247–284.

Østby, G. (2008). Horizontal Inequalities, Political Environment and Civil Conflict: Evidence from 55 Developing Countries. Stewart, F. (Ed.) *Horizontal Inequalities and Conflict: Understanding Group Violence in Multiethnic Societies*. New York: Palgrave Macmillan: 136–157.

Ostegaard-Nielsen, E. K. (2001). *The Politics of Migrants' Transnational Practices. Transnational Migration: Comparative Perspectives*. Princeton: Princeton University.

Özar, Ş., Uçarlar, N. & Aytar, O. (2013). *From Past to Present a Paramilitary Organization in Turkey. Village Guard System.* Diyarbakır: DİSA Publications (in Turkish, Kurdish and English).
Özcan, A. K. (2006). *Turkey's Kurds. A theoretical analysis of the PKK and Abdullah Öcalan*, London, New York: Routledge.
Özden, Ş. (2013). *Syrian Refugees in Turkey*. Florence: Robert Schuman Centre for Advanced Studies, European University Institute.
Özgen, H. N. (2004). *Sınır Kasabaları Sosyolojisi Projesi: 2001-2004*, İzmir: TÜBİTAK.
Özgen, H. N. (2007). "Devlet, Sınır, Aşiret: Aşiretin Etnik Bir Kimlik Olarak Yeniden İnşası". *Toplum ve Bilim,* No: 108: 239–261.
Özgen, H. N. (2013 Ocak 6). Sınırın Vatandaşlık Borcu: Roboski'nin Ölümleri Neden Kalplerde Yatar? *Birgün Gazetesi*, 1-6.
Özoglu, H. (2004). *Kurdish Notables and the Ottoman State, Evolving Identities, Competing Loyalties, and Shifting Boundaries*, Albany, NY: State University of New York Press.
Özsöz, M. (2012). *İlerlemenin Matematiği*. Brussels: İktisadi Kalkınma Vakfı.
Paasi, A. (2009). Bounded Spaces in a 'borderless world': Border Studies, Power and the Anatomy of Territory, *Journal of Power*, 2(2): 213-234.
Pantea, M.-C. (2012). From 'Making a Living' to 'Getting Ahead': Roma Women's Experiences of Migration. *Journal of Ethnic and Migration Studies*, 38(8), 1251-1268. doi: 10.1080/1369183x.2012.689185
Papastavridis, E. (2010). Fortress Europe" and FRONTEX: Within or Without International Law? *Nordic Journal of International Law*, 79 (1): 75-111.
Park, R., R.D. McKenzie and E. Burgess. (1925). *The City: Suggestions for the Study of Human Nature in the Urban Environment*, Chicago: University of Chicago Press.
Parnwell, M. (1993). *Why People Move?* in: J. D. S. Bale, *Population Movements and the Third World,* London, New York: Routledge: 71-100.
Peers, S. (2014). New EU Rules on Maritime Surveillance: Will They Stop the Deaths and Push-Backs in the Mediterranean. *Statewatch.*
Pérouse, J.F. (2014). Is Istanbul Entering the War in Syria? Some Notes regarding the Events that took place between 7 and 13 October 2014. Retrieved from: <https://www.academia.edu/8869504/Is_Istanbul_entering_the_war_in_Syria_Some_notes_regarding_the_events_that_took_place_betw_een_7_and_13_October_2014>
Peterson, S. (2000). Me against my brother. At war in Somalia, Sudan, and Rwanda: A journalistic report from the battlefields of Africa. New York: Routledge.
Pirbal, F. (2008). *The Apostrophe: Istanbul: the Capital city of Kurdish Literature*, The Kurdish Globe online: http://www.thefreelibrary.com/The+Apostrophe%3A +Istanbul%3A+ the +Capital+city+ of+Kurdish +Literature%3A...-a0180426162 [06.08.2012].
Portes, A. (2000). Social capital: Its origins and applications in modern sociology. *LESSER, Eric L. Knowledge and Social Capital. Boston: Butterworth-Heinemann*, 43-67.

Portes, A. (2010). Migration and social change: Some conceptual reflections. *Journal of Ethnic and Migration Studies, 36*(10), 1537-1563.

Portes, A., & Vickstrom, E. (2011). Diversity, social capital, and cohesion. *Annual Review of Sociology, 37,* 461-479.

Portes, A., & Zhou, M. (1993). The new second generation: Segmented assimilation and its variants. *The annals of the American academy of political and social science, 530*(1): 74-96.

Portes, A., Fernandez-Kelly, P., & Haller, W. (2005). Segmented assimilation on the ground: The new second generation in early adulthood. *Ethnic and racial studies, 28*(6): 1000-1040.

Putnam, R. (2001). Social capital: Measurement and consequences. *Canadian Journal of Policy Research, 2*(1): 41-51.

Putnam, R. D. (1995). Bowling alone: America's declining social capital. *Journal of Democracy, 6*(1): 65-78.

Putnam, R. D. (Ed.). (2002). Democracies in flux: The evolution of social capital in contemporary society. Oxford University Press.

Quartiersmanagement Reuterplatz (2011). *Integriertes Handlungs- und Entwicklungskonzept 2010* (mit Jahresbilanz 2010). Received from http://www.reuter-quartier.de/uploads/media/IHEK_2013_01.pdf available on: 30.04.2014.

Quartiersmanagement Reuterplatz (2013). *Integriertes Handlungs- und Entwicklungskonzept 2013* (mit Jahresbilanz 2011). Received from http://www.reuter-quartier.de/uploads/media/IHEK_2013_01.pdf available on: 30.04.2014.

Rabushka, A. & Shepsle, K. A. (1972). Politics in Plural Societies: A Theory of Democratic Instability. Columbus, OH: Merrill.

Rajkumar, D., Berkowitz, L., Vosko, L., Preston, V, and Latham, R. (2012). At the temporary-permanent divide: how Canada produces temporariness and makes citizens through its security, work and settlement policies. *Citizenship Studies 16*(3-4), 483-510.

Reed, J. S. (1972). Percent Black and Lynching: A Test of Blalock's Theory. *Social Forces,* 50 (3), 356-360.

Reeves, M. (2013). Clean fake: Authenticating documents and persons in migrant Moscow. *American Ethnologist,* 40(3), 508-524.

Regamey, A. (2010). Representations of migrants and migration policy in Russia. *Anthropologicheskiy Forum,* 13, 389-406.

Reid-Henry, S. M. (2013). An Incorporating Geopolitics: Frontex and the Geopolitical Rationalities of the European Border. *Geopolitics,* 18(1), 198-224.

Reisig, M. D., Holftfreter, K., & Morash, M. (2002). Social Capital among Women Offenders. *Journal of Contemporary Criminal Justice, 18*(2), 169-189.

Republic of Turkey (22 October 2014). Regulation No. 29153 on Temporary Protection. *Official Gazette.* Retrieved from:
<http://www.tkhk.gov.tr/DB/14/1673_gecici-koruma-yonetm>

Republic of Turkey (4 April 2013). Law No. 6458 on Foreigners and International Protection. *Official Gazette*. Retrieved from: http://gocdergisi.com/kaynak/2013_yabancilar_ve_uluslararasi_koruma_kanunu.pdf.

Romano, D. (2006). *The Kurdish Nationalist Movement. Opportunity, Mobilization, and Identity*, Cambridge and New York NJ: Cambridge University Press.

Romenlerin saldırısına uğrayan Kaplan'ın sağlık durumu ciddi [the health conditions of Kaplan who is exposed to attacks of Roma people are serious]. (2006). *Dicle Haber Ajansı*, 4 April. Received from http://www.diclehaber.com/ 1/4/5912/viewNews/62545 available on: 15/02/2012.

Rosen, G., & Razin, E. (2009). The Rise of Gated Communities in Israel: Reflections on Changing Urban Governance in a Neo-liberal Era. *Urban Studies*, 46(8): 1702-1722.

Rothschild J. (1981). *Ethnopolitics, a Conceptual Framework*. New York: Columbia University Press.

Sadan, M. (2010). *Review of the Art of Not Being Governed: An Anarchist History of Upland Southeast Asia*. Online article, available from: http://www.history.ac.uk/reviews/review/903. Date accessed: 20/03/2014

Sampson, R. J., & Laub, J. H. (1990). Crime and deviance over the life course: The salience of adult social bonds. *American Sociological Review*, 609-627.

Sampson, R. J., & Wilson, W. J. (1995). Toward a theory of race, crime, and urban inequality. *Race, crime, and justice: A reader*, 177-190.

Saraçoğlu, C. (2010). The changing image of the Kurds in Turkish cities: middle-class perceptions of Kurdish migrants in İzmir. *Patterns of Prejudice*, 44(3): 239-260.

Savitch, H., & Vogel, R. (2005). The United States: Executive Centred Politics. Denters, B. and Rose, L. E. (eds). Comparing Local Governance.Basingstoke: Palgrave: 211–228.

Schulman, M. D., & Anderson, C. (1999). The Dark Side of the Force: A Case Study of Restructuring and Social Capital1. *Rural Sociology*, 64(3): 351-372.

Scott, J. C. (2009). *The Art of Not Being Governed: An Anarchist History of Upland Southeast Asia*. New Haven: Yale University Press

Şekercioğlu E. & Arikan, G. (2008). Trends in party system indicators for the July 2007 Turkish elections. *Turkish Studies*, 9 (2): 213-231.

Serinci, D. (2014, May 21). The Candidates for EU Parliament: Kurdish Rights Should be Pre-condition for Turkey EU Accession. Retrieved July 21, 2014, from Rudaw: http://rudaw.net/english/world/21052014?keyword=European%20Union

Sezgin, D. & Wall, M. A. (2005). Constructing the Kurds in the Turkish press: a case study of *Hürriyet* newspaper. *Media, Culture & Society*, 27(5), 787–798.

Siebel, W. (2010). Die Zukunft der Städte. Bundeszentrale für politische Bildung (eds). AusPolitik und Zeitgeschichte 17/2010.Stadtentwicklung.Bonn: 5-9.

Sirkeci, I. (2000). Exploring the Kurdish Population in the Turkish Context, *Genus*, 56 (1-2): 149-175.

Sirkeci, I. (2002). The Ethnic environment of insecurity as a facilitating factor in asylum migration: the Turkish case, paper presented at UNU-WIDER

Conference on Poverty, International Migration and Asylum, 27-28 September, 2002, Helsinki, Finland. Received from http://www.mmo.gr/pdf/library/Balkans/Turkey%20and%20ethnic%20insecurity.pdf available on: 10.03.2014.

Sirkeci, I. (2003). *Migration, Ethnicity and Conflict.The Environment of Insecurity and Turkish Kurdish International Migration*, Doctoral dissertation, University of Sheffield.

Sirkeci, I. (2006). *The environment of insecurity in Turkey and the emigration of Turkish Kurds to Germany*. New York and Lampeter: Edwin Mellen Press.

Sirkeci, I. (2009). Transnational mobility and conflict. *Migration Letters*, 6(1): 3-14.

Sirkeci, I. & Cohen, J.H. (2016). Cultures of migration and conflict in contemporary human mobility in Turkey. *European Review*, 22(2) (forthcoming).

Sirkeci, I., Cohen, J. H., & Ratha, D. (Eds). (2012). *Migration and Remittances during the Global Financial Crisis and Beyond*. Washington, D.C.: The World Bank.

Sirkeci, I., Cohen, J. H., & Yazgan, P. (2012). Turkish culture of migration: Flows between Turkey and Germany, socio-economic development and conflict. *Migration Letters*, 9(1): 33-46.

Sirkeci, I. & Martin, P. L. (2014). Sources of Irregularity and Managing Migration: The Case of Turkey. *Border Crossing: Transnational Working Papers*, No.1401, 1-16.

Sjaastad, L. A. (1962). The Costs and Returns of Human Migration, *Journal of Political Economy* 70: 80-93.

Slater, T. (2006). The Eviction of Critical Perspectives from Gentrification Research.*International Journal of Urban and Regional Research, 30(4)*: 737–757.

Smith, N. (1996). *The New Urban Frontier: Gentrification and the Revanchist City*. New York: Routledge.

Smith, N. (2002). New Globalism, New Urbanism: Gentrification as Global Urban Strategy. *Brenner, N. and Theodore, N. (eds). Spaces of Neoliberalism.Urban Restructuring in North America and Western Europe*. Oxford: Blackwell, 80-103.

Soja, E. W. (1971). The Political Organization of Space, *Commision on College Geography Resource*, No: 8. Washington D.C.: Association of American Geographers.

Somer, M. (2005). Resurgence and Remaking of Identity Civil Beliefs, Domestic and External Dynamics, and the Turkish Mainstream Discourse on Kurds. *Comparative Political Studies,* 38(6), 591-622.

Sonnenschein, F. and van Meijl, T. (2014). Migration and the Dialogue of Multiple Identifications: Kurdish Migrants in the Tourist Industry of Istanbul. *Identities: Global Studies in Culture and Power*. 21(5): 481-497.

Soule, S. A. (1992). Populism and Black Lynching in Georgia, 1890-1900. *Social Forces*, 71 (2): 431-449.

Stark, O. (1991). *The Migration of Labor*, Cambridge MA: Basil Blackwell.

Stewart, F. (Ed.). (2008). Horizontal Inequalities and Conflict: Understanding Group Violence in Multiethnic Societies. New York: Palgrave Macmillan.

Stirling, P. (1951). *The social structure of Turkish peasant communities*. Institute of Current World Affairs.

Straßburger, G., & Wurtzbacher, J. (2010). *Mehr Demokratie: Sicherstellung der bürgerschaftlichen Beteiligung im Wohnquartier.* Abschlussbericht des gleichnamigen Forschungsprojektes mit einer Analyse des Quartiersbeirates Reuterkiez und Hinweisen zur Weiterentwicklung, im Auftrag der Katholischen Hochschule für Sozialwesen. Berlin.

Strik, T. (2013). Migration and asylum: mounting tensions in the Eastern Mediterranean. Report for the Committee on Migration, Refugees and Displaced Persons, Council of Europe. Doc. 13106, 23 January 2013

Subrahmanyam, S. (2010). "The View from the Top. Review of the Art of Not Being Governed: An Anarchist History of Upland South-East Asia by Scott, J. C." *London Review of Books* [online] vol. 32 no. 23 pp. 25-26. Available from: http://www.lrb.co.uk/v32/n23/sanjay-subrahmanyam/the-view-from-the-top. Accessed on 25/03/2014.

Sunata, U. (2002). Not a "Flight" From Home but 'Potential Brain Drain'. Published Master Thesis. METU.

Sunata, U. (2011). Highly Skilled Labor Migration: The Case of ICT Specialists from Turkey in Germany. Münster: LIT.

Sunata, U. (2014). "Tersine Beyin Göçünde Sosyal Ağların Rolü: Türkiyeli Mühendislerin Almanya'dan Geriye Göç Deneyim ve Algıları" *Türk Psikoloji Yazıları*, 17(34): 85-96.

Swanson, K. (2007). Revanchist Urbanism Heads South: The Regulation of Indigenous Beggars and Street Vendors in Ecuador. *Antipode, 39(4):* 708-728.

T.C. Avrupa Birliği Bakanlığı. (2011, July 01). Türkiye- AB İlişikilerinin Tarihçesi. Retrieved July 2, 2014, from T.C. Avrupa Birliği Bakanlığı: http://www.abgs.gov.tr/index.php?p=111&l=1

T.C. Avrupa Birliği Bakanlığı. (2012). Türkiye tarafından hazırlanan 2012 ilerleme raporu. Ankara: Avrupa Birliği Bakanlığı.

Tansel, A., & Güngör, N. D. (2003). "Brain drain" from Turkey: Survey evidence of student non-return. *Career Development International*, 8(2): 52-69.

Tekin, F. (2012). *Sosyolojik Açıdan Sınır: Hakkâri Örneği*, (The Border from a Sociological Perspective: The Case of Hakkâri), yayınlanmamış doktora tezi, Selçuk Üniversitesi Sosyal Bilimler Enstitüsü, Konya.

Tekin, F. (2013). Sınırın Çifte Anlamlılığı: Sınırdaki Merkezler ve Taşralar (The Double Meaning of the Border: Centres and the Countries on the Border) *Sosyoloji Divanı*, S:1, 57-63.

Temo, S. (2013). "Roboskî'ye Gidecekler İçin". *Radikal* 31.10.2013. Available from: http://www.radikal.com.tr/yazarlar/selim_temo/roboskiye_gidecekler _icin-1158196 Accessed on: 31.10.2013

Tezcür, G. M. (2010). The Moderation Theory Revisited: The Case of Islamic Political Actors. *Party Politics*, 16 (1): 69–88.

Tezcür, G. M. (2012). Trends and Characteristics of the Turkish Party System in Light of the 2011 Elections. *Turkish Studies* 13 (2): 117-134.

The Economist. (2005). *Can't they get along anymore?* online: http://www.economist.com/node/4389654 (8/9/2005) [06.08.2012]
The European Commission. (2011). *Turkey 2011 Progress Report*. Brussels.
The European Commission. (2013). *Turkey 2013 Progress Report*. Brussels.
Tilly, C. & Zambrano, R. (1989). *Violent Events in France, 1830-1860 and 1930-1960*. Inter-university Consortium for Political and Social Research.
Tilly, C. (1999). "Now Where?" In *State/Culture: State Formation After The Cultural Turn,* Edited By George Steinmetz, Cornell University Press, 1999; p. 407-420.
Tilly, C. (2003). *The politics of collective violence*. Cambridge: Cambridge University Press.
Tilly, C. (1966). *Intensive Sample of Disturbances in France, 1830-1860 and 1930-1960*. Vol. 51. Inter-university Consortium for Political and Social Research.
TimeTurk. (2010). *En büyük Kürt şehri, Istanbul* online: http://www.timeturk.com/tr/2010/03/25/en-buyuk-kurt-sehri-istanbul.html [06.08.2012].
Tirebolu'da Kürt öğrenciler linç edilmek istendi [Kurdish students in Tirebolu are attempted to be lynched]. (2010). *Dicle Haber Ajansı*, 28 June. Received from http://www.diclehaber.com/1/4/2519/viewNews/218189 available on: 13 February 2012.
TMMOB. (1998). *Bölgeiçi Zorunlu Göçten Kaynaklanan Toplumsal Sorunların Diyarbakır Kenti Ölçeğinde Araştırılması*. Ankara: TMMOB.
Todaro, M. (1969). A Model of Labor Migration and Urban Unemployment in Less Developed Countries. *American Economic Review*, 59: 138-148.
Toğral, B. (2011). Convergence of Securitization of Migration and 'New Racism' in Europe: Rise of Culturalism and Disappearance of Politics. Lazaridis, G. (ed.) *Security, Insecurity and Migration in Europe*. Surrey: Ashgate: 219-239.
Toğral Koca, B. (2013). *The Securitization of Migration in Europe in the Post-September 11 Era A Comparative Analysis of Germany and Spain*. Online-Published doctoral dissertation, University of Hamburg.
Tolnay, S. E., Beck, E. M. & Massey, J. L. (1989). Black Lynchings: The Power Threat Hypothesis Revisited. *Social Forces*, 67 (3): 605-623.
TOPOS Stadtforschung (2011). *Sozialstrukturentwicklung in Nord-Neukölln*. Im Auftrag der Senatsverwaltung für Stadtentwicklung. Dezember 2011.
Trager, L. (2005). Women Migrants and Hometown Linakges in Nigeria: Status, Economic Roles and Contributions to Community Development. In L. Trager (Ed.), *Society for Economic Anthropology monographs*, v. 22. (pp. 225-256). Walnut Creek: AltaMira Press.
Triandafyllidou, A. (2009). Sub-Saharan African immigrant activists in Europe: transcultural capital and transcultural community building. *Ethnic and Racial Studies*, 32(1): 93-116.
United Nations High Commissioner for Refugees (UNHCR) (2010). UNHCR recommends urgent measures to address the serious humanitarian needs in the Evros region. Received from http://www.proasyl.de/fileadmin/fmdam/ NEWS/2010/UNHCR_Urgent_Measures_Evros_Regionen.pdf available on: 02.07.2011.

Uslu, E. (2008). Ulusalcılık: The Neo-nationalist Resurgence in Turkey. *Turkish Studies*, 9 (1): 73-97.

Uuslararası Af Örgütü (UAÖ) (2014). Kale Avrupası'nın İnsani Bedeli: Avrupa Sınırlarında Göçmen ve Mültecilerin Karşılaştıkları İnsan Hakları İhlalleri. Londra: Uluslararası Af Örgütü Ltd.

van Bruinessen, M. (1998). Shifting National and Ethnic Identities: The Kurds in Turkey and the European Diaspora. *Journal of Muslim Minority Affairs*, 18(1): 39-54.

van Bruinessen, M. (1999). The Kurds in movement: migrations, mobilisations, communications and the globalisation of the Kurdish question, Working Paper no. 14, Islamic Area Studies Project, Tokyo, Japan.

van Bruinessen, M. (2013). Kurds and the City. In: H. Bozarslan and C. Scalbert-Yücel (eds.), *Joyce Blau, l'éternelle chez les Kurdes*, Paris: Institut Kurde de Paris: 273-95.

van Munster, R. (2009). Securitizing Migration: The Politics of Risk in the EU. Basingstoke: Palgrave.

van Oorschot, W., Arts, W., & Gelissen, J. (2006). Social capital in Europe measurement and social and regional distribution of a multifaceted phenomenon. *Acta sociologica*, 49(2): 149-167.

van Schendel, W. (2002). "Geographies of Knowing, Geographies of Ignorance: Jumping Scale In Southeast Asia." In *Environment and Planning D: Society and Space*. Vol. 20: 647-668.

Varshney, A. (2002). *Ethnic Conflict and Civic Life*. New Haven, CT: Yale University Press.

Vasquez, M. A. (2014). From Colonialism to Neo-Liberal Capitalism: Latino/A Immigrants in the U.S. and the New Biopolitics. *Journal for Cultural and Religious Theory*. 3 (1): 81-100.

Vazsonyi, A. T., & Killias, M. (2001). Immigration and crime among youth in Switzerland. *Criminal Justice and Behavior*, 28(3), 329-366.

Vertovec, S. (1999). Conceiving and researching transnationalism, *Ethnic and Racial Studies*, 22(2): 447-62.

Vertovec, S. (2005). The Political Importance of Diasporas. Oxford: Centre on Migration, Policy and Society. Retrieved July 26, 2014, from https://www.compas.ox.ac.uk/fileadmin/files/Publications/working_papers/WP_2005/Steve%20Vertovec%20WP0513.pdf

Vianello, F. A. (2013). Ukrainian migrant women's social remittances: Contents and effects on families left behind. *Migration Letters*, 10(1), 91-100.

w2eu (Welcome to Europe) (2014). Frontex in the Mediterranean: The border is the problem. Received from http://w2eu.net/frontex/frontex-in-the-mediterranean/ available on: 02.02.2014.

Waever, O. (2000). The EU as a Security Actor: Reflections from a Pessimistic Constructivist on Post Sovereign Security Orders. M. Kelstrup ve M. C. Williams (eds.) *International Relations Theory and the Politics of European Integration*. London: Routledge. pp. 250-294.

Wallerstein, I. (1974). The Modern World System. Capitalist Agriculture and the Origins of the European World Economy in the Sixteenth Century. New York: Academic Press.

Walther, U.-J., & Güntner, S. (2007). Vom lernenden Programm zur lernenden Politik? Stand und Perspektiven sozialer Stadtpolitik in Deutschland. *Informationen zur Raumentwicklung*, 34(6): 345-362.

Ware, V. (2012). Military Migrants: Fighting for YOUR Country. Palgrave Macmillan.

Watts, N. F. (1999). Allies and Enemies: Pro-Kurdish Parties in Turkish Politics, 1990-94. *International Journal of Middle East Studies*, 31(4): 631-656.

Weber, E. (1976). Peasants into Frenchmen: the modernization of rural France, 1870-1914. Stanford University Press.

Westin, C. (1983). Self-reference, Consciousness and Time. In: A. Jacobson-Widding (ed.), *Identity: Personal and Social-Cultural. A Symposium.* Uppsala: 93-110.

White, R. (2008). Disputed definitions and fluid identities: The limitations of social profiling in relation to ethnic youth gangs. *Youth Justice*, 8(2): 149-161.

Wilkinson, S. I. (2004). Votes and Violence: Electoral Competition and Ethnic Riots in India. New York: Cambridge University Press.

Wilmoth, J. M., & London, A. S. (Eds.). (2013). *Life course perspectives on military service*. Routledge.

Woodward, S. L. (1995). *Balkan Tragedy: Chaos and Dissolution after the Cold War*. Washington, D.C.: Brookings Institution.

Wright, J. P., Cullen, F. T., & Miller, J. T. (2001). Family social capital and delinquent involvement. *Journal of criminal Justice*, 29(1), 1-9.

Yağız, D. Ö., Amca, Y., Erdoğan, E.U. & Saydam, N. (2012). *Malan Barkirin. Zorunlu Göç Anlatıları*, Timaş.

Yavuz, M. H. (2001). "Five Stages of the Construction of Kurdish Nationalism in Turkey". In *Nationalism & Ethnic Politics*, Vol.7, No.3, Autumn 2001:1-24.

Yeğen, M. (1999). *Devlet Söyleminde Kürt Sorunu* [Kurdish Problem in State Discourse]. Istanbul: Iletişim Yayınları.

Yeğen, M. (2004). Citizenship and Ethnicity in Turkey. *Middle Eastern Studies*, 40(6): 51-66.

Yegen, M. (2009). Prospective-Turks or Pseudo-Citizens: Kurds in Turkey. *The Middle East Journal*, 63(4): 597-616.

Yıldız, K. (2005). The Kurds in Turkey. EU accession and Human Rights, London: Pluto Press.

Yinanç, B. (2013). 'Poor Transparency Shadow's Turkey's Syria Refugee Policy', *Hürriyet Daily News*.

Young, J. (2013). "This is My Life": Youth Negotiating Legality and Belonging in Toronto. In L. Goldring & P. Landolt (Eds.), *Producing and Negotiating Non-citizenship: Precarious Legal Status in Canada* (pp. 99-117). Toronto: University of Toronto Press.

Zeydanlıoğlu, W. (2008). "The White Turkish Man's Burden": Orientalism, Kemalism and the Kurds in Turkey. In: Rings, G. and Ife, A. (eds.) *Neo-colonial Mentalities in Contemporary Europe? Language and Discourse in the Construction of Identities*. Newcastle upon Tyne: Cambridge Scholars Publishing:155-174.

Zick, A., Wagner, U., Van Dick, R., & Petzel, T. (2001). Acculturation and prejudice in Germany: Majority and minority perspectives. *Journal of Social Issues*, *57*(3): 541-557.

Index

Abdullah Öcalan 64, 65, 174
acculturation.. 149
acts of terrorism 45
Ahmet Kaya 129, 133
Amnesty International.. 55, 58, 159, 160
Amsterdam Treaty............................... 68
Anders Rasmussen 66
Andreas Blätte..................................... 70
Angela Merkel..................................... 58
Ankara v, 98, 101, 102, 162, 165, 169, 172, 178, 179
Armenians... 103
Bedirxan.............................. 95, 116, 127
beri road 108
Berlin-Neukölln .... i, 5, 77-80, 87
biopolitics...................................... 45, 46
Birgül Ayman Güler........................... 98
boomerang effect...................... 148, 156
border controls . 45, 47, 51, 58, 160, 167
Bulgaria... 26
Cecilia Malmström..................... 53, 166
Cemil Çeto 89
Christian Democratic Party 84
citizenship iii, 12, 19-26, 33, 34, 68, 73, 74, 95, 137, 153, 154, 157, 167, 181
Ciwan Haco...................................... 129
Cold War... 43
community cohesion 78, 82
co-nationals.. 2
conflicts i, iv, 1, 3, 4, 5, 61, 77, 81, 97, 101, 120, 129, 136, 144
Conscription...................................... 149
Copenhagen i, iv, 4, 7, 8, 9, 12, 15, 16, 18, 43, 69
Council of the European Union 48, 49, 164, 166
criminal capital 4, 7, 8, 12, 14, 15, 17, 161
cultural integration 78
Damascus............................... 22, 28, 30
Denmark.................. vi, 7, 14, 15, 17, 18
difficulties 1, 30, 39, 83, 87, 105, 130
'Districts with Special Development Needs.. 77, 80
Eastern Anatolia............................... 110
Eastern Mediterranean 52, 53, 178
Eminê Ahmed 89
empowerment..................................... 78
environment of insecurity 120, 155, 169, 176, 177

European Anti-Fraud Office.............. 49
European Court of Human Rights 67, 107
European Parliament 49, 51, 67, 68, 69, 163, 166
EUROPOL 49
Feleknas Uca 68
Ferguson... 167
Forced migration of Kurds 102
Foucauldian approach.............. 5, 43, 45
Foucault...................................... 44, 166
France 89, 149, 150, 160, 166, 173, 179, 181
French model.................................... 149
Frontex 43, 45, 48-59, 165-170, 175, 180
Georgia 164, 177
Gerdi tribe 4, 35, 39, 40, 41, 42
Germany iii, v, 77, 80, 119, 150, 154, 172, 177-179, 182
governance 5, 44-48, 52, 57, 58, 77, 79, 80, 84, 88
Greece 52, 53, 54, 55, 56, 58, 159, 160, 161, 163, 166, 169
guerrilla children 110
Gupta... 167
Hacettepe University 102
Hakkari 102, 129
human insecurity 3, 115, 120, 121, 123, 127, 129, 130, 155
human mobility............................. 3, 177
Human Rights Association 102
insecurities................................. 1, 3, 4, 5
international vi, 1, 24, 35, 37, 44, 50, 53, 55, 58, 61, 62, 71, 120, 121, 140, 148, 150, 155, 157
Iraq 52, 115, 121, 169
Istanbul i, iii, iv, 4, 5, 19, 20, 21, 26-34, 101, 105, 113-117, 121-130, 144, 159-165, 170, 174, 177, 179, 181
İzmir 102, 174, 176
Justice and Development Party......... 151
Kavar 5, 101, 103, 104, 105, 106, 107, 109, 110, 112
Klaus Roesler 56, 165
Konya .... vi, 125, 127, 178
Kurdish diaspora.............. 61-68, 70-75
Kurdish question...................... 151, 180
Kurdistan 65, 66, 89-101, 115-118, 121, 127, 130, 131, 141, 162

Kurds from Syria .. 19-21, 25, 26, 32-34
Lebanon 29
Left-wing Party 84
Leyla Zana 66
Mardin 33, 102, 126, 127, 139, 140
Marginalisation .... i, 7, 10
Mexican migrants 26
Middle East .... v, 3, 52, 161, 173, 181
military migration 147, 148
military service 5, 147-150, 151-156, 181
Mir Bedirxan 95
neighbourhood management 78, 79, 81, 82, 83, 85
neofunctional models 1, 2
Neukölln-Reuterquartier 82
non-refoulement 51, 54, 57
Özgen 174
Paris Kurdish Institute 65, 66
Partiya Karkerên Kurdistan 101, 150
Peace and Democracy Party 109
peace process 110, 151
People's Republican Party 98
PKK 38, 64, 65, 70-74, 101-104, 107, 108, 110, 112-125, 131-133, 138, 139, 140-145, 150, 151, 165, 174
Portes, Alejandro 8
Puerto Ricans 26, 164
Qamishli 19, 22, 27-30, 32
Recep Tayyip Erdogan 58
remittances 156, 160, 167, 171, 180

rival gangs 7
Roboski 39, 128, 140, 174
Romano Prodi 66
S. Castles 163
Schengen Regime 45
September 11 .... 45, 47, 179
Sheikh Ubeydullah 95
Şivan Perwer 129
social agents 1
social capital 1, 2, 7, 8, 9, 10, 11, 12, 13, 14, 15, 16, 17, 18, 41, 79, 165, 167, 171, 172, 173, 175, 181
Social Democratic Party 84
Social exclusion 10, 162
Soziale Stadt 77-87, 161, 162, 166, 168, 169
Syria 19, 97, 125, 151, 174, 181
Syrian nationals 19, 24, 27
tensions 1, 15, 26, 54, 135, 136, 137, 141, 142, 144, 178
Treaty of Lausanne 72
Turkish International Migration Survey 150
Turkish-Greek border 5, 43, 45, 52, 55
Uğur Boran 106
United Kingdom .... v, 121, 150, 161
urban fragmentation 77
Village guards 103, 106
Wise Men committee 110
World War II 147, 152
Yüksekova 40, 41

www.ingramcontent.com/pod-product-compliance
Lightning Source LLC
Chambersburg PA
CBHW021842220426
43663CB00005B/370